Safeguarding the Health Sector in Times of Macroeconomic Instability

Safeguarding the Health Sector in Times of Macroeconomic Instability

Policy Lessons for Low- and Middle-Income Countries

Edited by
Slim Haddad, Enis Barış, Delampady Narayana

Africa World Press, Inc.

P.O. Box 1892
Trenton, NJ 08607

P.O. Box 48
Asmara, ERITREA

International Development Research Centre
Ottawa • Cairo • Dakar • Montevideo • Nairobi • New Delhi • Singapore

Africa World Press, Inc.

P.O. Box 1892
Trenton, NJ 08607

P.O. Box 48
Asmara, ERITREA

Copyright © 2008 International Development Research Centre (IDRC)
First Printing 2008

Jointly Published by
AFRICA WORLD PRESS
P.O. Box 1892, Trenton, New Jersey 08607
awprsp@verizon.net/www.africaworldpressbooks.com

and the
International Development Research Centre
PO Box 8500, Ottawa, ON Canada KIG 3149
info@idrc/www.idrc.ca
ISBN (e-book): 978-1-55250-370-6

The findings, interpretations and conclusions expressed in this study are entirely those of the authors and should not be attributed in any manner to the institutions with which they are, or have been, affiliated or employed.

Book and cover design: Saverance Publishing Services

Library of Congress Cataloging-in-Publication Data
Safeguarding the health sector in times of macroeconomic instability : policy lessons for low- and middle-income countries / editors: Slim Haddad, Enis Baris, Delampady Narayana.
    p. ; cm.
Includes bibliographical references and index.
ISBN-10: 1-59221-596-3 (hardcover)
ISBN-10: 1-59221-597-1 (pbk.)
1. Health care reform--Economic aspects--Developing countries. 2. Medical policy--Economic aspects--Developing countries. 3. Public policy--Developing countries--Finance. 4. Structural adjustment (Economic policy)--Developing countries. 5. Economic stabilization--Developing countries. 6. Medical economics--Developing countries. I. Haddad, Slim. II. Baris, Enis. III. Narayana, D.
    [DNLM: 1. Health Care Reform--economics. 2. Developing Countries. 3. Public Policy. 4. Socioeconomic Factors. WA 530.1 S128 2007]

RA395.D44S34 2007
362.109172'4--dc22
                        2007028214

In memory of our friend and esteemed colleague
Stephen Chandiwana,
an ardent advocate for health policy and systems research
as a key ingredient in improving the health of sub-Saharan
African communities.

TABLE OF CONTENTS

FOREWORD

Structural adjustment, macroeconomic adjustment, and health sector reform are loaded terms. Each has become a kind of shorthand for diverse and frequently opposing health and development constituencies, signalling for each constituency a very different constellation of goals, assumptions, values, ideologies, methodologies, technical content and results. At one fundamental level, these differences reflect very different visions of how societies should function. Recent and ongoing debates about globalization, market-based approaches to service delivery, and roles of the state and active civil society are helping to sharpen these alternative visions and continue to play an important role in unpacking the contents of such seemingly bland terms as macroeconomic adjustment and health sector reform. At another level, the debates and growing evidence base around globalization highlight how entangled national and local policy and practice are with decisions and political and economic imperatives elsewhere. Yet at a third level, the level on the ground where macroeconomic policies and realities, health policies, health-care delivery systems, and people intersect, we see a much more complex and subtle situation unfolding.

At this third level, contexts, policy choices, personalities, policy-implementation capabilities, cultural and social norms, and political and economic history interact to produce outcomes that are both promising and troubling. It is this reality on the ground that is too often neglected or avoided by sweeping triumphalist or catastrophist narratives, the reality where governments must make choices in circumstances they may ardently wish were different, where ministries and clinics alike are short of skilled staff, where sudden shifts in commodity prices or weather may precipitate a crisis with which a health department must somehow deal, where both noble and venal motives and actions are in evidence, but where there may just be ways to safeguard the health sector while the higher-level debates about politics and vision continue both in-country and around the world. It is this third level which the researchers of the MAPHealth study so rigorously and thoughtfully address, and the result is an exceptional collection of analyses, reflections, and recommendations. Some of the results confirm prior findings, while others are surprising and on the surface may be counterintuitive. The conclusions and recommendations within each case study, and of the overall comparative work, make for sobering but also hopeful reading. There are no easy answers. The continued importance of political will points to the critical role that broad-based public debate and real—not pro forma—civic engagement play in informing and shaping power and politics, in and between societies, to the benefit of all, especially the poor. "Governance" is indeed political, despite what the more technocratic among us might wish. But as all the case studies show, action to safeguard the health sector *is* possible, even in countries as poor as Burkina Faso, as crisis-ridden during the period examined here as Zimbabwe, Mexico, Colombia, and Thailand, or as complex as India. The vision is crucial but the devil, as always, is in the details—hence the importance of the careful, systematic work presented here.

This book and other studies support the view that some kinds of imposed policy choices, such as the first generation of structural adjustment, leave very little room for action or mitigation at the country level. However, neither the study design nor the analysis presented here are aimed specifically at these macro-level political and philosophical debates, though the reader will find frequent, thoughtful, and challenging contributions to these debates throughout the chapters. The debates are longstanding, with modernization and dependency theory still being played out under new names as the pendulum swings back and forth in global development policy.

It is perhaps worth noting, in the foreword to a book which reports on many years of careful effort to collect and interpret evidence of policy impact, how seldom these sweeping and enthusiastic policy shifts are actually informed by careful ex ante analysis, or even concurrent rigorous evaluation of implementation and impact. This is one admonition the book's authors delicately avoid making, but which needs to made. Fortunately, recent initiatives around the world reflect a growing impatience with making the developing world a kind of global social policy laboratory, minus the careful lab science. We hope the methodological challenges experienced by these and other researchers, discussed in Chapter 3, will become less of an obstacle to future researchers and decision-makers.

As this book goes to press, the WHO Commission on Social Determinants of Health is winding up its deliberations—a fortuitous marker for the end of this chapter of the work described in this book, which also coincided with the work of the WHO Commission on Macroeconomics and Health. While the latter Commission played a seminal role in shifting the world's attention to the importance of health not only as an outcome of development and economic growth, but also as an essential input, our growing understanding of the social determinants of health equips us to address better some of the challenging findings and recommendations of the MAPHealth study. Research on population health and the social determinants of health has repeatedly demonstrated that social and income inequalities translate into health and mortality inequalities along the full gradient of inequality (and not just between the ends), as biological and social processes interact and are embodied in vulnerability or resilience to illness and death. However, recent data, notably from Canada, also demonstrate that deliberate social policies to transfer wealth and protect broad-based social benefits can significantly, or even entirely, flatten this gradient effect. This is good news because it suggests that, even in the absence of the more complete social and economic equity to which many of us are committed, there is room for action and significant gains in health. This news is echoed by several of the chapters in this book, though tempered at times with the sobering reality that good intentions—or even individually good policies—are no guarantee of good outcomes.

The MAPHealth team put into practice a key desideratum of current health policy and global health research thinking: that country work should be led as much as possible by national teams and that both Southern and Northern research partners should collaborate in the intellectual effort of global policy research and analysis. The collegial and collaborative spirit among all the country teams and with the *Université de Montreal* research team is in evidence throughout the book. The International Development Research Centre is privileged to have been able to support and participate in this important work.

This is an important and challenging book. If you are looking for a broad, high-level diagnosis or an easy-to-swallow generic prescription to immunize health systems against macroeconomic instability or crisis, this book is not for you. If, however, you are ready to tackle the complexities of understanding real health systems, real policies, and real politics in six very different countries facing similar constraints, this analysis of a collaborative, comparative, multi-year initiative is an invaluable contribution.

Christina Zarowsky, MD, PhD
Research for Health Equity
International Development Research Centre

ACKNOWLEDGMENTS

The Editors and the members of the MAPHealth team extend their heartfelt thanks to all those persons who provided invaluable support in the preparation and execution of this research program across the several countries involved. The Editors also gratefully acknowledge the important contribution of the International Development Research Centre (IDRC), which provided both technical and financial support for the studies, and offer our warmest appreciation to Randy Spence, Christina Zarowsky, Marie-Claude Martin, Rohinton Medhora, Rosemary Kennedy, and Marta Melesse, who were a constant source of support over the years and without whom this work would not have been possible. Special thanks go to Donna Riley, our editor, translator and overall coordinator for her invaluable assistance in the production of this work. Publication of this book was also made possible in part by the Quebec Population Health Research Network.

CHAPTER 1

THE MAPHEALTH PROJECT: A MULTI-COUNTRY INITIATIVE

Slim Haddad, Enis Barış, Delampady Narayana

Health sector reform has been a recurring theme over the past two decades in many low- and middle-income countries, especially in the broader context of macroeconomic instability. Although countries have adopted both macroeconomic and health policies to stimulate growth and improve health system efficiency, implementations and outcomes have varied considerably depending upon several factors: the origin, extent, and duration of the instability; the relative importance of economic, social, and political factors at play; and the scope and severity of sectoral challenges in health and health care. These policies, termed macroeconomic adjustment policies (MAPs), often involved adopting short-term austerity measures and longer-term structural and sectoral adjustment programs with financial assistance and policy guidance from international finance institutions (IFIs). MAPs have since been the subject of intense debate and remain controversial not only in terms of the scope and nature of policy dialogues, interventions, and implementation processes, but also because of their purported effects on the overall economy, on the poorest and most vulnerable households, and on the financing and provision of social services such as education and health.

Despite the existence of several studies, the outcomes of this unique natural experiment also remain controversial. Data are often unreliable and results vary widely. This is not surprising, given the great diversity of policies that vary from one country to another in terms of content, severity, implementation, and, of course, the contexts within which they are applied. Divergence of opinions is also to be expected for reasons ranging from ideology and underlying values to more credible ontological and epistemological explanations. More specifically, as described in Chapter 2, these studies differed not only in scope and purpose, but also in their design and methodology. Here it should simply be noted that the usual problems of validity and inference in attributing causes and effects proved to be more daunting in the health sector, where the reasons for—and the timing, sequencing, and degree of implementation of—sectoral reforms seldom lend themselves to a thorough and rigorous evaluation.

Not surprisingly, even if the consequences of MAPs on the overall economy in developing countries are relatively well documented, their impacts on the health sector proper, and more specifically on access to health care, utilization, and quality—and indeed on health outcomes—are still debated. Many policy analysts, researchers, and activists claim that the health sector in adjusting countries has been seriously undermined either as a direct result of MAPs or due to the deterioration of socioeconomic conditions associated with their stabilization measures. Following UNICEF's 1987 report *Adjustment with a Human Face*, many studies demonstrated a disturbing deterioration in health conditions in countries facing stringent adjustment policies, generating an intense debate regarding the real origin of this decline. Some ascribed it to the adjustment itself, and others, notably the IFIs, attributed it to the original crises that led to the need for adjustment, or else to an implementation of MAPs that was too timid or inappropriate. In this way, with examples at the ready, each side was able to delve into the diversity of experiences and the heterogeneity of situations in the countries under adjustment to support their arguments either that the adjustments were intrinsically deficient or that the original economic crisis was to blame, or to label those countries "poor adjusters."

Given that these adjustment policies were largely recycled within the context of recently resuscitated strategies in the war against poverty, our proposal is not, in this text, to re-examine these arguments and the value of the premises underlying them.

It must be noted that in the great majority of cases, analysis of the effects of MAPs on the health sector was primarily focused on one specific consequence—health conditions—and on one specific mechanism, i.e., deterioration of households' living conditions as the agency by which adjustment policies led to decline in the conditions of health. This perspective was justifiable in terms of studying the social consequences of adjustment and their impacts on health. However, this approach also served to distract attention away from the influence of MAPs and socioeconomic context on the health-care system itself, and on its performance in terms of its principal functions of regulation, financing, and provision of services.

Conversely, these questions have been at the heart of research into the effects of sectoral reform undertaken over the past 15 years by the Southern countries. However, the tendency has been to observe these transformations through a primarily sectoral lens, which does not sufficiently take into account the socioeconomic context within which health sector reform takes place, nor the influence and roles of various non-sectoral stakeholders in its design and implementation.

Whether integral to or concomitant with MAPs, health sector reform initiatives often arise from sectoral needs to improve the health status of the population and to improve system performance. Yet the timing, extent, and scope of health sector reform vary across countries. Therefore, a thorough impact assessment of health-care outcomes—such as accessibility, utilization, and quality of care—would require not only examining relationships between the reform parameters and the outcomes, but also carrying out a comparative assessment of the macroeconomic and sectoral contexts within which they occur in various countries. With this information, we would be better able to draw lessons from both failures and successes.

The research initiative that led to this book was designed to provide a comparative ex-post evaluation of health sector reform initiatives in middle- and low-income countries so as to document which measures, and which policy environments, are more likely to be successful in safeguarding the health sector. This evaluation is intended to offer some perspective on how and why changes in the health-care system manifested in the ways they did in different countries under similar adjustment policies. It also provides evidence to help in defining the appropriate mix of policy instruments and adaptations to be made according to the particularities of each country. As such, this book provides a fresh look at the relationships between public policies and the health system in general, and presents new and detailed observations to inform policy choices within the health-care sector worldwide.

The results presented here come out of studies carried out by researchers in Africa, Latin America, Asia, and Canada within the framework of a research initiative entitled "Macroeconomic and adjustment policies and health care: studying the macro-micro links," also referred to as the MAPHealth project. This initiative was developed through a cooperative network of eight participating countries, the International Development Research Centre (IDRC), which initiated and funded the project, and the *Groupe de recherche interdisciplinaire en santé* (GRIS) at the *Université de Montréal*.

The MAPHealth project examined the evolution of policies and health services in eight Southern countries (of which six are presented in this book) in light of transformations in their macroeconomic environments, and especially with regard to the crises and sectoral adjustment policies they faced, i.e., how health systems responded, at different times and in different contexts, to

major transformations of their environments. The countries associated with this IDRC initiative were Burkina Faso, Colombia,
India, Kenya, Mexico, Thailand, Uganda, and Zimbabwe. Given
that the majority of these countries had begun or carried out, in
the previous 20 years, one or more health system reforms, particular attention was given to analyzing the links between these
reforms, macroadjustment policies, and the services provided.

Chapter 2 surveys the literature for two key areas of study—the
effects of MAPs on health outcomes and the effects of health sector
reform on system performance. The impacts of MAPs are considered from both the demand side (e.g. health, nutritional status,
education) and the supply side (e.g. health expenditures, access
to good quality care). The evidence on the effects of health sector
reforms is reviewed for three core measures: financing, decentralization, and integrating competition into the health sector. The
literature, while significant, indicates a need for stronger evidence
on the impacts of reforms driven by macroeconomic instability, as
well as for a better understanding of how health systems are influenced by various factors within and external to the health sector.

Chapter 3 focuses on methods. In that chapter, we present
briefly the main features of multiple-country and single-country
studies used to assess the effects of reforms and adjustment
policies in the health sector. We examine the challenges faced in
evaluating outcomes of large-scale policies, with special attention
to issues related to the assessment of counterfactual situations,
the attribution of observed changes to specific measures or global
policies, and the choice of appropriate designs and measurement
tools. We then describe the methodology of the MAPHealth
project, which builds upon our efforts to draw lessons in methodology from studies carried out over the past 15 years on the
effects on health of structural adjustment.

The experiences of the six countries, summarized in the following paragraphs, are presented in greater detail in chapters 4
through 10 of this book. Note that, in India, the experience of

the state of Kerala was found to be sufficiently informative that it has been described in a chapter of its own.

BURKINA FASO

To move from a state-dominated to a market-based economy, the government of Burkina Faso decided, in 1991, to implement a structural adjustment program (SAP) with the aid of the International Monetary Fund (IMF) and the World Bank. This involved stabilization measures as well as structural and sectoral reforms. The most significant measure was the deep devaluation the CFA franc BCEAO (XOF) in 1994 to one-half its value.

Health sector reform was one of the sectoral reforms within the adjustment package. It focused on decentralization and implementation of cost-recovery mechanisms, the supply of essential generic drugs, the liberalization of health services, and the hospital sector. Laws and regulations were passed giving public facilities a great deal of management autonomy and establishing the principle of cost recovery through fees for services, and particularly for essential drugs. Within a few years, fees for services were generalized in public facilities.

Chapter 4 studies the implementation and the outcomes of the ambitious health sector reform initiated with the SAP in 1992. The authors look at decentralization and the other elements of the health system reform: development of the private health sector, reform of the pharmaceutical sector and hospital reform. They examine the impacts of the reform on the allocation of financial resources and on the availability and distribution of personnel, facilities, and services; they also consider the effects on prices, economic barriers, and access to health care services. The analysis includes an assessment of the economic burden of health care on families and of the impoverishing effects of out-of-pocket expenditures in urban and rural areas.

COLOMBIA

Colombia underwent adjustment programs during the 1980s in the areas of fiscal exchange, trade, and foreign debt, but adjustment was less drastic compared to other countries. Health sector reform was not an immediate consequence of MAPs, but was rather the product of a new Constitution (1991) that led to a profound transformation from a highly centralized government to a decentralized one. The new Constitution authorized the participation of the private sector in the provision of public services, set the basic rights to education, health, and social security, and made decentralization a constitutional mandate. In 1993, a wide and ambitious "pro-equity" social security reform aimed at increasing health insurance coverage and ensuring access to a basic package of services was adopted and has been progressively implemented.

The Colombian study, in Chapter 5, analyzes the equity effects of health system reform, looking especially at the decentralization of the system with social participation by local health committees and at the social security reform. In particular, the study focuses on whether coverage of the poor has improved under the subsidized system, where there has been an increase in public health expenditure in a context of low overall economic growth.

INDIA

A national MAP was implemented in 1991 in India in response to the balance of payment crisis following the Gulf War. Reform measures were undertaken in fiscal policy, industrial and trade policy, exchange rate policy, foreign investment, and technology import policy. State governments, which have a significant degree of autonomy in the Indian federal system of governance, have taken their own policy stances. They have been led to reform the state apparatus, invest in infrastructure, and provide incentive frameworks for private enterprise.

With the support of the World Bank, seven states have initiated health sector reforms, called Health Systems Development

Projects: Andhra Pradesh, Karnataka, Maharastra, Orissa, Punjab, Uttar Pradesh, and West Bengal. Although these projects have been implemented differently and at different times, they have objectives in common such as strengthening the performance, accountability, and efficiency of health systems. The projects seek to improve not only access to health care, but also the quality of health services, by renovating and expanding district, subdistrict, and community hospitals.

The Indian study, presented in Chapter 6, focuses on the issue of public expenditure. Trends in expenditure are analyzed over a long period—before MAPs and after—across the diverse states. Public health expenditure during the adjustment period is compared between two groups of states, i.e., those that implemented the World Bank-funded Health Systems Development Projects and those that did not. The study looked at questions such as whether the states used the World Bank loans for capital spending in the health sector and whether the hope of external funding for disease control programs led to reductions in allocation from state budgets, with possible adverse effects on programs.

While the Indian study focused on an inter-state analysis of public health-care expenditures, Chapter 7 takes up the analysis of utilization and quality of health care and out-of-pocket health-care expenditures in the state of Kerala. Kerala is often taken as a model of good health at low cost. But creeping privatization can lead to private financing of health care, with an attendant heavy burden and impoverishment of vast segments of population. Decentralization of the public health-care sector does not help greatly in mitigating this situation. The chapter explores the reasons for high utilization of private health care facilities in Kerala in terms of quality differences between the public and private sectors and analyzes the burden of health care costs.

MEXICO

Several adjustment packages have been implemented in Mexico since the early 1980s, each lasting about five years. In 1994, a severe financial crisis led the government and the international community to set up a financial rescue package, conditional upon a stringent adjustment program under IMF control. This crisis and subsequent adjustments led to a decline in general public expenditures and a profound deterioration in socioeconomic conditions among the population, prompting the authorities to implement social policies targeting the most vulnerable groups. A new program was created—Progresa (Program of Education, Health and Nutrition)—to improve maternal and child nutritional conditions and the quality of health and education services, as well as to provide financial support to families in the program. Expanding services to the poor and decentralizing public health services to the state level were major directions of the National Development Plan of 1995–2000, with health sector reform aimed at improving quality and efficiency and extending coverage, especially among the uninsured.

Chapter 8 examines the role of the state in providing primary care and a basic package of services to the poor. It analyzes the variation in access to primary care across the regions of Mexico and differences in access to secondary care between the poor and the rich. The perceived quality of service among private, social insurance, and SSA providers is also assessed.

THAILAND

In recent history, Thailand experienced three macroeconomic crises, all followed by structural reforms: the first (1973–1975) and second (1979–1985) oil crises and the 1997–1999 currency crisis. The latter led to a severe contraction of the economy. The government's response was to implement a strict stabilization program supported by the IMF. However, after being criticized for following the IMF program, which was deemed inappropriate for the Thai situation, the government reversed its macroeconomic policy and launched a stimulation package intended to bring the economy out of recession and resume economic growth.

There have been three cycles of health sector reform (1975–1980, 1990–1995, and 1996 to the present), each following a period of economic adjustment. The most recent cycle included autonomous management of public hospitals, reform of the Civil Servant Medical Benefits Scheme (CSMBS), and introduction of the Universal Coverage Scheme, or the so-called 30 Baht Scheme, offering a comprehensive benefits package for 45 million Thais.

Chapter 9 examines these three cycles of health sector reform in relation to Thailand's major economic and social transformations and, in particular, the three economic crises of 1973, 1979, and 1997. The authors explore the linkages between macroeconomic policies and changes in financing, resource allocation, coverage, and provision of services. Special attention is given to successful strategies adopted to mitigate the adverse effects of external shocks.

ZIMBABWE

After severe foreign currency shortages, the Zimbabwe government launched, in 1991, its first Economic Structural Adjustment Programme (ESAP). The package was aimed at increasing investment and restoring economic growth through a market-based economy. This was followed, in 1995, by a second phase of reforms embodied in the Zimbabwe Programme for Economic and Social Transformation (ZIMPREST) that were designed to stimulate broad-based macroeconomic stability, accelerate poverty reduction, and alleviate hardships arising from ESAP.

In the period following independence, the health sector became the target of ambitious and proactive public policies, health being seen as a key component of the development process. Under pressure from the World Bank, the IMF, and bilateral agencies, health system reform was introduced in the late 1980s. Its main objective was to decentralize power and decision-making in health services to the operational level. Cost-recovery and market-based mechanisms were promoted favouring the private and non-governmental sectors.

Chapter 10 analyzes the detrimental effects of MAPs on access to and utilization and quality of health care services in Zimbabwe and the government's strategy for mitigating adverse impacts on the poor. The authors assess structural changes within the health-care system resulting from socioeconomic pressures arising out of MAPs, such as the migration of skilled health manpower and the requirement of using foreign currency to acquire the inputs for drugs.

These six countries represent diverse cases in terms of population size, level of income, human development, and implementation of MAPs and health system reforms. At one end are medium-income countries like Mexico, Colombia, and Thailand, and at the other end is the extremely poor country of Burkina Faso, with India and Zimbabwe lying in between. The diversity of cases and of health system characteristics allows for useful and informative comparisons within the framework of a common approach evolved through numerous interactions among the researchers involved in the MAPHealth project.

CHAPTER 2

MACROECONOMIC ADJUSTMENT POLICIES AND HEALTH SECTOR REFORM: SURVEYING THE LITERATURE

Katherine S. Mohindra

INTRODUCTION

By the time the MAPHealth initiative was launched in the mid-1990s, an extensive body of literature had accumulated on macroeconomic adjustment policies (MAPs) and health sector reform. Two major streams of research had emerged. The first focused on the impacts of adjusting economies on health outcomes. In the late 1980s, UNICEF sounded a warning bell in its report *Adjustment with a Human Face* (Cornia et al. 1987), that captured the attention of the international community. UNICEF pointed out that the earlier gains of the 1970s in child nutrition and health were eroding under poor economic conditions. Public health activists and researchers responded with a call to protect the health of communities, particularly poor and vulnerable populations such as children. For this, MAPs would need to take into account social aspects.

Increasingly, studies have been aimed at deepening our understanding of MAPs and their impacts on equity, health, and social welfare. Since the late 1980s, researchers have attempted to assess whether MAPs have had negative consequences on health, either through the deterioration of socioeconomic conditions or the dismantling of public health-care systems. Surveying the literature, we encounter proponents of MAPs and (more often) opponents, both of whose arguments are often ideologically driven rather than empirically based. The literature, sometimes referred to as "inconclusive and often contentious" (Anand and Chen 1996, p.1), is peppered with lamentations of the lack of timely and reliable data, as well as of the methodological difficulties impeding the research process (Birdsall and Hecht 1995; Costello et al. 1994; Lundy 1996; Peabody 1996).

The other stream of research concentrated on changes in health-care systems among countries undergoing health sector reforms. During the 1980s and 1990s, health-care systems, particularly in sub-Saharan Africa, were collapsing (Simms et al. 2001; Turshen 1999). Multiple pressures, including deteriorating economic conditions, demographic transitions, HIV/AIDS, and other emerging or re-emerging diseases, were too much of a burden on already strained health-care systems. Health sector reforms, the new imperative, encompassed a range of strategies aimed at improving the financing, organization, and delivery of health services. The World Bank offered a number of policy ideas to mobilize resources and improve the efficiency of the systems (World Bank 1987, 1993).

By the 1990s, the World Bank had become a major player in the field of international health, both as donor and as policy adviser (Fournier et al. 2001). In 1998, Kamran Abbasi interviewed Richard Feachem, former director of the Bank's Health, Nutrition, and Population (HNP) sector, about the World Bank's engagement in health. Feachem gave three reasons for this new interest:

> The first one is that, in all countries, health sector expenditure is a major slice of GDP. And therefore for an organisation interested in macroeconomic policy it matters. The second factor comes from the fact that the two main parts of the bank, IBRD and IDA [the International Bank for Reconstruction and Development and the International Development Associa-

tion], lend to governments; and that leads us into those sectors where the free market cannot work without major government involvement ... Thirdly, investment in people and the formation of "human capital" is an essential prerequisite for sustained economic growth and social development (Abassi 1999, p. 1206).

Not everyone celebrated the entrance of the World Bank into the health sector. Many feared that its market-driven approach created more problems than solutions for under-resourced health-care systems (Banerji 1994; Laurell and Arellano 1996; Loewenson 1994; Simms et al. 2001). Researchers turned to studying the effects of health-care reforms to assess changes in access and utilization of health services and to see whether their quality was improving.

However, these two areas of study—the effects of MAPs on health outcomes and the effects of health sector reform on system performance—did not tend to intersect. Comparatively less attention was paid to how MAPs transformed health-care systems in terms of access, utilization, and quality of care. Nor was there sufficient analysis of health sector reforms within the broader context of MAPs (Sen and Koivusalo 1998). The research has been criticized for being "technocratic," ignoring the wider social, economic, and political contexts (Berman 1995).

In this chapter, we do not present an exhaustive review of the material to date. Rather, we re-examine the literature, highlighting these two important knowledge gaps, from which the theoretical underpinnings of the MAPHealth conceptual framework are derived (see Chapter 3). First, we present an overview of MAPs and health sector reforms. Then, we consider the impacts of MAPs from both the supply and demand sides. We then look at health sector reforms and at strategies and assumptions most often espoused in their formulation. In conclusion, we point out areas where outstanding issues remain.

MACROECONOMIC AND SECTORAL REFORMS: AN OVERVIEW

Macroeconomic adjustment policies (MAPs)

Proposed as a cure for economic woes, MAPs allowed international lenders to support a country's balance of payments on the condition that certain economic policy interventions were undertaken (World Bank 1994a). These may be divided into two main types. The first were measures, typically guided by the IMF, to correct for internal and external macroeconomic disequilibria over the short term and were aimed at contracting demand, principally through restricting public expenditures. Once an economy had stabilized, policies could then be implemented to address structural barriers to production (Husain 1994). This involved medium- to long-term measures for stimulating economic growth. These "supply" policies relied on a variety of directions recommended by the World Bank that included, among others, liberalization, privatization, and deregulation. MAPs varied with respect to their content, scope, intensity, duration, and ultimate outcomes, leading authors to propose different approaches to classifying MAPs and the countries adopting them, for purposes of comparison.

One approach used a *conceptual* classification to provide a framework for understanding the evolution of policies. Cornia (1992) described the progression of MAPs over time, distinguishing among three different generations. During the early 1980s, a first generation of MAPs maintained purely fiscal and monetary objectives. The main goals were to stabilize the economy and liberalize the market. There were no stipulations to protect social sectors or vulnerable populations. The second generation expanded supply policies across sectors, including industry, agriculture, energy, finance, banking, health, and education. In their 1990 World Development Report, the World Bank officially recognized the need for social funds (Cornia 2001), and by 1991, MAPs included at least one condition specific to health (Van der Gaag and Barham 1998). Certain policies included compensatory measures for temporary relief from the costs of reforms. Finally, the third generation aimed to integrate economic and social objectives, with explicit intentions of protecting health and education.

An *operational* approach was used by two sets of authors in their respective cross-country studies looking at conditions that enabled MAPs to be operationalized. Kakwani's (1995) system divided countries according to whether they underwent adjustment or not. He further divided adjusting countries according to whether they had received single or multiple loans. This approach measured the intensity of MAPs. Van der Gaag and Barham (1998) divided countries into four groups. The first two included adjusting countries, further subdivided by time period: Early Adjusting Countries (EAC) and Other Adjusting Countries (OAC). Countries that did not implement MAPs were divided between those having achieved positive economic growth and those where growth had been negative. This system also captured the intensity of MAPs. Although these systems of classification facilitate comparisons among countries by capturing certain characteristics of MAP implementation, they fail to represent the complexity and diversity of country experiences and ultimately provide limited perspectives in terms of political and social contexts.

A third approach categorized MAPs according to outcomes, using a *normative* classification system based on judgments related to the adherence to MAPs, as illustrated in a World Bank evaluation study of the period 1980–1993 (Jayarajah et al. 1996). Countries were classified into four categories according to their experiences with policy instruments. The first, labeled "good cases," included those countries that followed the "right" policy and achieved the "right" outcome. The second, called "bad cases," followed the "wrong" policy and got the "wrong" outcome. The third and fourth categories are the "ugly cases," which included "unlucky" countries that implemented the "right" policy but achieved the "wrong" outcome and "lucky" countries that pursued the "wrong" policy but got the "right" outcome. The "ugly cases" were a result of exogenous events—the unlucky cases faced negative circumstances, such as adverse trade conditions, while the lucky cases experienced favourable events. The rather unfortunate and simplistic labeling of the cases (the good, the bad, and the ugly) fails to acknowledge that governments can autonomously design and implement policies leading to positive outcomes and makes it impossible to extract lessons from these cases. Nor does this system address the shortcomings of MAPs and the crucial dimension of country diversity in shaping public policies.

These approaches—conceptual, operational, and normative—illustrate the complexity associated with the analysis of MAPs. Although policy differences should be considered in evaluating MAPs, none of these approaches sufficiently takes into account the diversity of country experiences.

Health sector reform

Most countries that underwent MAPs during the 1980s and 1990s also initiated health sector reform. Sometimes these reforms were stimulated by problems related to the economy, or by specific causes within the health sector, or combinations of both. Financial crises in the public sector led to severe consequences, such as deterioration of public health infrastructures and quality of health services, and declining capacities of governments to provide free health care for their citizens. Policies shaping the organization and delivery of quality health services were inadequate, focusing largely on curative care within hospital settings.

Health sector reforms adopted different forms and varied with respect to content, timing, and implementation. Generally, these reforms were aimed at increasing health sector financing; reallocating public budgets to promote primary health-care services; reorienting public funds to benefit the poor; improving the quality and range of services; increasing utilization; decentralizing the public sector through institutional reforms; reinforcing managerial capacities; and liberalizing the health sector by expanding private sector involvement (Gilson and Mills 1995).

In some countries, health sector reform was an integral part of adjustment. In others, reforms were undertaken independently, although MAPs could either precede or follow. In certain rare cases, MAPs were implemented without concomitant reforms of the health sector. In studying the first two types, particular efforts are required to dissociate influences arising from MAPs and from health sector reforms.

IMPACTS OF MAPS ON THE HEALTH SECTOR

The effects of MAPs on the health sector are multiple and interrelated, affecting the macro (e.g. macroeconomic or sectoral policies), meso (e.g. health-care systems, communities), and micro levels (e.g. households, individuals). MAPs may operate through either the supply or demand side (Anand and Chen 1996; Costello et al. 1994). Many studies explored the impacts of MAPs on the demand side, specifically by assessing changes in health outcomes. Comparatively less effort was made to understand change processes in the health sector by analyzing factors influencing health, including both medical and non-medical determinants of health. The supply side of MAPs was also explored. However, except for a few notable studies on changes in quality of care, most concentrated on the evolution of public health-care expenditures. Assessing the health impacts of MAPs is plagued with methodological difficulties; weighing the evidence requires explicit knowledge of methods employed, data sources used, and the context in which the study took place.

A recent review of the literature prepared for the World Health Organization (WHO) Commission on Macroeconomics and Health surveyed the debate, including the empirical evidence and methodological approaches adopted (Breman and Shelton 2001). Several trends are worth mentioning. First, of the 72 articles reviewed, although normative articles generally argued that MAPs had negative consequences on health, the empirical evidence presented both negative and positive outcomes. Second, among 28 empirical studies, the two most widely studied outcome variables were public health expenditures and child mortality. Other variables studied were malnutrition, life expectancy, and maternal mortality. A few studies also analyzed quality of health care. Both positive and negative outcomes were described in these empirical studies. Third, studies were divided evenly into whether a case study approach or cross-country analysis was used. Negative effects tended to be reported in case studies, whereas cross-country comparisons illustrated both positive and negative outcomes on health. Finally, there were no discernible trends with respect to region, except in Africa, the most widely studied region, that generally displayed negative outcomes. The review does not highlight differential impacts of MAPs on distinct populations such as women, indigenous populations, or people living in urban versus rural areas, hiding possible inequalities arising from, or worsened by, the implementation of MAPs. This omission is most likely due to a lack of disaggregate data at the time, but these potential inequalities should be kept in mind when assessing the health impacts of MAPs.

Demand-side effects of MAPs

As highlighted by the review of Breman and Shelton, the impacts of MAPs on health status and malnutrition, particularly among children, were intensively studied. Child mortality and malnutrition are indicators sensitive to changes in health policies and programs, and these indicators are generally available in poor countries (Garenne and Gakusi 2000; Musgrove 1986). The results were, however, mixed. The literature is complicated by disagreements among researchers at two different levels. First, the evidence diverges on whether health status deteriorated or improved following the period of adjustment. This may be related, in part, to regional or local conditions. For example, increases in malnutrition were noted, at least for a short period, in most African countries during the 1980s (Stewart and Van der Geest 1995), while in Latin America, nutritional status improved in some countries but declined in others (Tardanico and Larín

1997). UNICEF (1984) found increasing malnutrition in Costa Rica and Bolivia during the early 1980s, while in Chile and Cuba, child nutritional status was improving and infant mortality rates were declining (Musgrove 1986).

Different results may also arise depending on how health or nutritional status is measured. Even though many studies indicated that health deteriorated in sub-Saharan Africa (Breman and Shelton 2001), Garenne and Gakusi (2000) found child survival either stabilized or improved among 10 African countries using "innovative methodology." Positive and negative outcomes were often found within a single study, illustrating the challenges of assessing "health." For example, a survey of child nutritional status in a community in the Congo noted an increase in wasting but a decline in levels of stunting (Cornu et al. 1995). This type of pattern, demonstrated elsewhere, can be explained by the fact that the indicators measure different dimensions of malnutrition; wasting captures short-term impacts, whereas stunting is an indication of long-term undernutrition (Mohindra 1999). This reaffirms that, in studying the impacts of MAPs on health, distinction must be made between short-term and long-term effects (Musgrove 1986).

Another area of disagreement among researchers is in how changes in health status are explained. Certain authors attributed deterioration of health and nutritional status directly to MAPs (Kanji et al. 1991; Loewenson 1993), whereas other, more nuanced, interpretations inferred that MAPs did not protect populations from wider economic conditions (Cornu et al. 1995). MAPs have also been credited with stimulating improvements in health. For example, a multicase study of African countries argued that health improved because "positive forces associated with SAP's were at work," particularly better governance and management (Garenne and Gakusi 2000, p.15). Some argued that causal links could not be made because the study designs were incapable of discounting rival hypotheses. Other explanations were offered for the reversal of trends in health gains. For example, the World Bank proposed that improvements in health status (measured as life expectancy) of populations in countries undergoing adjustment were declining because infant and child mortality rates were stabilizing (World Bank 1996).

The lack of clear evidence makes it difficult to formulate general statements about the health effects of MAPs. Methodological difficulties in linking MAPs to health status are extensive (see Chapter 3). Measuring health status is not enough. Explicit pathways between MAPs and health outcomes must also be described and analyzed.

Health is determined by a number of factors both within and external to the health sector (Evans et al. 1994; Kjellstrom et al. 1992). Although deterioration in living conditions was recognized as a potential link between MAPs and health outcomes, a more complex analysis of how MAPs influenced the determinants of health was lacking (Yach and von Schirnding 1994). There were, however, a number of studies outside of public health that examined the impact of MAPs on key inputs for both health and health care, such as economic status, employment, and education. Not surprisingly, the evidence was contradictory and inconclusive.

Increases in poverty have enormous implications for health; poverty is both a fundamental cause of disease and a barrier to health care (Wagstaff 2001). Increased poverty is especially associated with malnutrition, and some argued that MAPs led to higher food prices and reductions in subsidies, affecting the diet of the poor (Schoepf et al. 2000). Poverty studies varied in their results and were hindered by methodological problems and data deficiencies. As in the health sector, studies diverged on the nature and severity of changes in poverty and on the extent to which these could be linked with MAPs. Differences occurred both across and within countries and depended on how the poor were defined and measured. While certain studies reported increases in poverty, particularly during the early stages of MAPs (ECLAC 1996; Stewart and Van der Geest 1995), World Bank studies showed that poverty was declining in countries undergoing adjustment (Jayarajah et al. 1996). Sahn and colleagues found not only that the poor did not suffer from the effects of MAPs, but also that their lives improved slightly. They analyzed 10 African countries and concluded that:

> ... reforms primarily hurt those who receive rents that arise when goods are rationed, benefit from guaranteed public employment, gain a disproportionate share of subsidies on poorly targeted public services, and profit from interference in agriculture and food markets. Africa's poor rarely belong to these groups. As a result, policies that reduce or eliminate these privileges in the name of economic efficiency are not usually prejudicial to the poor (Sahn et al. 1997, p. 247).

Others have indicated that MAPs created a new class of poor, the "adjustment poor," as opposed to the "chronic poor," who were poor before MAPs. The adjustment poor spurred the development of social funds (Cornia 2001). Eventually, the distinction between the two types of poor became blurred and the social funds required expansion because the chronic poor were being excluded from employment and welfare programs. Although debates continue regarding the impact of MAPs on the poor, whether pre-existing or newly created, it is clear that MAPs had a large influence on poverty through changes in employment policies (Gershman and Irwin 2000).

In many low-income countries, particularly in sub-Saharan Africa, agriculture was the most important employment sector during the 1980s (Basu and Stewart 1995). The informal sector played an increasingly important role in the 1980s and 1990s, providing an important refuge for people during times of economic crisis and restructuring. Following the implementation of MAPs, there were reports of declining wages and increasing levels of unemployment. For example, declining wages were observed in Latin America during the 1980s, and although they began to reverse in the 1990s, unemployment rates remained high (ILO

1991; Morley 1995). Using general equilibrium models, a multicase study on MAPs also noted increasing unemployment, to the extent that the number of unemployed would have tripled if people had not moved over to the informal sector (Bourguignon and Morrisson 1992). Changes in the workforce affect women in particular, in two ways. First, due to male bias in the labour market, women are more vulnerable to declining wages and loss of jobs (Elson 1992; Stewart 1992). Second, they are more likely to spend their time coping with reductions in household income and increasing health needs of family members. Many case studies demonstrated women not only continued their unpaid functions, such as domestic chores and care of family members, but also took on paid employment to supplement family income, often at the expense of abandoning educational goals (Garcia and Oliveira 1997; Gindling 1993; Lam and Levison 1997; Minujin 1992).

The effect of MAPs on education is also a controversial issue. It was argued that, as in the health sector, education was protected (Ferroni and Kanbur 1990; Sahn et al. 1997). However, others suggested that MAPs had negative impacts on the education sector (Reimers 1994; Reimers and Tiburcio 1993). Reimers (1994) argued that cuts in recurrent expenditures lessened the quality of education systems, thereby reducing demand for schooling. The combined effects of MAPs on the demand and supply of education reduced primary school enrolment rates, particularly among girls (Cornia et al. 1987; Jayarajah et al. 1996). Reimers (1994) noted that, at the primary level, enrolment rates were twice as high in non-adjusting than in adjusting countries, but that this trend was not found at secondary and tertiary levels. Grootaert (1994) underscored the importance of analyzing differences in area of residence, socioeconomic status, and gender when assessing the impact of adjustment on education. He studied the Ivory Coast, often cited as an example of a country that invested heavily in education and was superior to other countries in protecting this sector following adjustment. The analysis of household survey data between 1985 and 1988 indicated there were important inequalities in school enrolments. School attendance declined, but only among poor households, and particularly for girls, and in urban areas.

Declining participation of girls in the education system is particularly troublesome to the development community, because education of women is one of the key determinants of household health and a major contributor to lowering fertility rates (World Bank 1993). Education also improves women's chances of participating in stable and well paid jobs (Buchmann 1996). Removing girls from school became an important coping strategy for households under financial constraints, either because of increasing school fees or declining household incomes.

When school expenses increase dramatically (as government subsidies are eliminated), parents may decide to keep their daughters at home. If parents know that women have limited opportunities in the formal market, they may reason that the benefit of educating their daughters no longer outweighs the expense. Moreover, daughters may be kept at home to help with the increasing amount of household labour. Thus, household strategies to survive during periods of austerity may inhibit female access to education (Buchmann 1996, p. 8).

Supply-side effects of MAPs

Studying changes in public health expenditures was popular among researchers, particularly at the World Bank and IMF. These studies were facilitated by the relatively wide availability of this data (Costello et al. 1994). During the early 1980s, governments were supposed to cut expenditures, including health, to improve their economy. The World Bank suggested that these cuts would not necessarily be detrimental because a more efficient use of resources would improve health outcomes (Alderman and Lavy 1996; World Bank 1993). A number of authors pointed to a decline in public health expenditures following the adoption of MAPs during the 1980s (Cornia et al. 1987; Kanji et al. 1991; Stewart 1989; Woodward 1992). Others concluded that, in countries where public health expenditures declined, there was no evidence this was caused by budget cuts related to MAPs (Sahn 1992; Sahn and Bernier 1995; World Bank 1993).

Jayarajah and colleagues (1996) found that between 1980 and 1993, expenditures declined in most countries, although considerably less among the "good adjusters" compared to both non-adjusting countries and those that did not adjust properly. The World Bank argued that MAPs had evolved to consider social sectors, such that public health expenditures were protected during later generations (World Bank 1990). A study comparing health expenditures among non-adjusting and adjusting countries that differentiated "early" adjusters from others came to the same conclusion (Van der Gaag and Barham 1998). This study found that health expenditures declined more in adjusting countries than in non-adjusters during the 1980s, but that this was reversed during the 1990s. However, these results should be interpreted with caution, as the authors themselves mention their data was of poor quality. The evidence is conflicting across studies, and within studies there are differences across countries. Several explanations have been proposed, including government's level of commitment to protecting the health sector, the severity of the economic crisis, and the manner in which the MAPs were implemented (Breman and Shelton 2001).

The picture is clearer with respect to the impact of MAPs on the allocation of public health resources. Most studies, including those of the World Bank, concluded that MAPs did not improve allocative efficiency in the health sector. The World Bank observed that hospital care continued to receive the lion's share of health resources at the expense of primary care, even in countries where there was a decline in health-care expenditures (Jayarajah and Branson 1995). In the African context, Sahn and Bernier (1995, p. 254) concluded that "while not being able to resolve the accounting and definitional problems, our review of existing data paints a picture that despite the assertions of most governments, and years of engaging in structural adjustment, preventive and promotive care remains neglected at the expense of curative care." This is problematic because most of the health needs in the South, particularly among the poor, require primary health care.

Studies examining the supply of health services were overwhelmingly centred on health expenditures, with studies linking MAPs to access, utilization, and quality of health care being more rare. Two studies demonstrated associations between perceived declines in quality and the implementation of MAPs. One examined nurse professionalism, patient satisfaction, and quality of care in Zimbabwe following a structural adjustment program in 1991, and others demonstrated drops in utilization rates (Bassett et al. 1997). Bassett and colleagues conducted focus groups with nurses and with community members, in which there was consensus that people were dissatisfied with clinic service fees, drug shortages, and long waiting times for care. Although such problems were not new, the participants perceived a notable increase. There were also more conflicts between nurses and patients. Patients felt nurses were indifferent toward them, and nurses complained of being overworked and undervalued. The worsening patient–nurse relationship was clearer to patients than nurses. The authors argued that these conflicts were not created, but rather exacerbated, by adjustment.

Lundy (1996) examined the case of Jamaica, conducting semi-structured interviews with various health professionals, as well as clinic interviews, and surveying participants' observations of clinic conditions. Most described a deterioration of public health services, which they associated with Jamaica's debt crisis and specifically with MAP-related cuts to social expenditures. Although the departure of health personnel had already been problematic, this exodus intensified following adjustment. Informants observed that patients had become disillusioned with public services, complaining of longer waiting times and shortages of supplies. They also noted declining standards among health professionals and increasing environmental health risks. Bassett and Lundy documented important declines in quality of care, although it is difficult to ascertain the specific role of MAPs as opposed to economic crisis.

HEALTH SECTOR REFORM

Even if health sector reform does not include any "consistently applied, universal package of measures" (Haran 1998, p. 768), it generally comprises three core measures: financing reforms, decentralization, and integrating competition into the health sector (McPake and Machray 1997).[1] We examine each of these in turn, beginning with financing reforms, which have accumulated the most evidence thus far.

Financing reforms

Driven by a scarcity of resources in the health sector, governments faced the dilemma of how to provide adequate health services to their citizens. The solution proposed by the World Bank (1987) was to encourage governments to apply a user fee at the point of service delivery, both to increase revenue and to create a greater rationalization of services, because the cost would incite people to "think twice about demanding it" (Shaw and Griffin 1996). The World Bank further argued that cost recovery would improve equity because as the contributions of households (especially richer ones) increased, there would be more money in the system, making possible more and better services for all people, including the poor (Griffin 1992; World Bank 1993). The severity of the financial crisis in the health sector and, in certain cases, explicit loan conditions left governments little choice but to follow the route of cost recovery. In 1987, African Ministers of Health launched their own cost-recovery program, with the support of UNICEF and WHO, known as the Bamako Initiative (UNICEF 1992). This initiative sought to mobilize resources through community financing to improve primary health-care services and especially to ensure availability of essential drugs. The scarcity of resources for African health systems led UNICEF to campaign for a selective approach to primary health care, by improving people's health through a limited number of targeted interventions. UNICEF was criticized for following in the ideological footsteps of the World Bank, and it was argued that the Bamako Initiative undermined poor people's access to health services (Kanji 1989).

Before the merits of cost recovery had been sufficiently proven, however, governments across the developing world were implementing this policy. In 1997, over 30 African governments were operating cost-recovery programs (Watkins 1997). The hasty introduction of user fees raised concerns, particularly regarding equity (Gilson et al. 1995), and the dialogue became focused not on *whether* but on *how* user fees should be implemented. The vast array of practical cost-recovery experiences has provided fertile ground for testing the efficiency and equity claims made in the 1980s. These claims were based on a number of assumptions, of which the following four are most prominent.

Assumption 1: Demand for health care is price inelastic

Early World Bank proponents of user fees argued that the demand for health care was price inelastic, such that implementing or increasing costs did not deter people from using health services when in need (de Ferranti 1985; World Bank 1987). Since then studies, including those by the World Bank, have repeatedly demonstrated that demand for health care is in fact price elastic, especially among the poor (Creese 1994; de Béthune et al. 1989; Gertler and Van der Gaag 1990; Haddad and Fournier 1995; Mwabu and Wang'ombe 1995; Sauerborn et al. 1996; Sahn et al. 2003; Waddington and Enyimayew 1989; Yoder 1989). Studies of the demand for health care illustrated that user fees were sensitive to price, but other alternatives for increasing resources were scarce. Some authors proposed that the focus be shifted toward minimizing the regressive nature of cost recovery and, in particular, to improving quality (McPake 1993).

Assumption 2: User fees will be offset by improvements in quality

User fees were supposed to increase resources in the health sector that could subsequently be used to improve the range and quality of services (World Bank 1987). It was further argued that better quality of health care would lead to increased use of services, including among the poor (Alderman and Lavy 1996). A review of user charges noted that early studies largely ignored the question of quality, focusing instead on financial gains (McPake 1993). Later studies considering quality, notably the often-cited study by Litvack and Bodart (1993) in Cameroon, observed higher utilization when quality improvements accompanied the introduction of user fees. Some studies supported the notion that quality improvements can negate rising fees (Chawla and Ellis 2000; Diop et al. 1995; Knippenberg et al. 1997). Others, however, suggested the issue is more complex. For example, in a longitudinal study in Zaire, utilization rates declined by 40% within a five-year period, even with quality improvements (Haddad and Fournier 1995). Cost of care explained 18–32% of the drop.

Assumption 3: Exemption policies will be effective in practice

Effective exemption policies would ensure that the poor would not have to pay the full cost of care. Equity would improve because richer patients would subsidize the poor through user fees at public health-care facilities, thereby raising quality to the benefit of all users. Although many governments designed exemption policies, they were difficult to put into action (Kaddar et al. 1997). Administrative costs were high, and many countries had neither the capacity nor the political will to put in place exemption policies (Watkins 1997). More importantly, the systems were simply ineffective (Gilson and Mills 1995; Gilson et al. 1995; Watkins 1997). Exemptions were only weakly linked to the poverty status of users (Ensor and Bich San 1996; Newbrander et al. 2000; Nolan and Turbat 1995). For example, in Kenya, only 1–5% of users were exempted because of their poverty status, although 11–34% of the population fulfilled the criteria for exemption (Huber 1993). In a multi-country study, fees were not waived among the poor because either the poor were unaware of such waivers or an exemption system was not in place (Newbrander et al. 2000). Leakage also occurred, such that non-eligible users were being exempted (Gilson et al. 1995). For example, one study found the non-poor benefited from exemptions in 88% of cases in Senegal, 75% in Burkina Faso, and 73% in Niger (Leighton and Diop 1995). Thus, without effective exemption policies, gains in equity become illusory.

Assumption 4: People are willing to pay

Cost recovery relies on the principle that people are willing to pay for health services (Shaw and Griffin 1995). It was argued that people were already paying for health care, whether for private services or unofficial fees. Furthermore, studies indicated that people were willing to pay for health services if there were quality improvements and that utilization rates did not necessarily decline among the poor following the implementation of user fees and quality improvements. This was considered to be sufficient evidence that there were no equity trade-offs to cost recovery. There was, however, conceptual confusion between the concepts of willingness to pay and ability to pay (Russell 1996; Watkins 1997). Watkins (p. 14) observed that "markets do not reflect human need, but monetised consumer preference, as expressed through the price system." Russell urged that studies should analyze the impact of user fees not only on utilization, but also on household processes. This has been corroborated empirically. For example, a study in Vietnam concluded that "while charges may have a relatively small impact on current willingness to pay, they do have a substantial impact on income, wealth and the ability to pay for treatment in the future" (Ensor and Bich San 1996, p. 79).

In examining the equity impacts of user fees, the financial burden of care must also be considered. Studies have demonstrated that, in countries where no effective national health insurance system is in place, the poor have a greater financial burden of health care than the non-poor because they pay proportionately more of their household income for health care. In Vietnam, about 19% of household incomes of the very poor was allocated to health care, compared to almost 4% for the rich (Ensor and Bich San 1996). This phenomenon has been noted in a number of countries (Berman 1995; Fabricant et al. 1999; Pannarunothai and Mills 1997; Sen 1997).

Furthermore, studies have shown that user fees elicit household coping strategies that can be destructive to families, particularly over the long term. These include delaying or not seeking treatment, seeking informal care, or self-treatment (Sahn et al. 2003). Health services may be obtained at the expense selling off assets, removing children from school, reducing food consumption, or borrowing from friends and relatives. Gender-based coping strategies also contribute to increasing inequalities. During periods of financial stress, girls were more likely to be removed from school than boys (Buchman 1996). Also, women were more likely to take on employment to raise income for families, while continuing unpaid work, such as domestic chores, child rearing, and caring for family members who had fallen ill (Garcia and Oliveira 1997; Gindling 1993). Kanji emphasized that our understanding of user fees will depend on the questions asked. For example, "How much would you be willing to pay for an x% reduction in the risk of dying?" elicits different information than "How much can you afford to pay for a particular treatment without getting into debt or cutting down on your food bill?" (Kanji 1989, p. 118). To assess the full impact of user fees, studies must recognize "the multi-faceted nature of vulnerability and responses" (Watkins 1997, p. 15), by considering not only impacts on health-seeking behaviours, but also the concessions made by the poor to cope with costs.

In sum, cost recovery has not proven to be a panacea for cash-strapped health systems in poor countries. Equity and efficiency are current objectives in improving health-care systems, and access to health care for the poor is at the forefront of policy discussions (Kaddar et al. 1997). Certain governments are beginning to reverse the policy on cost recovery. For example, in 2001 the Ugandan government removed their cost-sharing program and supplemented the health budget with funds from a World Bank project (Burnham et al. 2004). Some argue that cost recovery remains essential but must be done humanely (Van der Geest et al. 2000), and others argue that cost recovery is simply not the best policy option for poor countries and that other financing mechanisms should be considered, such as community health insurance (Arhin-Tenkorang 2001).

Decentralization

According to Gilson and Mills "the main public sector organizational reform ... is the decentralization of planning and management, which aims to push responsibility for at least some decisions down the administrative hierarchy" (Gilson and Mills 1995, p. 292). The four main objectives of decentralization were to improve planning and management of services, to create a more effective and efficient organization of services, to increase accountability, and to encourage community participation in decision-making (Gilson and Mills 1995). Although not a new concept, decentralization received enormous support during the late 1980s and 1990s from donor institutions, including the World Bank, WHO, and USAID. Even if decentralization is purported to be inherently good, benefits remain for the most part speculative (Bossert 1998; Collins 1996). It is possible that decentralization merely provides a channel for central governments to shift financial and administrative burdens to lower levels because of limited resources at the national level (Sahn and Bernier 1995), as illustrated in Nicaragua (Birn et al. 2000).

Because decentralization involves reshaping institutional arrangements and redistributing powers and tasks within the health sector, it was difficult to link impacts with changes in access to and utilization of services (World Bank 1994b). Decentralization is best viewed as a complement to other reform measures, such as user fees and increased market competition. Although there are few studies linking decentralization with health system performance (Bossert 1998), various experiences with decentralization do offer lessons by highlighting problems and successes that arose in practice.

To ensure proper functioning and acceptance by health workers, roles and regulations related to decentralization must be clear. A review of 10 countries highlighted this as a problematic issue (Kolehmainen-Aitken 1998). The problem is amplified by the number of organizations involved. Larbi (1998) noted that the multiplicity of institutions involved in Ghana—Ministry of Health, Ministry of Finance, Auditor General, Bureau Chief, and Commission of Public Services—contributed to policy confusion, conflicts of authority, and other administrative problems and consequently led to only a partial decentralization. Conflicts also arose in Uganda between the Ministry of Health and district staff, particularly related to budget priorities (Jeppsson 2001). These conflicts were further exacerbated by conditions imposed on the districts by central government.

Decentralization also provoked resistance. In some countries, the Ministry of Health was less than enthusiastic, partly because this reform was externally imposed, entailing a shift in powers (Collins 1996). Health providers, such as hospitals and NGOs, also resisted coming under the control of districts or municipalities and losing privileges they had enjoyed under the Ministry of Health (Prud'homme 1995). In Nicaragua, the central government had to withdraw local control of five hospitals because of problems between hospital directors and local health authorities (Kolehmainen-Aitken 1998).

To improve efficiency, resources were to be decentralized to the periphery. However, political obstacles presented significant challenges to the equitable redistribution of resources. Also, many governments did not possess sufficient information to complete such transactions, nor were procedures, such as planning and budgeting, properly in place. Tanzania was a case in point, where communities continued to rely on central government funding after decentralization (Gilson et al. 1994). Decentralization in Papua New Guinea led to resources being allocated to economically and politically stronger regions (Campos-Outcalt et al. 1995). In contrast, decentralization in Bolivia resulted in the creation of 200 new municipalities that adopted a per capita formula for reallocating resources that enabled previously disadvantaged areas to receive more resources (Holley 1995).

Other important concerns continue to be raised about decentralization. Community participation, advocated by the World Bank (1994), was often a top-down process, such that formal consultations with communities were largely absent (Smithson et al. 1997). Decentralization also had negative impacts on human resources (Kolehmainen-Aitken 1998) and information systems, which were already ineffective in poor countries (Collins et al. 1999; Thomason et al. 1991). Studies are also emerging on experiments with autonomous hospitals, a form of decentralization in which hospitals are given greater authority to pursue their own goals (Collins et al. 1999).

In sum, although decentralization has had many proponents, concerns remain. In situations where reforms have led to lesser forms of decentralization, the question may not be whether to decentralize, but rather how to ensure that "whether or not authority and accountability for health services delivery are fully transferred to subnational levels, parallel changes in financing and organization must not be ignored" (Birn et al., p. 126).

Introducing and expanding competition

The World Bank encouraged reducing the role of the state and introducing competition into the health sector by expanding the private sector. This strategy is based on the belief that the market is a more efficient producer of goods and services.

For some health services provided by the public sector, the system of provision is so grossly inefficient that it is unlikely to be cost-effective no matter what interventions the system tries to provide. Such inefficiencies have been criticized so clearly and for so long that it is evident they will only be overcome by radical changes in the organization of the health care—such as a shift in the government's role from providing care to financing care and stimulating competition among providers (World Bank 1993, p. 65).

The World Bank also argued that private health expenditures were already high in the South and that many people would be willing to pay for better quality services in the private sector, freeing up resources for the poor. Unfortunately, a lack of even basic data, such as on levels and composition of private health care provision, has hampered a better understanding of the private sector in the South (Hanson and Berman 1998). Several authors point out the important and growing role of the private sector in many poor countries (Berman 1998; Bhat 1996; Gilson and Mills, 1995; Ogunbekun et al. 1999; Sahn and Bernier, 1995; World Bank, 1994b). Two types of privatization, passive (or incremental) and active, have been identified in the literature (Uplekar 2000). Passive privatization is largely unplanned and is a result of public sector failure, whereas active privatization is advanced by purposeful public policy. The deterioration of public health services in many countries has also contributed to more people seeking health care in the private sector, including the poor (Bloom and Lucas 2000; Bloom and Standing 2001).

A number of strategies have been used to stimulate private sector involvement, including subsidizing NGOs (Gilson et al. 1994; Laffont and Tirole 1993), contracting out (McPake and Ngalande-Banda 1994; Mills 1998), introduction of managed care (Iriart et al. 2001), integration into planning processes (Bennett et al. 1994; Larbi 1998); and institutional reforms (Bossert et al. 1998; PAHO 1998). There are few studies evaluating the impact of increased competition in the health sector on access and quality of care. Concerns have been raised about increasing private participation, particularly when this occurs rapidly without proper regulation in place.

These concerns may be illustrated by two examples from the literature. First, looking at countries that have integrated contracting, we consider the claim that there will be efficiency gains in the private sector. Second, we look at the quality of private provider practices in the management and treatment of tuberculosis (TB) in India. Such examples highlight the important counterbalancing role of regulation.

Governments can stimulate private sector involvement by contracting the services of private providers. In a study done in South Africa, Thailand, and China of contracting-out practices, efficiency gains were partially or completely offset by administrative costs (Mills 1998). Large transaction costs were also found in Chile and the Philippines, on the order of 30% and 45%, respectively (Tollman, Schopper, and Torres 1990).

Negotiating, preparing, and managing contracts also add to the strain on human resources, because these skills were not needed when health care was publicly provided (McPake and Ngalande-Banda 1994). It is not clear that public services are less efficient than private services. Mills (1998, p. 39) wrote that "it is far from self-evident that efforts to establish contracting will provide greater returns than efforts to improve public service provision." Transaction costs must also be included in any comparison of efficiency between the private and public sectors (Hsiao 1995).

The profit motive can encourage unethical practices of private providers (Bennett et al. 1994). Providers may cut costs by reducing quality of care, or create profits by doing more expensive tests. Uplekar (2000) provided an interesting example in his studies of private providers and tuberculosis (TB) in India. TB is manageable and curable if diagnosis is accurate and treatments closely monitored. There were positive observations, such as proximity of private providers to patients, patients' confidence in their providers, and acceptance of services despite costs. There were also a number of what Uplekar called "ignorant practices." For example, private providers tended to use X-rays instead of sputum examinations for testing, thereby increasing costs and reducing reliability of diagnosis. Many providers did not reveal the prognosis of TB to their patients. Many inappropriate and costly drugs were prescribed and follow-up with patients was minimal. Record-keeping was also not a strong point. There were discrepancies between provider advice and patient behaviors, and essential records were not kept. Uplekar also cited similar performance of providers in other countries. For example, in Korea, in a study of 923 private providers, 50% stated that sputum examinations were not essential, 75% said treatments did not need to be monitored, 73% gave non-recommended regimens, and 16% provided unacceptable regimens. It is clear that state involvement is required through regulative practices to discourage poor quality and unethical practices.

The state is recognized as playing an important role in addressing problems arising from market involvement, particularly through regulation (Söderlund and Tangcharoensathien 2000; World Bank 1997). Regulation involves control through either incentives or legal restrictions. However, even when regulations are in place, they are often outdated and rarely effective (Hongoro and Kumaranayake 2000; Kumaranayake 1997). In Zimbabwe and Tanzania, legislative regulation existed but important gaps remained, particularly related to consumer protection and development of new private markets (Kumaranayake et al. 2000).

In sum, despite increased marketization of the health sector, there is still no evidence that the private sector is more efficient. Furthermore, marketization has rarely been accompanied by effective regulation, thereby failing to protect patients, particularly the poor, from inappropriate care. More resources are needed to improve regulatory practices to keep up with the growing private sector (Kumaranayake 1997).

CONCLUSION

Improving health sectors in the South remains a critical issue for the 21st century. The 1990s produced a vast number of publications but, curiously, attention has since waned even as more data become available and better tools are developed for evaluating macroeconomic and sectoral policies. One editorial stated that "it seems as if the academic community lost interest in writing about health sector reform at about the same time that it became possible to study its results" (Blas and Hearst 2002, p. 2). Many questions remain in understanding the full impact of MAPs on the health sector, although certain knowledge gaps are perhaps more pressing. Sen and Koivusalo summarized a number of priority issues:

> It is important to develop case studies from different regions of the world allowing comparison of the processes and possible impacts of changes upon vulnerable groups and health systems as a whole. In view of the evidence already emerging, there is also a need to support evaluations and descriptive studies of process rather than focusing on single measures of outcomes such as clinic attendance, drug availability or waiting times, in order to assess the overall impact of these changes. Furthermore, the cumulative effects of these changes need to be better understood. More information is needed on the meso and macro-level impacts of the reforms on health systems development, as well as on micro level impacts at the household level, analysed by gender and socio-economic status over a long-term perspective (Sen and Koivusalo 1998, pp. 209–210).

Two areas for further study would be the differential impact of reforms on rural and urban areas with respect to issues such as ability to pay and use of services and the impact of reforms on indigenous populations.

The MAPHealth initiative grew out of a need to gather stronger evidence on the impacts of reforms driven by macroeconomic instability. Protecting the health sector requires a better understanding of how health systems are influenced by factors within and external to the health sector at both national and international levels. Insights gained from the experiences of countries undergoing macroeconomic and health reforms are a valuable resource for policymakers, international donors, and civil society, by highlighting which policies are most equitable and effective in turbulent economies.

Note

1. Other authors have provided further breakdowns of reform measures. See especially Cassels (1995).

References

Abbasi, K. 1999. The World Bank and world health: interview with Richard Feachem. British Medical Journal, 318, 1206–1208.

Alderman, H.; Lavy, V. 1996. Household responses to public health services: cost and quality tradeoffs. The World Bank Research Observer, 11(1), 3–22.

Anand, S.; Chen, L. 1996. Health implications of economic policies: a framework of analysis. Discussion paper series, no. 3. United Nations Development Program, Office of Development Studies, New York, NY, USA. 34 pp.

Arhin-Tenkorang, D. 2001. Mobilizing resources for health: the case for user fees revisited. CID Working paper no. 81. Center for International Development (CID), Harvard University, Cambridge, MA, USA. 21 pp.

Banerji, D. 1994. A simplistic approach to health policy analysis: the World Bank team on the Indian health sector. International Journal of Health Services, 24(1), 151–159.

Bassett, M.T.; Bijlmakers, L.; Sanders, D.M. 1997. Professionalism, patient satisfaction and quality of health care: experience during Zimbabwe's structural adjustment programme. Social Science and Medicine, 45(12), 1845–1852.

Basu, A.; Stewart, F. 1995. Structural adjustment policies and the poor in Africa: an analysis of the 1980s. In Stewart, F., ed., Adjustment and poverty: options and choices. Routledge, London, UK. pp. 138–170.

Bennett, S.; Dakpallah, G.; Garner, P.; Gilson, L.; Nittayaramphong, S.; Zurita, B.; Zwi, A. 1994. Carrot and stick: state mechanisms to influence private provider behaviour. Health Policy and Planning, 9(1), 1–13.

Berman, P.A. 1995. Health sector reform: making health development sustainable. *In* Berman, P.A., ed., Health sector reform in developing countries: making health development sustainable. Harvard University Press, Boston, MA, USA. pp. 13–36.

_____ 1998. Rethinking health care systems: private health care provision in India. World Development, 26(8), 1463–1479.

Bhat, R. 1996. Regulation of the private health sector in India. International Journal of Health Planning and Management, 11(3), 253–274.

Birdsall, N.; Hecht, R. 1995. Swimming against the tide: strategies for improving equity in health. Inter-American Development Bank, Human Resources Development and Operations Policy (HRO), Washington, DC, USA. 23 pp.

Birn, A.; Zimmerman, S.; Garfield, R. 2000. To decentralize or not to decentralize, is that the question? Nicaraguan health policy under structural adjustment in the 1990s. International Journal of Health Services, 30(1), 111–128.

Blas, E.; Hearst, N. 2002. Health sector reform and equity – learning from evidence? Health Policy and Planning, 17, 1–4.

Bloom, G.; Lucas, H. 2000. Health and poverty in sub-Saharan Africa. IDS Working Paper no. 103, Institute of Development Studies, Brighton, UK. 44 pp.

Bloom, G.; Standing, H. 2001. Pluralism and marketisation in the health sector: meeting health needs in contexts of social change in low and middle income countries. IDS Working Paper no. 136, Institute of Development Studies, Brighton, UK. 36 pp.

Bossert, T. 1998. Analyzing the decentralization of health systems in developing countries: decision space, innovation and performance. Social Science and Medicine, 47(10), 1513–1527.

Bossert, T.; Hsiao, W.; Barrera, M.; Alarcon, L.; Leo, M.; Casares, C. 1998. Transformation of ministries of health in the era of health reform: the case of Colombia. Health Policy and Planning, 13(1), 59–77.

Bourguignon, F.; Morrisson, C. 1992. Adjustment and equity in developing countries: a new approach. Development Centre of the Organisation for Economic Co-operation and Development. OECD Publications and Information Centre, Washington, DC, USA. 111 pp.

Breman, A.; Shelton, C. 2001. Structural adjustment and health: a literature review of the debate, its role-players and presented empirical evidence. Commission on Macroeconomics and Health (CMH), Working Paper Series, no. WG6:6, World Health Organization, Cambridge, MA, USA. 53 pp.

Buchmann, C. 1996. The debt crisis, structural adjustment and women's education: implications for status and social development. International Journal of Comparative Sociology, 37, 5–30.

Burnham, G.M.; Pariyo, G.; Galiwango, E.; Wabwire-Mangen, F. 2004. Discontinuation of cost sharing in Uganda. Bulletin of the World Health Organization, 82(3), 187–195.

Campos-Outcalt, D.; Kewa, K.; Thomason, J. 1995. Decentralization of health services in Western Highlands Province, Papua New Guinea: an attempt to administer health service at the subdistrict level. Social Science and Medicine, 40(8), 1091–1098.

Chawla, M.; Ellis, R.P. 2000. The impact of financing and quality changes on health care demand in Niger. Health Policy and Planning, 15(1), 76–84.

Collins, C. 1996. Decentralization. *In* Janovsky, K., ed., Health policy and systems development: an agenda for research. World Health Organization, Geneva, Switzerland. pp. 161–178.

Collins, C.; Green, A.; Hunter, D. 1999. Health sector reform and the interpretation of policy context. Health Policy, 47(1), 69–83.

Cornia, G.A. 2001. Social funds in stabilization and adjustment programmes: a critique. Development and Change, 32, 1–32.

Cornia, G. A.; Jolly, R.; Stewart, F., ed. 1987. Adjustment with a human face. Clarendon Press, Oxford, UK. 340 pp.

Cornia, G.A.; van der Hoeven, R.; Mkandawire, T. 1992. Africa's recovery in the 1990s: from stagnation and adjustment to human development. St. Martin's Press, New York, NY, USA. 375 pp.

Cornu, A.; Massamba, J.P.; Traissac, P.; Simondon, F.; Villeneuve, P.; Delpeuch, F. 1995. Nutritional change and economic crisis in an urban Congolese community. International Journal of Epidemiology, 24(1), 155–164.

Costello, A.; Watson, F.; Woodward, D. 1994. Human face or human facade? Adjustment and the health of mothers and children. Centre for International Child Health, Institute of Child Health, London, UK. 68 pp.

Creese, A.L. 1994. User charges for health care: a review of recent experience. Health Policy and Planning, 6(4), 309–319.

de Béthune, X.; Alfani, S.; Lahaye, J.P. 1989. The influence of an abrupt price increase on health service utilization: evidence from Zaire. Health Policy and Planning, 4(1), 76–81.

de Ferranti, D. 1985. Paying for health services in developing countries: an overview. Staff Working Paper no. 721. World Bank, Washington, DC, USA. 140 pp.

Diop, F.; Yazbeck, A.; Bitran, R. 1995. The impact of alternative cost recovery schemes on access and equity in Niger. Health Policy and Planning, 10(3), 223–240.

ECLAC (Economic Commission for Latin America and the Caribbean). 1996. Preliminary overview of the economy of Latin America and the Caribbean 1996. United Nations, Santiago, Chile. 53 pp.

Elson, D. 1992. From survival strategies to transformation strategies: women's needs and structural adjustment. In Beneria, L.; Feldman, S., ed., Unequal burden: economic crises, persistent poverty, and women's work. Westview Press, Boulder, CO, USA. pp. 26–49.

Ensor, T.; Bich San, P. 1996. Access and payment for health care: the poor of northern Vietnam. International Journal of Health Planning and Management, 11(1), 69–83.

Evans, R.; Barer, M. 1994. Producing health, consuming health care. In Evans, R.; Barer, M.; Marmor, T., ed., Why are some people healthy and others not? The determinants of health of populations. Aldine de Gruyter, New York, NY, USA. pp. 27–66.

Fabricant, S.J.; Kamara, C.W.; Mills, A. 1999. Why the poor pay more: household curative expenditures in rural Sierra Leone. International Journal of Health Planning and Management, 14(4), 179–199.

Ferroni, M.; Kanbur, R. 1990. Poverty-conscious restructuring of public expenditures. Working Paper no. 9, Social Dimensions of Adjustment and Development Unit, Africa Technical Unit. World Bank, Washington, DC, USA. 34 pp.

Fournier, P.; Haddad, S.; Mantoura, P. 2001. Réformes des systèmes de santé dans les pays en développement : l'irrésistible emprise des agences internationales et les dangers de la pensée unique. *In* Rainhorn, J.; Burnier, M., ed., La santé au risque du marché. Incertitudes à l'aube du XXIe siècle. Presses Universitaires de France, Paris, France. pp. 71–84.

Garcia, G.; Oliveira, O. 1997. Economic recession and changing determinants of women's work. *In* Tapinos, G.; Mason, A.; Bravo, J., ed., Demographic responses to economic adjustment in Latin America. Clarendon Press, Oxford, UK. pp. 229–251.

Garenne, M.G.; Gakusi, E. 2000. Health effects of structural adjustment programs in sub-Saharan Africa. Working paper, French Center for Population and Development Studies (CEPED), Paris, France. 26 pp.

Gershman, J.; Irwin, A. 2000. Getting a grip on the global economy. *In* Irwin, A.; Kim, J.Y.; Gershman, J.; Millen, J.V., ed., Dying for growth: global inequality and the health of the poor. Common Courage Press, Monroe, ME, USA. pp. 11–43.

Gertler, P.; Van der Gaag, J. 1990. The willingness to pay for medical care: evidence from two developing countries. Johns Hopkins University Press, Baltimore, MD, USA. 139 pp.

Gilson, L.; Kilima, P.; Tanner, M. 1994. Local government decentralization and the health sector in Tanzania. Public Administration and Development, 14, 451–477.

Gilson, L.; Mills, A. 1995. Health sector reforms in sub-Saharan Africa: lessons of the last 10 years. *In* Berman, P.A., ed., Health sector reform in developing countries: making health development sustainable. Harvard University Press, Boston, MA, USA. pp. 277–316.

Gilson, L.; Russell, S.; Buse, K. 1995. The political economy of user fees with targeting: developing equitable health financing policy. Journal of International Development, 7(3), 369–402.

Gilson, L.; Sen, P.D.; Mohammed, S.; Mujinja, P. 1994. The potential of health sector non-governmental organizations: policy options. Health Policy and Planning, 9(1), 14–24.

Gindling, T.H. 1993. Women's wages and economic crisis in Costa Rica. Economic Development and Cultural Change, 41(2), 277–297.

Griffin, C. 1992. Welfare gains from user charges for government health services. Health Policy and Planning, 7(2), 177–180.

Grootaert, C. 1994. Education, poverty, and structural change in Africa: lessons from Côte d'Ivoire. International Journal of Educational Development, 14(2), 131–142.

Haddad, S.; Fournier, P. 1995. Quality, cost and utilization of health services in developing countries. A longitudinal study in Zaire. Social Science and Medicine, 40(6), 743–753.

Hanson, K.; Berman, P. 1998. Private health care provision in developing countries: a preliminary analysis of levels and consumption. Health Policy and Planning, 13(3), 195–211.

Haran, D. 1998. Health sector reform. Journal of Epidemiology and Community Health, 52(12), 768–769.

Holley, J. 1995. Estudio de descentralización de la gestion de los servicios de salud. Territorio de Capinota, Bolivia. Latin American Health and Nutrition Sustainability Project. University Research Corporation, Washington, DC, USA.

Hongoro, C.; Kumaranayake, L. 2000. Do they work? Regulating for-profit providers in Zimbabwe. Health Policy and Planning, 15(4), 368–377.

Hsiao, W.C. 1995. Abnormal economics in the health sector. In Berman, P.A., ed., Health sector reform in developing countries: making health development sustainable. Harvard University Press, Boston, MA, USA. pp. 161–179.

Husain, I. 1994. Structural adjustment and long-term development in sub-Saharan Africa. In van de Hoeven, R.; van de Kraaij, F., ed., Structural adjustment and beyond in sub-Saharan Africa: research and policy issues. James Curry, London, UK. 290 pp.

ILO (International Labour Organization). 1991. Employment policies in the economic restructuring of Latin America and the Caribbean. Tripartite Symposium on Structural Adjustment and Employment in Latin America and the Caribbean. WEP 1-4-07 (Doc. 2), Geneva, Switzerland.

Iriart, C.; Merhy, E.E.; Waitzkin, H. 2001. Managed care in Latin America: the new common sense in health policy reform. Social Science and Medicine, 52(8), 1243–1253.

Jayarajah, C.; Branson, W. 1995. Structural and sectoral adjustment: World Bank experience, 1980–92. World Bank, Washington, DC, USA. 358 pp.

Jayarajah, C.; Branson, W.; Sen, B. 1996. Social dimensions of adjustment: World Bank experience, 1980–93. Operations Evaluation Division, World Bank, Washington, DC, USA. 218 pp.

Jeppsson, A. 2001. Financial priorities under decentralization in Uganda. Health Policy and Planning, 16(2), 187–192.

Kaddar, M.; Schmidt-Ehry, B.; Stierle, F.; Tchicaya, A. 1997. Indigence et accès aux soins de santé en Afrique sub-saharienne: situation et perspective d'action. Gesellschaft für Technische Zusammenarbeit (GTZ), Eschborn, Germany. 65 pp.

Kakwani, N. 1995. Structural adjustment and performance in living standards in developing countries. Development and Change, 26(3), 469–502.

Kanji, N. 1989. Charging for drugs in Africa: UNICEF's Bamako Initiative. Health Policy and Planning, 4(2), 110–120.

Kanji, N.; Kanji, N.; Manji, F. 1991. From development to sustained crisis: structural adjustment, equity and health. Social Science and Medicine, 33(9), 985–993.

Kjellstrom, T.; Koplan, J.P.; Rothenberg, R.B. 1992. Current and future determinants of adult ill-health. In Feachem, R.G.A.; Kjellstrom, T.; Murray, C.J.L.; Over, M.; Philips, M.A., ed., The health of adults in the developing world. Oxford University Press, New York, NY, USA. pp. 209–260.

Knippenberg, R.; Reinke, W.; Hopwood, I. 1997. Sustainability of primary health care including expanded program of immunizations in Bamako Initiative programs in West Africa: an assessment of 5 years' field experience in Benin and Guinea. International Journal of Health Planning and Management, 12(suppl.), S9–S28.

Kolehmainen-Aitken, R.-L. 1998. Decentralization and human resources: implications and impact. Human Resource Development Journal, 2(1), 1–16.

Kumaranayake, L. 1997. The role of regulation: influencing private sector activity within health sector reform. Journal of International Development, 9(4), 641–649.

Kumaranayake, L.; Lake, S.; Mujinja, P.; Hongoro, C.; Mpembeni, R. 2000. How do countries regulate the health sector? Evidence from Tanzania and Zimbabwe. Health Policy and Planning, 15(4), 357–367.

Laffont, J.-J.; Tirole, J. 1993. A theory of incentives in procurement and regulation. MIT Press, Cambridge, MA, USA. 705 pp.

Lam, D.; Levison, D. 1997. Structural adjustment and family labour supply in Latin America. In Tapinos, G.; Mason, A.; Bravo, J., ed., Demographic responses to economic adjustments in Latin America. Clarendon Press, Oxford, UK, pp. 201–228.

Larbi, G.A. 1998. Institutional constraints and capacity issues in decentralizing management in public services: the case of health in Ghana. Journal of International Development, 10(3), 377–386.

Laurell, A.C.; Arellano, O.L. 1996. Market commodities and poor relief: the World Bank proposal for health. International Journal of Health Services, 26(1), 1–18.

Lavy, V.; Germain, J.-M. 1994. Quality and cost in health care choice in developing countries. Living Standards Measurement Study, Working Paper no. 105. World Bank, Washington, DC, USA. 48 pp.

Leighton, C.; Diop, F. 1995. Protecting the poor in Africa – impact of means testing on equity in the health sector in Burkina Faso, Niger, and Senegal. Health Financing and Sustainability (HFS) Project, Abt Associates Inc., Bethesda, MD, USA. 29 pp.

Litvack, J.I.; Bodart, C. 1993. User fees plus quality equals improved access to health care: results of a field experiment in Cameroon. Social Science and Medicine, 37(3), 369–383.

Loewenson, R. 1993. Structural adjustment and health policy in Africa. International Journal of Health Services, 23(4), 717–730.

_____ 1994. World Bank policy and health policy in Africa. Paper presented at the Economic Policy and Health Network Conference, 27–29 June 1994, Johannesburg, South Africa, 12 pp.

Lundy, P. 1996. Limitations of quantitative research in the study of structural adjustment. Social Science and Medicine, 42(3), 313–324.

McPake, B. 1993. User charges for health services in developing countries: a review of the economic literature. Social Science and Medicine, 36(11), 1397–1405.

McPake, B.; Machray, C. 1997. International comparisons of health sector reform: towards a comparative framework for developing countries. Journal of International Development, 9(4), 621–630.

McPake, B.; Ngalande-Banda, E. 1994. Contracting out of health services in developing countries. Health Policy and Planning, 9(1), 25–30.

Minujin, A. 1992. From "secondary workers" to breadwinners: poor and non-poor women facing the crisis. Paper presented at the IUSSP (International Union for the Scientific Study of Population) Seminar on Demographic Consequences of Structural Adjustment in Latin America, 29 September – 2 October 1992, Ouro Preto, Brazil.

Mills, A. 1998. To contract or not to contract? Issues for low and middle income countries. Health Policy and Planning, 13(1), 32–40.

Mohindra, K. 1999. Socio-economic determinants of child growth in five developing countries: implications for health and development. Unpublished MSc. thesis. University of Northern British Colombia, Department of Community Health Science, Prince George, BC, Canada. 112 pp.

Morley, S.A. 1995. Poverty and inequality in Latin America: the impact of adjustment and recovery in the 1980s. Johns Hopkins University Press, Baltimore, MD, USA. 222 pp.

Musgrove, P. 1986. The impact of the economic crisis on health and health care in Latin America and the Caribbean. WHO Chronicle, 40(4), 152–157.

Mwabu, G.; Wang'ombe, J. 1995. User charges in Kenya: health service pricing reforms in Kenya: 1989–93. International Health Policy Program, Washington, DC, USA. 16 pp.

Newbrander, W.; Collins, D.; Gilson, L. 2000. Ensuring equal access to health services: user fee systems and the poor. Management Sciences for Health, Boston, MA, USA. 187 pp.

Nolan, B.; Turbat, V. 1995. Cost recovery in public health services in sub-Saharan Africa. EDI Technical Materials Report no. 14520, World Bank, Washington, DC., USA. 118 pp.

Ogunbekun, I.; Ogunbekun, A.; Orobaton, N. 1999. Private health care in Nigeria: walking the tightrope. Health Policy and Planning, 14(2), 174–181.

PAHO (Pan American Health Organization). 1998. The response of the health systems. *In* Health in the Americas. PAHO, Washington, DC, USA. pp. 210–337.

Pannarunothai, S.; Mills, A. 1997. The poor pay more: health-related inequality in Thailand. Social Science and Medicine, 44(12), 1781–1790.

Peabody, J.W. 1996. Economic reform and health sector policy: lessons from structural adjustment programs. Social Science and Medicine, 43(5), 823–35.

Prud'homme, R. 1995. The dangers of decentralization. The World Bank Research Observer, 10(2), 201–220.

Reimers, F. 1994. Education and structural adjustment in Latin America and sub-Saharan Africa. International Journal of Educational Development, 14(2), 119–129.

Reimers, F.; Tiburcio, L. 1993. Education, adjustment and reconstruction: options for change. UNESCO, Paris, France. 116 pp.

Russell, S. 1996. Ability to pay for health care: concepts and evidence. Health Policy and Planning, 11(3), 219–237.

Sahn, D.E. 1992. Public expenditures in sub-Saharan Africa during a period of economic reform. World Development, 20(5), 673–693.

Sahn, D.E.; Bernier, R. 1995. Has structural adjustment led to health sector reform in Africa? *In* Berman, P.A., ed., Health sector reform in developing countries: making health development sustainable. Harvard University Press, Boston, MA, USA. pp. 247–275.

Sahn, D.E.; Dorosh, P.; Younger, S. 1997. Structural adjustment reconsidered: economic policy and poverty in Africa. Cambridge University Press, New York, NY, USA. 304 pp.

Sahn, D.E.; Younger, S.D.; Genicot, G. 2003. The demand for health care services in rural Tanzania. Oxford Bulletin of Economics and Statistics, 65(2), 241–260.

Sauerborn, R.; Nougtara, A.; Hein, M.; Diesfeld, H.J. 1996. Seasonal variations of household costs of illness in Burkina Faso. Social Science and Medicine, 43(3), 281–290.

Schoepf, B.G.; Schoepf, C.; Millen, J. 2000. Theoretical therapies, remote remedies: SAPs and the political ecology of poverty and health in Africa. In Irwin, A.; Kim, J.Y.; Gershman, J.; Millen, J.V., ed., Dying for growth: global inequality and the health of the poor. Common Courage Press, Monroe, ME, USA. pp. 91–125.

Sen, B. 1997. Health and poverty in the context of country development strategy: a case study on Bangladesh. Macroeconomics, Health and Development Series, no. 26. World Health Organization, Geneva, Switzerland. 25 pp.

Sen, K.; Koivusalo, M. 1998. Health care reforms and developing countries – a critical overview. International Journal of Health Planning and Management, 13, 199–215.

Shaw, R.P.; Griffin, C.C. 1995. Financing health care in sub-Saharan Africa through user fees and insurance. World Bank, Washington, DC, USA. 99 pp.

Simms, C.; Rowson, M.; Peattie, S. 2001. The bitterest pill of all: the collapse of Africa's health systems. Medact and Save the Children Fund, London, UK. 27 pp.

Smithson, P.; Asamoa-Baah; Mills, A. 1997. The case of the health sector in Ghana experience. University of Birmingham Series, The role of government in adjusting economies, Paper 26. University of Birmingham, Birmingham, UK. 48 pp.

Söderlund, N.; Tangcharoensathien, V. 2000. Health sector regulation – understanding the range of responses from government. Health Policy and Planning, 15(4), 347–348.

Stewart, F. 1989. Recession, structural adjustment and infant health: the need for a human face. Transactions of the Royal Society of Tropical Medicine and Hygiene, 83, 30–31.

_____ 1992. Can adjustment programmes incorporate the interests of women? In Afshar, H.; Dennis, C., ed., Women and adjustment policies in the Third World. Macmillan, Hong Kong. 291 pp.

Stewart, F.; Van de Geest, W. 1995. Adjustment and social funds: political panacea or effective poverty reduction? In Stewart, F., ed., Adjustment and poverty: options and choices. Routledge, New York, NY, USA. pp. 108–137.

Tardanico, R.; Larín, R.M. 1997. Global restructuring, employment and social inequality in urban Latin America. North-South Center Press, Coral Gables, FL, USA. 320 pp.

Tollman, S.; Schopper, D.; Torres, A. 1990. Health maintenance organizations in developing countries: what can we expect? Health Policy and Planning, 5(2), 149–160.

Turshen, M. 1999. Privatizing health services in Africa. Rutgers University Press, Piscataway, NJ, USA. 200 pp.

Uplekar, M.W. 2000. Private health care. Social Science and Medicine, 51(16), 897–904.

UNICEF. 1984. The state of the world's children, 1984. Oxford University Press, New York, NY, USA. 126 pp.

_____ 1992. The Bamako Initiative: progress report, UNICEF Executive Board 1992 session. E/ICEF/1992/L.6, 3 February 1992. UNICEF, New York, NY, USA. 40 pp.

Van der Gaag, J.; Barham, T. 1998. Health and health expenditures in adjusting and non-adjusting countries. Social Science and Medicine, 46(8), 995–1009.

Van der Geest, S.; Macwan'gi, M.; Kamwanga, J.; Mulikelela, D.; Mazimba, A.; Mwangelwa, M. 2000. User fees and drugs: what did the health reforms in Zambia achieve? Health Policy and Planning, 15(1), 59–65.

Wagstaff, A. 2001. Poverty and health. Commission on Macroeconomics and Health Working Paper no. WG1:5. World Health Organization, Geneva, Switzerland. 52 pp.

Waddington, C.; Enyimayew, K. 1989. A price to pay. Part 1: the impact of user charges in Ashatin-Akim district, Ghana. International Journal of Health Planning and Management, 4, 17–47.

Watkins, K. 1997. Cost-recovery and equity in the health sector: issues for developing countries. Paper presented at World Institute for Development Economics Research (WIDER) Project on Provision and Financing of Public Goods in Developing Countries,

27 February 1997, London, UK. Oxfam, Oxford, UK, and Ireland Policy Department. 31 pp.

Woodward, D. 1992. Debt, adjustment and poverty in developing countries: national and international dimensions of debt and adjustment in developing countries, vol. 1. Save the Children Foundation (SCF) and Pinter Publishers, London, UK. 300 pp.

World Bank. 1987. Financing health services in developing countries: an agenda for reform. World Bank, Washington, DC, USA. 108 pp.

_____ 1990. World development report 1990: poverty. Oxford University Press, New York, NY, USA. 272 pp.

_____ 1993. World development report: investing in health. Report no. 12183. Washington, DC, USA. 344 pp.

_____ 1994a. Adjustment in Africa: reforms, results, and the road ahead. Oxford University Press, New York, NY, USA. 304 pp.

_____ 1994b. Better health in Africa: experience and lessons learned. Report no. 13488. World Bank, Washington, DC, USA. 304 pp.

_____ 1996. World development report: from plan to market. Report no. 15892. World Bank, Washington, DC, USA. 260 pp.

_____ 1997. World development report: the state in a changing world. Oxford University Press, New York, NY. 354 pp.

Yach, D.; von Schirnding, Y.E.R. 1994. Towards a higher priority for health on the development agenda. Public Health Review, 22, 339–374.

Yoder, R.A. 1989. Are people willing and able to pay for health services? Social Science and Medicine, 29(1), 35–42.

CHAPTER 3

Methodological Issues in Evaluating Public Policy

Slim Haddad, Enis Barış, and the MAPHealth team:
Katherine S. Mohindra, Delampady Narayana, Jeannie Haggerty, Luis
Durán, Stephen K. Chandiwana, Francisco José Yepes, Sanguan
Nittayaramphong, Adrien Nougtara, Barthélémy Kuate Defo

INTRODUCTION

Producing a solid base of factual evidence to use in assessing the impacts of reforms and adjustment policies is a complex undertaking fraught with difficulties. These have to do mainly with the attribution, in an uncontrolled context, of cause–effect relationships between public interventions and dimensions of health and well-being that are themselves the products of multiple processes. There are also difficulties inherent in isolating the interventions from their presumed consequences, as well as in generalizing observations from very specific contexts and environments. The issue of methodology is therefore central to any evaluation of public policy. There would no doubt be considerable divergence of opinion on the social consequences of structural adjustment even without these difficulties, although the terms of the debate would probably be greatly simplified.

Before introducing the MAPHealth project, we review briefly, in the following section, the methodological approaches currently used to evaluate the effects of macroeconomic adjustment on the health-care sector.[1] We then examine the challenges in identifying counterfactual situations and in choosing appropriate measurement tools for evaluating the impacts of public policies. We draw lessons in methodology from studies carried out over the past 15 years on the effects on health of structural adjustment that inform and enrich the final design and methodology of the MAPHealth project, as described in the latter part of the chapter.

STUDYING THE RELATIONSHIPS BETWEEN ADJUSTMENT AND HEALTH

Studies on structural adjustment policies in relation to health have been carried out in single as well as multiple countries, with single-country studies being more frequent. Table 1 presents the main features of each approach and the elements that may vary among studies. For each type, examples are drawn from the literature. Single case studies are often based on before–after approaches, i.e., pretest–posttest non-experimental designs, and some use simulation approaches based on modeling techniques such as CGE (computable general equilibrium). Interrupted time series are eventually part of the analyses. Both primary and secondary data may be used, and we found an increasing use of primary data in the later 1990s. Some surveys, such as Patricia Lundy's (1996) in Jamaica, use qualitative approaches, employing semi-structured interviews and participant observation to assess the quality of health-care services. A well-known case study in Zimbabwe used complex, multiple methods that combined quantitative and qualitative data with household and clinic data (Bijlmakers et al. 1998).

In multiple-country studies, there are many factors to be considered, including the number of countries, the specificity of each case, and the types of generalizations that can be made. For this discussion, we have categorized multiple-country studies into two types. The first, Type I, compare outcomes levels between adjusting and non-adjusting countries. Typically, a limited number of outcomes is examined among a large number of countries. The evaluation is broad, in that it does not look at specific policies or macroeconomic measures, but at adjustment policies as a whole.

TABLE 1. COMPARISON OF RESEARCH APPROACHES

Approach	Typical features	Differences among studies	Examples
Case study	Before–after Primary and secondary data Quantitative and/or qualitative Several specific outcomes Sponsored by international organizations, universities Low to high cost	Use of modeling and econometric tools (e.g. CGE – computable general equilibrium)	Bijlmakers, Bassett, Sanders 1996 Cornu 1995 Lundy 1996
Multiple country studies Type I	With–without Posttest-only designs Secondary data from countries and IFI sources Quantitative Limited number of outcomes Sponsored by IFIs Low cost	Number of countries Regional diversity Statistical tools Outcome types	Garenne and Gakusi 2000 Jayarajah et al. 1996 Kakwani 1995 Makinen et al. 2000 Mwabu 1996 Noorbakhsh 1998 Van der Gaag and Barham 1998
Multiple country studies Type II	Shared methodology between countries Complex designs Primary and secondary data Quantitative and qualitative Multiple outcomes Sponsored by international organizations, universities Large teams High cost	Number of countries Regional diversity Use of qualitative techniques Level and type of collaboration between teams Household surveys Health facility surveys	Bourguignon and Morrisson 1992 Hanson 1999 Newbrander et al. 2000 Reed 1999 Sahn et al. 1997

Based on posttest-only designs, these studies draw upon secondary data taken mostly from international financial institution (IFI) sources. These are low-cost studies conducted by individuals or single teams from IFIs, other organizations, or universities. Often, they aggregate countries from widely divergent contexts, making generalizations difficult. Typical studies of this approach include Mwabu's (1996) cross-country regression analysis of 103 countries. The author used aggregated household data from the

World Bank, the International Monetary Fund (IMF), and the United Nations, performing econometric estimations to complete missing data from these sources. Four outcome variables were included in the analysis: life expectancy, child mortality, infant mortality, and maternal mortality. Another example is Van der Gaag and Barham's (1998) study of health and health expenditures in adjusting and non-adjusting developing countries.

Type II multiple-case studies also compare countries but adopt a different approach. These studies have a smaller number of cases (each country being a case) but analyses are more in-depth, and specific aspects of public policies are analyzed. Methodologies are often multiple and more complex than Type I studies. Study designs are shared by the cases, and efforts are made to compile and synthesize results. These studies often rely on before–after observations, collecting primary as well as secondary data. Extensive investments in time and money are needed, particularly for initiatives involving a high level of country collaboration. Country teams often conduct their own research, with the assistance of a technical advisory committee. The topics covered are variable. For example, Sahn and his colleagues (1997) examined trade, exchange rate, fiscal, and agricultural policy outcomes related to macroeconomic adjustment policies (MAPs) among 10 African countries, using CGE modeling. A study by UNICEF coordinated an eight-country team effort to examine health sector reform in Africa, where teams used qualitative approaches (Hanson 1999). Reed's comparative survey (1999) estimated structural adjustment impacts on the environment. These three studies resulted in in-depth analysis of a relatively small number of cases that synthesized results and extracted common policy lessons. Other examples include a study of user fees and access to health care among five countries, using a common methodology under the guidance of a technical advisory committee (Newbrander et al. 2000). This study also demonstrated the inter-country variation and the role of local context, while providing a synthesis of results and policy recommendations.

ESTIMATING FACTS AND COUNTERFACTS: THE "CRUX OF IMPACT ANALYSIS"[2]

The primary challenge is to assess appropriately which effects are attributable to the reforms, i.e., given a set of outcomes, to differentiate between the situation post-intervention and the situation that would have prevailed had the intervention not occurred (Shadish et al. 2001). It is a relatively simple task to assess the post-intervention situation. On the other hand, one can never observe, nor accurately measure, what the situation might have been without the intervention—the counterfactual situation that "remains forever in the darkness of the unfulfilled" (Thomas Hardy, quoted by Mohr, 1995, p. 4.) We are thus constrained to develop a source of counterfactual inference to serve as a plausible foundation from which to determine those changes that might be attributed to the policies implemented. We will generally find this source in one or another of the following situations: (i) the situation as it existed in the same place, before intervention (the before situation); (ii) the situation observed elsewhere, where the intervention did not occur (the situation without); (iii) a virtual situation, neither observed before nor elsewhere, but rather simulated (the as-if situation); and (iv) a virtual situation derived from repeated observation of the evolution of states similar to that in which the intervention was implemented, that represents the natural evolution of the situation (the situation as it might have been).

The "before" situation as a source of counterfactual inference

The "before" situation is that which prevailed immediately before the implementation of the changes under evaluation. For every indicator of a presumed outcome, the effect of a policy is derived by comparing the indicator before and after the policy's implementation. Thus, the effect of the adjustment on the health of a population would correspond to the average of the changes in health status of individuals in that population. This approach forms the basis of the simplest quasi-experimental evaluations, based on before–after observations but without control groups. These types of assessments are very common because of their appealing simplicity and because of the great advantage of using as the source of counterfactual inference the same as that used to assess the situation after the intervention. However, these advantages are also their greatest weakness, in that their internal validity is poor and their findings are generally considered to be less robust.

The primary threat to internal validity lies in the possibility that changes that occurred between the two points of observation are the result either of events other than the intervention itself (history bias) or of the natural evolution of the phenomena under consideration (maturation bias) (Campbell and Stanley 1963; Cook and Campbell 1979). These assessments also do not take into consideration changes induced by exogenous factors—political, economic, climatic, social, etc.—that inevitably arise, nor the long-standing tendencies of existing natural cumulative processes, whether social or physiological. Therefore, although the approach may be appealing in its simplicity, it cannot, in itself, guarantee acceptable scientific results (Bourgignon and Morrisson 1992).

The situation "without" as a source of counterfactual inference

In this approach, for a given indicator, the effect is deduced from differences observed between countries that have been exposed to reforms and those that have not.[3] The appeal of this approach is that it offers a control group of non-adjusting countries to test the counterfactual argument (Costello et al. 1994) and also offers the possibility, at least in principle, of generating more generalized findings than single case studies. Even here, there are major weaknesses in the design. The internal validity is undermined by the heterogeneity of the exposed and non-exposed groups, the inability to control for selection bias, and the excessive simplification of comparisons based on aggregate data.

The first problem encountered is that situations differ greatly among countries making up any one particular group, whether they are the early adjusters, the late adjusters, the non-adjusters, or any other grouping of countries. Among the adjusting countries, there are differences in the conditions leading to adjustment, the policies implemented, the rhythms of implementation, and, of course, the economic and sociopolitical contexts in which they occur. Thus, in aggregating the data from these heterogeneous groups of countries, the specific realities of each are masked by the resulting forced homogeneity, as are the unique features of their reforms and the conditions that prevailed at their implementation (Sahn et al. 1997). In other words, many key endogenous factors are overlooked that determine, in large measure, the economy, the level of well-being, and the living conditions of the country. In so doing, there is the risk that the analysis of the presumed effects of reform will be biased.

Another problem may be found in the conditions under which countries are designated as *exposed-adjusters* and *controls-non-adjusters* and the resulting selection biases that may emerge from the start (P selection bias) or during the course of implementation of the reforms (Q selection bias). The adjusting countries have had to deal with critical situations from which most non-adjusting countries have been spared. Often they have experienced turbulent cycles of crisis and reform. Their starting conditions and their particular histories set them apart from those who have never entered into structural adjustments. As such, the two groups of countries present distinctly different profiles with regard to external conditions and the outcomes of interest that tend to become accentuated during reform. It is not entirely reasonable to believe, as this type of approach would require, that adjusting and non-adjusting countries differ only in terms of their policies and the adjustment measures implemented; therefore, it is difficult to see the non-adjusting countries as constituting a plausible counterfactual base of reference. Additionally, selection biases can be reinforced by the non-availability of data. It frequently happens, as Reed found in his multi-country survey on adjustment and environment, that those countries for which there is little or no data have particular profiles that in themselves are associated with specific levels of health or well-being; very poor countries, or countries under reconstruction where the public statistical apparatus is not functioning, are also likely to be performing less well in terms of human development (Reed 1999).

A third problem is the frequent existence of contamination bias. The fact that certain countries have not received formal adjustment credits from IFIs does not mean they have not, or would not, put in place policies or measures emanating from the same reasoning. During the 1980s, for example, Burkina Faso undertook a so-called *auto-adjustment policy* that is comparable in many respects to those promoted by the Bretton Woods institutions.

In the end, what are the consequences, in these multi-country studies based on aggregate data, of such threats to internal validity? For some authors, these approaches result in reducing the sensitivity of the results, as well as introducing systematic bias "in a positive direction, so that favourable effects are overstated and unfavourable results are understated" (Costello et al. 1994, p. 9). This assertion is supported in a recent review of studies on health and adjustment, in which the authors demonstrate, notably, that in multi-country studies of the with–without type, there is less tendency to highlight negative impacts of adjustment on health than in single-country studies, that more often use a before–after design (Breman and Shelton 2001).

To produce acceptable evidence using with–without approaches, a number of conditions would have to come together that are difficult to achieve: a significant sample of countries regrouped into homogeneous categories; natural histories that are similar; data of sufficiently good quality; and information that is both longitudinal and transversal (Bourguignon and Morrisson 1992, Lundy 1996). Another condition would be that the countries' economies behave in similar ways, which is an unrealistic hypothesis (Bourguignon and Morrisson 1992). For these reasons, contrary to the IFIs, most scientific researchers look suspiciously upon these approaches based on minimalist counterfacts, which produce tenuous results (Sahn et al. 1997; Lundy 1996; Narayana and Navaneetham 1998). "While such aggregate analysis is very valuable, it does not help much in determining whether the effects that we believe are caused by structural adjustment actually happen" (Peabody 1996, p. 827).

The "as-if" situation as a source of counterfactual inference

Simulation studies attempt to compare the post-adjustment situation with that which would have prevailed if the adjustment had not occurred. Thus, these are one-group designs in which the validity is strengthened by the addition of a counterfactual situation created through modeling. With the development of CGE modeling techniques, this approach is now commonly used to evaluate or predict the consequences of macroeconomic policies. The study may focus on a single country, or, if there is sufficient available data, on multiple countries, as in the OECD's international study (Bourguignon and Morrisson 1992). The popularity of simulation is explained by its advantages. First, it is easier to control biases that would threaten internal validity. The result is somewhat like having a with–without study that controls for history and maturation biases, but in which, furthermore, the country being studied is matched to itself. As in a before–after study, this matching would eliminate the problem of designating exposed and control groups, thereby limiting selection biases. Next, the evaluation possibilities are nearly infinite because once the causal structure has been defined, it is possible not only to define a counterfactual scenario, but also to elaborate upon it and evaluate any number of alternative scenarios. Finally, these analyses require only secondary data and can, insofar as the base data is available, be carried out at a limited cost.

It is important to keep in mind that any simulation is based upon a causal structure derived from a series of hypotheses about the mechanisms of *macro-meso-micro* transmission. Therefore, predictions are necessarily limited by the validity of these hypotheses and the ability of the researchers to produce a good scaled-down model of reality (Bourguignon and Morrisson 1992). This requires a deep understanding of the functioning of causal mechanisms and, more generally, of the world being modeled, that is really only possible in areas where there is a substantial base of empirical knowledge (Rossi and Freeman 1993). This is true, to a point, for general modeling of an economy. However, it is less true when it comes to the social sector, and it is not true at all when it comes to modeling functions of individual and collective production in health or the behaviour of the health services market. Therefore, although promising, simulations are still not very useful for evaluating the effects of public policy on health.

The situation "as it might have been" as a source of counterfactual inference

The fourth approach to building a counterfactual scenario is to base it upon a series of historical observations. Using appropriate statistical techniques, the impact is deduced by comparing several time series before and after the intervention (*interrupted time series*). The main advantage to this approach is in the enriched information that makes it possible to construct a more elaborate and credible counterfactual scenario. Biases that could undermine internal validity are minimized. Maturation bias is controlled, and even if historical bias is still possible, it is significantly reduced in comparison with before–after designs. In practice, historical bias can be nearly completely eliminated through the use of *comparative time series*, which are more demanding but always possible (Mohr 1995). In this case, the analysis is based on the comparative analysis of several chronological series, each related to a specific result.

One of the primary advantages of time series is their capacity to integrate temporal dimensions into the analysis. In the first place, they make it possible to take into account the temporal nature of the response to the intervention. Some interventions will have immediate, or near-immediate, impacts, as with devaluation and the price of imported medicines. However, this is not always the case, and it is very useful to be able to take into account delayed responses when studying phenomena such as health. Sometimes the response is intrinsically delayed because the action mechanisms take time, or the changes require a long exposure, or several other prerequisite mechanisms or mediators need to be activated first. In other cases, the response is shifted because of adaptive strategies, as in the case, for example, of households real-locating their resources to protect themselves from the negative effects on their service consumption of a reduction in revenue or in the number of professionals (Costello et al. 1994). As long as these adaptive strategies work, no change in outcomes may be observed. The first changes emerge when the adaptive strategies become ineffective. In some cases, transformation occurs but the changes are modest or progressive and the effects are not imme-diately measured or even measurable. Finally, when it comes to health, past investments in infrastructure, education, vaccina-tion, etc., because of their long-term influence, can obstruct, modify, or delay changes that might result from any modifica-tion of the economic environment and public policies (Grosh 1990). Certain legacies are long-lasting and even irreversible, such as vaccinal immunity, and are therefore not susceptible to changes in context or policy. Other indicators, such as mortality, are known not to be very sensitive in the short or long term.

Chronological series also make it possible to test differ-ent hypotheses regarding the permanent or temporary nature, cumulative or not, of the effects. However, it is not always pos-sible to draw full advantage of these possibilities and assessing the medium- and long-term effects of reforms remains difficult. First, the reforms are often undertaken intermittently (Reed 1999) and precise temporal reference points are not always available for analyzing response times or cause–effect relation-ships, nor for projecting a counterfactual scenario. To be fully exploitable statistically, temporal series must be sufficiently long and based on a large number of observation points, both before and after the intervention. Nevertheless, even short time series with only summary statistical analyses are preferable to simplistic before–after designs, and it is therefore unfortunate that the use of chronological series for evaluating public policies is still somewhat limited. Finally, the researcher generally has only a limited number of time series available, most often built upon routine administrative data whose reliability is questionable.

We can see that none of the counterfactual scenarios is completely satisfactory and that recourse to research designs combining multiple approaches is inevitable. There are also practical considerations to this decision. The available quantitative indicators are often quite limited and their reliability doubtful, such that they need to be complemented with both quantitative and qualitative primary data. The problem of reliability in data is particularly acute when it comes to aggregate measures of health status. A recent review of maternal mortality in Africa demonstrated that aggregate estimates can be extremely imprecise and require great caution when used for evaluation (WHO 2004). Maternal mortality estimates varied from one to five times for the African region of the World Health Organization (390–1 500 per 100 000) and up to twice for the WHO American region (82–210 per 100 000). The same databases can give rise to very different estimates, as is demonstrated by the following example. To estimate differences in infant mortality in Burkina Faso, Lachaud used data from the 1998 Demographic and Health Survey (Lachaud 2001). He estimated the coefficient of concentration to be −0.241. The World Bank, using the same data, estimated this coefficient to be −0.06. The former group concluded that post-adjustment differences in infant mortality were significant, whereas the latter found that there were no differences!

LESSONS

First of all, we cannot ignore what has already been learned from two decades of studies on the social effects of adjustment, given that so much of the controversy surrounding these effects stems from the disputed internal validity of the studies (White

1996) and their tenuous results. As was pointed out by Brennan et al., methodology effects are generally present in any study of the links between adjustment and health, as "the outcome depends on the variable used in the study, the method and whether or not it is a country specific case study or a cross country study" (Breman and Shelton 2001, p. 14).

The second lesson is the importance of specifying the object of the evaluation. Reforms are generally made up of a variety of macroeconomic measures that affect different elements of the economy or the health-care system. Using generic terms related to adjustment and reform can mask that plurality, leading researchers to question whether they should be evaluating policies in general or specific components. The idea of carrying out a comprehensive evaluation of the reforms is obviously appealing. However, this is not always possible, nor even desirable: first, because being policy-specific makes creating the counterfactual easier and certainly better (Sahn et al. 1997); then, because it is more informative and more efficient to establish the links between specific measures and their presumed consequences than to determine the aggregate effects (sometimes antagonistic) of the changes, which themselves may be staggered over several years. A good example of this concept is the analysis of the effects of public policy reforms on access to medications. Certain macroeconomic measures, such as a correction of the exchange rate and a reduction in public subsidies, when combined, may converge and result in an increase in the price of medications, thus reducing access to the poorer population. Let us then imagine that, several months later, still in the context of adjustment, the government introduces other measures designed to promote the offer of generic medications at lower cost. The result will likely be a reduction in the cost of medications in the market and a lowering of financial barriers to access. An evaluation looking at the comprehensive results of the reforms would probably not render adequately the effects on access of the various measures undertaken. It is therefore more efficient to concentrate on concrete aspects of reform policies. However, this being said, when implementation is progressive, or if reforms overlap or are carried out intermittently, this dissociation is not always possible. This is illustrated in Figure 1, which shows the principal measures carried out in Thailand over the course of three crises, three macroeconomic reforms, three sectoral reforms, and numerous changes affecting the health-care system since 1974. The search for specific links between measures and consequences in this case is greatly impeded by the multiplicity of changes and the rapid pace of events and reforms.

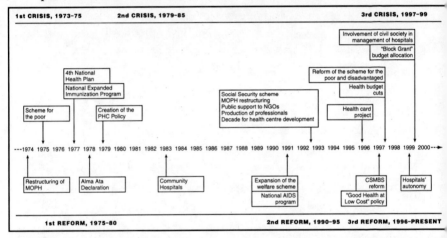

FIGURE 1. CRISES, MACROECONOMIC REFORMS, AND HEALTH SECTOR REFORMS IN THAILAND (1974–2000)

The third lesson is that it is vital to take into account the contingent nature of reforms. They are many-sided, with components that are very diverse in terms of context, scope, and the extent of transformation they generate. The initial conditions from which the reforms emerged vary from one country to another, as do the conditions within which the interventions are carried out. Some reforms extend over more than five years; others have a more limited duration. As is shown in Figure 2, some countries have engaged in a single reform, whereas others have experienced several adjustment cycles, with measures implemented at different times and at varying levels of intensity. Finally, all reforms undergo some type of amendment once they are put in place. Governments modify them, and it is not uncommon for the initial reforms to be substantially transformed in the wake of adjustments and debt rescheduling. This has two consequences for evaluation. First, of course, this obliges us to recognize the circumstantial nature of reforms. Given that public policies are embedded within a specific reality, it is not reasonably possible to judge their results outside of this context and without taking into account their specific characteristics and their own pace of implementation, if we are to retain their essence. This therefore restricts, as we have seen, the use of comparative quantitative studies based on aggregate data. Again, this touches upon the objectives of the evaluation; we must decide whether it should consider only the impact of what was actually implemented or also the processes—and particularly any discrepancies between the initial program and the implementation of the policies. We also must consider whether to limit ourselves to those consequences expected at the start or also to take into account the unexpected effects of modifications introduced during the course of implementation. Reforms are dynamic, some

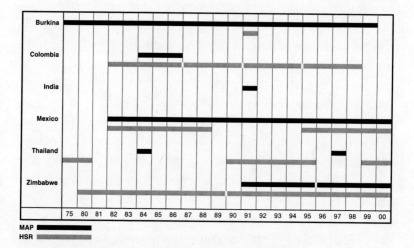

FIGURE 2. STRUCTURAL ADJUSTMENT AND HEALTH SECTOR REFORM IN THE MAPHEALTH COUNTRIES OF STUDY.

measures are unforeseen, and "the expected can give way to the unexpected" (Peabody 1996, p. 828).

The fourth lesson is that we must consider the influence not only of macroeconomic reforms, but of sectoral reforms as well. Setting aside sectoral reform, the effects of MAPs can be analyzed relatively independently. If, however,—as happens in most countries—the implementation of MAPs at any time precedes, follows, or is concurrent with reform of the health sector, this duality must be taken into account. What would we make of an analysis of the effects of adjustment on health that disregards the coexistence of a sectoral reform that, as seen in the previous chapter, greatly affects the allocation of resources, system performance, and equity of access? Conversely, any study that purports to examine the effects of health system reform would have little credibility if it were to disregard the contingent effects of adjustment on the general economy and household demand, as well as the multiple impacts—whether direct, indirect, immediate, or staggered—on the health sector of the tax system, the government's rate of expenditure, foreign exchange policies, reforms in the labour market, i.e., on the whole ensemble of macroeconomic adjustment measures. The regulation and distribution of supply, the allocation of resources, the price of services, and ultimately the production and consumption of health inputs are, in effect, largely influenced by government arbitrations and economic policies. It is therefore imperative that this double perspective (sectoral and macroeconomic) be integrated to avoid the inevitable distortions that would result from a myopic evaluation centred on purely endogenous or exogenous causes of change in the health sector.

The fifth lesson is that it is essential to be able to identify the causal pathways linking public policies with their possible consequences. Generally, measuring the micro effects of an adjustment requires modeling of macro–meso–micro links, i.e., the mechanisms by which the macroeconomic environment is internalized, through a variety of incentives and constraints, by those acting at the microeconomic level (Morrissey 1997). This is fundamental. To guide the analysis and the search for consistencies and to restrict the universe of alternative explanations, we require a system of reference that makes it possible to retrace the effects of adjustment on the constraints and behaviours of the actors and on the opportunities available to them. We come close to achieving this in accounting for the effects of adjustment on a country's economy. However, the problem expands when it comes to identifying and understanding the multiple causal pathways and leverage mechanisms, both direct and indirect, that are mobilized in health production and assessing the consequences of adjustment outside of the strictly economic sector. The complexity of this undertaking is illustrated by Sahn and colleagues, on the link between adjustment and poverty: "To understand how a particular adjustment policy affects the poor, we need to trace a complex path accounting for direct and indirect effects. In doing so, we must recognize the mediation of policy change by various economic institutions and account for other exogenous influences before we can understand the distributional and poverty effects" (Sahn et al. 1997, p.7). In other words, to assess the effects on health, we first need to identify the direct and indirect mechanisms that link macroeconomic developments with the production and consumption of health inputs.

However, to uncover these transmission mechanisms is a complex undertaking, particularly because we must take into account the many causal influences, as well as the interconnectedness of the causal pathways that may have been set in motion. As Chen puts it, "cause and effect linkages between the dynamics of the macro-economy and the health of populations are multiple, difficult to pinpoint and undoubtedly complex" (Chen 1986, p. 279). Certainly, public policies, through a variety of mechanisms, will model the opportunities for being in good or poor health. But these opportunities arise from a tangle of complex influences in which are interwoven public policies, lifestyles, characteristics of individuals and families, households' allocation decisions, etc. Then we must be able to distinguish between the changes that have come out of the reforms and the causes that provoked the reforms in the first place, i.e., the crises and imbalances that the adjustment programs were intended to correct (Sahn et al. 1997). Even there, the undertaking is complex, because what we are observing is the cumulative effect of the crises and the institutional responses to them (Genberg 1995). The interconnected nature of crises and reforms lends a certain artificiality to their separation, and, much as we might wish to, it is not always possible to distinguish their respective contributions to any eventual deterioration in health status.

The challenge, however, is not only in the multiplicity of causal mechanisms involved in health production; it is also in their interconnectedness and overlapping. We would need not only to model the causal links, but also to anticipate the consequences of the coexistence and interaction of the mechanisms of health production and the additive or synergistic, agonistic or antagonistic, nature of their behaviours. Ideally, we would also need to be able to judge the effects of (i) the intensity of the changes implemented, looking for possible dose–effect relationships; (ii) the sequence of implementation of macroeconomic measures; (iii) any interference from exogenous variables (e.g. natural disasters, social troubles, changes in governments, etc.); and (iv) the time delay between the adoption of a measure and the expression of its consequences. We also need to consider the recursive nature of certain causal mechanisms, as when changes at the micro level (poverty, productivity, input factors availability, etc.) feed back to the macro level.

All of this makes it especially complicated to estimate what the situation would have been in the absence of reforms (Behrman 1995), and identifying effects that are specific to the adjustment presents formidable methodological problems that some consider absolutely insoluble: "Changes in economic policy and Health Sector Reform are only a part of this very large set of forces influencing health outcomes, isolating the effect of which is virtually intractable" (Narayana and Navaneetham 1998, p.15).

The analysis of public reforms in relation to health status is thus strongly limited in terms of both internal validity and generalizability. It may seem more productive to concentrate on the study of modifications that, although not addressing changes in well-being, provide more prosaic information on institutional responses. This means judging the effects of reforms less on the basis of outcomes and more on outputs, i.e., changes induced in the production of services (availability, price, quality) and their interface with populations (accessibility, utilization). These indicators are, in fact, more specific, more sensitive, and more rapidly reactive to institutional changes and structural reforms, especially those targeting supply, than are health and well-being. Even this approach, however, has its limitations. Of course, it helps lift some of the constraints that weigh upon the analysis of causal links between adjustment and the health sector.

However, to a certain extent, what applies to the production of health (outcomes) applies as well to the production of health systems (outputs). Because these influences can also be numerous, any study of the effects of adjustment on system outputs and of the resulting snowball effect must disaggregate the mechanisms having direct or indirect influence on supply and demand in health services (Figure 3). The supply response to production incentives (e.g. devaluation, easing of price restrictions) is conditioned by many contextual factors such as the degree of liberalization of internal markets; the tax system; the quantity and quality of existing infrastructures; access to credit; the efficiency of financial institutions; the mobility of the labour force; the concentration and distribution of property; or again, the strength of the private sector and the extent of the informal sector. Similarly, the effects on demand are also dependent upon context, economic situation, political and institutional factors, and other factors.

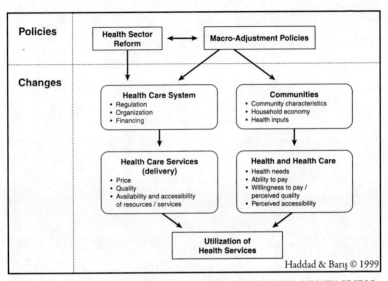

FIGURE 3. LINKING MACROECONOMIC ADJUSTMENT POLICIES, HEALTH SECTOR REFORMS, AND HEALTH SYSTEMS OUTCOMES.

In practice, no evaluation design is perfectly satisfactory. However, by triangulating different designs and methodologies and using a conceptual base that allows us to anticipate and understand macro–micro links, we can strengthen the internal validity of the evaluation. Our aim is to go well beyond the superficial approach of comparing aggregate indicators between adjusting countries and non-adjusters and to ensure a more serious analysis that recognizes the diversity of sociopolitical contexts, the content and pace of implementation of public policies, and the intercurrence of a variety of exogenous factors.

To be able to document policy outcomes and formulate recommendations, country-focused studies are primordial. However, any study that relies only on before–after analyses will have insufficient internal validity (Sahn et al. 1997). By using data and analytical tools that allow us to model, through simulation, multivariate analyses or, with the help of time series, the likely counterfactual scenario, we can greatly improve the quality of our results. Also, doing multiple-case studies, as proposed by Yin (1984), makes it possible to bring more depth to single case studies, identify potential recurrences, and avoid inferences based on anecdotal results.

With regard to evaluation criteria, it is important to measure the absolute consequences of the reforms and their effects in terms of how they respond to needs. Experience shows, however, that these consequences are differently distributed among economic sectors, social groups, or territories. Some persons will see their situation deteriorate, whereas others may not be affected by the reforms or may even benefit from them. Therefore, it is also important to be able to assess the distributive effects of the policies. Finally, as we have seen, the available quantitative indicators are often limited and poorly reliable and must be complemented by quantitative and qualitative primary data (Lundy 1996).

THE MAPHEALTH PROJECT

Objectives and country selection

The MAPHealth project is an international study that aims to contribute to a better understanding of the links among macroeconomic policies, health sector reform, and the organization and delivery of health services in developing countries. The project has a set of interwoven objectives. Its primary objective is to obtain as clear a picture as possible of the health systems of Southern countries whose economic environments, after a succession of crises and structural reforms, are considered to be turbulent. This picture includes an examination of health reforms undertaken in these countries—reforms that preceded the upheavals in some cases and followed in others. We were also interested in articulating these diverse elements and in studying how health systems responded, at different times and in different contexts, to major transformations of their environments. For the reasons mentioned earlier, the project is focused on the healthcare system, and particularly on the aspects of quality, accessibility, and utilization of health services. The study of changes attributable to the implementation of overall or sectoral policies is therefore centred on the organization and delivery of services, both within each country and between participating countries.

The study originally included eight countries: four African (Burkina Faso, Kenya, Uganda, Zimbabwe); two Latin-American (Colombia, Mexico); and two Asian (India, Thailand). Clearly, this selection is not fully representative of all situations of turbulent environments or of crisis–adjustment cycles. This would be extremely difficult to achieve, given the vast heterogeneity of situations and contexts among countries. The group is nevertheless sufficiently demonstrative of the great diversity of public policy reforms, particularly in the health sector, carried out in recent years. These countries embarked on this project in response to the invitation of the International Development Research Centre (IDRC). This development agency, which initiated and funded the study, invited research teams in Africa, Asia, and Latin America with an interest in the proposed area of study to submit research proposals. These proposals were subsequently evaluated by a peer review committee and eight teams were selected based on numerous criteria, including multi-disciplinary research capacity, political stability, availability and reliability of country-level data, level of country development, and background and experiences with MAPs and health sector reform. Six of these teams, with the support of a team of researchers from the *Université de Montréal*, in Québec, Canada, undertook and completed the process that has resulted in this report. Although case studies were carried out in Uganda and Kenya, the teams in these countries did not complete the process that would have led to inclusion in this book. Therefore, the material presented in the remainder of this chapter and in subsequent chapters refers only to six countries.

Participating countries

The participating countries, with some key development indicators, are listed in Table 2. Three countries fall within the group of intermediate economies (Colombia, Mexico, Thailand), and one, Burkina Faso, is among the least advanced countries. These countries have different development profiles and experiences with the implementation of MAPs and health sector reform. All of them were led to implement structural reforms of their economies, preceded or followed by more or less drastic reforms of their health-care systems. These reforms, whose intensity, content, and conditions of implementation are presented in the following chapters, are summarized in Table 3.

TABLE 2. SELECTED DEVELOPMENT INDICATORS FOR THE MAPHEALTH STUDY COUNTRIES, 2000

Country	Type of government	Population (000)	Human development index	Human poverty index	Illiteracy rate-adults	Infant mortality rate	Corruption perception index rank*	% of poor
Burkina Faso	Parliamentary Republic	11 553	0.325	58.4	76	105	65	61
Colombia	Republic	43 035	0.772	9	8	20	60	18
India	Federal republic	1 032 355	0.577	34	43	68	69	35
Mexico	Federal republic	99 420	0.796	10	9	25	59	10
Thailand	Constitutional monarchy	61 184	0.762	14	5	25	60	13
Zimbabwe	Parliamentary democracy	12 821	0.551	41	11	73	65	26

* out of 90 countries.

Source: All data except corruption perception index: UNDP, Human Development Report (2000). Corruption perception index: Transparency International (2000).

Project design

The project design was developed by the team leaders within a framework of close collaboration and with the support of the IDRC. Based on Yin's terminology, this is a multiple-case, multiple-level study. It is multiple-case, in that each country is considered a case in which an in-depth analysis of changes is conducted. It is multiple-level because it has, in each of the cases, three levels of observation and analysis (macro, meso, and micro) conducted at the national, regional, and local levels.

Together, the team leaders developed a methodology having one part in common and the other part specific to the case, taking into account the particular objectives and contexts encountered.

TABLE 3. IMPLEMENTATION OF MACROECONOMIC ADJUSTMENT POLICIES AND HEALTH SECTOR REFORMS IN THE MAPHEALTH STUDY COUNTRIES

Country	Implementation of IMF/World Bank-assisted MAPs	Health Sector Reform (HSR)
Burkina Faso	**1991:** First IMF/WB structural adjustment package implemented, aimed at integrating country into market economy. Measures included simplification of taxation system; compression of public expenditures; liberalization; rationalization; reform on price-fixing; restructuring of banking sector; currency devaluation. Five sectoral reforms: agriculture, public enterprise, environment, transport, human resources.	**1991:** HSR initiated as integral part of SAPs: *Decentralization*, with emphasis on health districts; *Cost recovery*, introduction of user fees in health centres; *Rationalization* of supply and distribution of generic medications at an affordable price; *Reform of hospital sector* to improve effectiveness; Promotion of *private medicine*; Collaboration between *traditional* and modern medicine; *Liberalization* of health services substantially increased during past decade.
Colombia	**1984–86:** Severe adjustment programs implemented in fiscal, exchange, and trade areas, and to address foreign debt. Measures included tax increases; administrative budget cuts; adjustment of public employees' wages to below inflation; import surcharges; devaluation; domestic inflation. **1986–1990:** Sustained MAP, focus on competitive exchange rate, fiscal and current account deficits. **1990–1994:** Structural reforms: foreign trade, labour, financial. Constitution of 1991: Important decentralization process, large transfers of powers and resources to municipalities.	**1993:** Law 100 passed, to increase insurance coverage and ensure universal access to basic packages of services. Four stages of HSR: **1982–86:** *Reform foundations* – Improvement of health system; incentives for private enterprises in health technology. **1986–90:** *Partial reform* – Administrative decentralization; integration of public, private, and social security organizations; participation of private sector discussed for the first time. **1990–94:** *Radical reform* – Creation of new health system supported by social security schemes for health and demand subsidies; adoption of primary care model. **1994–98:** *Reform implementation* – Establishment of contributive and subsidized regimes.
India	**1991:** MAPs implemented in monetary, external, and fiscal sectors under supervision of IMF. Structural reforms undertaken in industrial, trade, and financial liberalization, to stimulate market-led growth .	HSR is a state-level issue, e.g.: Orissa among a number of states that borrowed from WB to restructure their health sector. Kerala decentralized health sector as part of broader decentralization effort.

Mexico	**Since 1982:** Several classical packages implemented, each accompanied by reductions in the public budget for health; usual duration of packages five years.	**1982–1988:** Health services integrated to form a national health system; universal right to health protection incorporated into the Constitution in 1983. **1995–2000:** Intense transformation of health, social security, and private sectors; provision of basic packages of services for marginalized groups; introduction of competition among service providers; provision of family health insurance; decentralization and encouragement of local participation via the national healthy *municipios* program.
Thailand	**1985:** IMF loan obtained in response to second oil crisis of **1979–85:** foreign exchange and external debt policies implemented. **1997:** Second IMF loan sought after Asian crisis. Flexibility brought to interest rate, tax revenue raised, government budget cut and current account surplus maintained.	**1975–1980:** Primary health care policy, free medical scheme for poor. **1990–1995:** Expansion of health welfare program; promotion of public–private health care mix; health card scheme. **1999–present:** Reforms of civil servant medical benefits and payment scheme for the poor; implementation of universal health insurance.
Zimbabwe	**1991–1995:** *Phase I* (ESAP– Economic Structural Adjustment Program): to increase investment and restore economic growth. Measures include trade and labour market liberalization; deregulation; devaluation of local currency; removal of subsidies; restructuring of parastatals; reduction of government budget deficit; privatization and rationalization of public sector employment. **1996–2000:** *Phase II* (ZIMPREST–Zimbabwe Program for Economic and Social Transformation): selective price controls; increases in tariffs; pegging of the exchange rate; suspension of foreign currency accounts; tobacco levy; export incentives in budget.	**1980–89:** "Equity in health" policy adopted to address inequalities; primary health care approach advocated for service provision. **1990–2000:** Broad-based health sector reforms implemented: decentralization; cost recovery; health financing; regulation of private medical sector; strengthening of management; contracting out. Social Development Fund introduced to cushion potentially deleterious effects on the poor.

The general principles of the country studies are that they are cross-sectional and retrospective (over the past 15 years) and that they use both quantitative and qualitative data based on multiple primary and secondary sources, including national and regional surveys (Table 4). The finest unit of observation is the household, and the units of analysis are the country, regions, households, and individuals.

TABLE 4. GENERIC STUDY DESIGN PROPOSED TO, AND SUBSEQUENTLY ADAPTED BY, PARTICIPATING MAPHEALTH STUDY COUNTRIES

Level	Study, survey	Data collection sources		Instruments
		Primary	Secondary	
National	Health system study (HSS)	Interviews, focus groups	Policy plans, reports, previous surveys, system data, statistics	Health systems kit
	MAPHealth study	Interviews, focus groups	Policy plans, reports, previous surveys, system data, statistics	MAPHealth kit
Regional	Community survey (CS)	Interviews	Reports, previous studies, system data, statistics	Community checklist
	Health facilities survey (HFS)	Interviews, observations	System data, statistics, reports	Health facility questionnaires
	Household surveys (HHS)	Interviews	Databases	Household questionnaires

The national-level studies are concerned with the health system and the implementation of MAPs. Each country team selected two or three states or regions based on analyses of the country situation and regional differences in the implementation of reforms. Within these regions, a limited number of administrative units, communities, and health districts were surveyed. Finally, community, household, and health facility surveys were conducted locally. The methodology was piloted in India and Mexico and refined based on the findings and experience of those teams.

Framework of the study

A common framework was proposed for the different teams to facilitate the process of analysis and future comparative approaches. It was, in fact, useful most of all in developing a common vision of the mechanisms by which macroeconomic policies can influence health systems and, later, in the formulation of specific research hypotheses by the country teams. The mechanisms through which adjustment can drive changes in health systems are both complex and deeply tied to the characteristics of these MAPs (measures of implementation, duration, intensity, and conditions of their introduction). Following Peabody's (1996) suggestions, these mechanisms are seen as both direct and indirect:

— Expenditures on health constitute the main lever through which adjustment can directly influence the health system. Adjustment and the eventual sector reforms that accompany it can directly affect the total spending, the distribution, and the allocation of expenditures. The relative prices of imported health goods (equipment, medications, consumables) constitute a second important lever. Equally, the positioning, adjusting, and directing of the general organization of the health system can be profoundly remodeled by institutional reforms and measures looking to promote the private sector. These different measures will also influence the system of care and play on diverse health services, in terms of their availability, quality, price, financial autonomy, geographical and financial accessibility, etc.

— Similarly, the demand for health care can be modified by different mechanisms. Austerity measures directly influence numerous determinants of health and of the ability to pay: employment, disposable income, education, consumption, nutrition, etc. The engendered price-level modifications of the quality and availability care in turn affect individual and household perceptions of quality and price, their willingness to pay for health services, and the capacity to reach these services, all of which will subsequently modify the behaviour of people seeking care. The most vulnerable social groups—the poor, women, and children—are also particularly exposed to the risk of exclusion.

As part of the framework, some key intermediate variables were identified, with implementation of macro policies being the main variable of interest. We distinguished:

— three levels of effects: (i) of macroeconomic adjustment programs, including health sector reform, on the health system and communities; (ii) of previous changes on the supply of health services and on the demand for health care among susceptible households; and (iii) of all these modifications on the geographical and financial accessibility of the services, and consequently, on the utilization of health services (Figure 1).

— three types of effects: (i) on the supply side, i.e., on health policies (regulations, organization, financing) and services (availability, price, quality); (ii) on the demand side, i.e., on determinants of health (employment, income, nutrition, education) and on the demand for health care (needs, preferences, budget constraints); and (iii) on accessibility and utilization of health services, resulting from the interaction of the first two groups of factors (Figure 3).

Levels of measurement and instruments

Macro variables include both contextual variables (demographic, epidemiological, social structure, political dynamic, economic data) and variables related to MAPs (importance, implementation, impact, duration, etc.). Meso variables concern both the health-care system (organization, regulation, financing, and delivery of care and health services) and communities (social and economic organization, political and community environments, local resources, needs and health behaviours, inequities, and gender-specific issues). Micro variables include information on access, quality, and utilization of care, and on household capabilities and well-being.

To facilitate the analyses, the group developed a set of instruments that were then adapted by each country team (Table 4) and made available in three languages (French, English, and Spanish). The three levels of measurement are reflected in three general tools: macro- and meso-level instruments with a guide, health facilities questionnaire with supplements and guide, and household questionnaires.

The macro- and meso-level kits were organized into four components: economic indicators, analysis of structural adjustment, health system indicators, and a community checklist. The economic indicators component included grids for data on population, human development, macroeconomics, public expenditures, households, and employment. The section on the analysis of structural adjustment provided researchers with guidance on evaluating macroeconomic measures, suggestions on the presentation of structural adjustment policies, and a matrix for analyzing the impact of MAPs. The evaluation of the performance of the health-care system was centred on four qualities or attributes: effectiveness, efficiency, equity, and sustainability. The section on health-system indicators included grids for data on baseline indicators, health resources, service coverage, health expenditure, prices of care and services, and utilization. Teams were encouraged to consult national sources as well as statistical yearbooks and publications from international agencies and to augment this quantitative data with qualitative information from key informants. Finally, the community checklist provided a list of factors guiding researchers to describe the general background of the location, sociocultural characteristics of the community, and details of the local health-care system.

The tool for the evaluation of health centres consists of three questionnaires plus a guide. The principal questionnaire elicits data about the centre and the accessibility, quality, and utilization of services, as well as information on the impact of macroeconomic policies and health reforms on the centre. The first appendix is a questionnaire to be administered to centres with hospital beds, with more in-depth questions on services offered, physical plant, equipment, drugs, financial data, cultural data, types of activities, reasons for hospitalization, quality indicators, and the impact of health reforms. The second appendix is a questionnaire to be completed by health-care personnel. It asks questions on the personnel profile, their degree of satisfaction with work conditions, and their opinions regarding the evolution of certain parameters with respect to the health centre and its environment.

The largest tool in the methodology is the set of four household questionnaires. The first collects information on household composition, income, assets, expenses, education, and utilization of health-care services. The second asks about community participation, perceived health status, accessibility of health-care services, willingness to pay, perceptions of the quality of health care, and health problems experienced during the previous four weeks. Questions on women's and children's health and on women's workload are found in the third, and the last one asks specific questions about health care utilization.

Analyses

The case studies evolved rapidly into research centred on country-specific issues. As such, the analyses were carried out separately by each of the country teams and the scope of comparative analyses initially envisioned was necessarily substantially reduced, insofar as the pace at which the studies were carried out tended to vary considerably from one team to another.

As a general pattern, the analyses paid special attention to the effects of reforms on specific subgroups of the population, on both the supply (e.g. health practitioners) and the demand (e.g. women, poor) sides. Because of local concerns, almost all the teams focused the analyses on the implementation and the consequences of health sector reforms. Special attention was paid to structural adjustment or external shocks by the teams in Burkina Faso, Mexico, Thailand, and Zimbabwe. The teams in federal countries (India and Mexico) gave more attention to the possible mediating effects of state- or province-specific policies and regulations. In general, more attention was devoted to the analysis of household questionnaires (demand side) than to the health facility questionnaires, which could undoubtedly be further explored.

Notes

1. For a more complete inventory, the reader may consult Bourguignon and Morrisson (1992); Behrman (1995); Costello et al. (1994); Genberg (1995); Lundy (1996); Peabody (1996); Sahn et al. (1997); and White (1996).
2. Phrase borrowed from Mohr (1995).
3. The category of countries "exposed to reform" could be divided into several subcategories to distinguish between different levels of exposure, or periods during which adjustment occurred (see Chapter 2).

References

Behrman, J.R. 1995. Santé et croissance économique: théorie, réalité et politique. *In* Environnement macro-économique et santé. Avec études de cas dans les pays les plus démunis. Organisation mondiale de la Santé (World Health Organization), Geneva, Switzerland. pp. 17– 50.

Bijlmakers, L.A.; Bassett, M.T.; Sanders, D.M. 1996. Health and structural adjustment in rural and urban Zimbabwe. Research report no. 101. Nordiska Afrikainstitutet, Uppsala, Sweden. 78 pp.

Bijlmakers, L.A.; Bassett, M.T.; Sanders, D.M. 1998. Socioeconomic stress, health and child nutritional status in Zimbabwe at a time of economic structural adjustment. Research report no. 105. Nordiska Afrikainstitutet, Uppsala, Sweden. 123 pp.

Bourguignon, F.; Morrisson, C. 1992. Adjustment and equity in developing countries: a new approach. Development Centre of the Organisation for Economic Co-operation and Development.

OECD Publications and Information Centre, Washington, DC, USA. 111 pp.

Breman, A.; Shelton, C. 2001. Structural adjustment and health: a literature review of the debate, its role-players and presented empirical evidence. Commission on Macroeconomics and Health (CMH), Working Paper Series, no. WG6:6, World Health Organization, Cambridge, MA, USA. 53 pp.

Campbell, D.T.; Stanley, J.C. 1963. Experimental and quasi-experimental designs for research. Rand McNally, Chicago, IL, USA. 84 pp.

Chen, L.C. 1986. Health policy responses: an approach derived from the China and India experiences. In Bell, D.E.; Reich, M.R., ed., Health, nutrition, and economic crisis: approaches to policy in the Third World. Auburn House, Dover, MA, USA. pp. 279–305.

Cook, T.D.; Campbell; D.T. 1979. Quasi-experimentation: design and analysis issues for field settings. Rand McNally, Chicago, IL, USA. 405 pp.

Cornu, A.; Massamba, J.P.; Traissac, P.; Simondon, F.; Villeneuve, P.; Delpeuch, F. 1995. Nutritional change and economic crisis in an urban Congolese community. International Journal of Epidemiology, 24(1), 155–164.

Costello, A.; Watson, F.; Woodward, D. 1994. Human face or human facade? Adjustment and the health of mothers and children. Centre for International Child Health, Institute of Child Health, London, UK. 68 pp.

Garenne, M.G.; Gakusi, E. 2000. Health effects of structural adjustment programs in sub-Saharan Africa. Working paper, French Center for Population and Development Studies (CEPED), Paris, France. 26 pp.

Genberg, H. 1995. Ajustement macro-économique et secteur de la santé. In Environnement macro-économique et santé. Avec études de cas dans les pays les plus démunis. Organisation mondiale de la Santé (World Health Organization), Geneva, Switzerland.

Grosh, M.E. 1990. Social spending in Latin America: the story of the 1980s. World Bank discussion paper no. 106. World Bank, Washington, DC, USA. 163 pp.

Hanson, K. 1999. Implementing health sector reform in Africa: a review of eight country experiences. UNICEF, Division of Evaluation, Policy and Planning, New York, NY, USA. 92 pp.

Jayarajah, C.; Branson, W.; Sen, B. 1996. Social dimensions of adjustment: World Bank experience, 1980–93. Operations Evaluation Division, World Bank, Washington, DC, USA. 218 pp.

Kakwani, N. 1995. Structural adjustment and performance in living standards in developing countries. Development and Change, 26(3), 469–502.

Lachaud, J.P. 2001. Dynamique de pauvreté et inégalité de la mortalité des enfants au Burkina Faso. Documents de travail, no. 66, Centre d'Économie du Développement de l'Université Montesquieu Bordeaux IV. Pessac, France. 20 pp.

Lundy, P. 1996. Limitations of quantitative research in the study of structural adjustment. Social Science and Medicine, 42(3), 313–324.

Makinen, M.; Waters, H.; Rauch, M.; Almagambetova, N.; Bitran, R.; Gilson, L.; McIntyre, D.; Pannarunothai, S.; Prieto, A.L.; Ubilla, G.; Ram, S. 2000. Inequalities in health care use and expenditures: empirical data from eight developing countries and countries in transition. Bulletin of the World Health Organization, 78(1), 55–65.

Mohr, L.B. 1995. The theory of impact analysis: experiments and the elementary quasi-experiments. *In* Impact analysis for program evaluation. Sage Publications, Thousand Oaks, CA, USA. 311 pp.

Morrissey, O. 1997. Micro-macro linkages: an economist's perspective. Journal of International Development. 9(5), 755–760.

Mwabu, G. 1996. Health effects of market-based reforms in developing countries, UNU/WIDER Research Paper no. 120. World Institute for Development Economics Research, Helsinki, Finland. 53 pp.

Narayana D.; Navaneetham, K. 1998. Impact of structural adjustment programme and health sector reforms on reproductive health and family planning services in South Asia. Study sponsored by the United Nations Fund for Population Activities. Centre for Development Studies, Thiruvananthapuram, Kerala, India.

Newbrander, W.; Collins, D.; Gilson, L. 2000. Ensuring equal access to health services: user fee systems and the poor. Management Sciences for Health, Boston, MA, USA. 187 pp.

Noorbakhsh, F.; Paloni, A. 1998. Stuctural adjustment programmes and export supply response. Journal of International Development, 10, 555–573.

Peabody, J.W. 1996. Economic reform and health sector policy: lessons from structural adjustment programs. Social Science and Medicine, 43(5), 823–835.

Reed, D. 1999. Ajustement structurel, environnement et développement durable. Editions L'Harmattan, Paris, France. 377 pp.

Rossi, P.H.; Freeman, H.E. 1993. Evaluation: a systematic approach, 5th ed. Sage Publications, Newbury Park, CA, USA. pp. 215–260.

Sahn, D.E.; Dorosh, P.; Younger, S. 1997. Structural adjustment reconsidered: economic policy and poverty in Africa. Cambridge University Press, New York, NY, USA. 304 pp.

Shadish, W.R.; Cook T.D.; Campbell, D.T. 2001. Experimental and quasi-experimental designs for generalized causal inference. Houghton Mifflin Company, Boston, MA, USA. 623 pp.

Transparency International. 2000. TI corruption perceptions index 2000. http://www.transparency.org/policy_research/surveys_indices/cpi/previous_cpi__1/2000, cited April 2006.

UNDP. 2000. Human development report 2000. United Nations Development Programme, New York, NY, USA, http://hdr.undp.org/reports/global/2000/en/, cited April 2006.

Van der Gaag, J.; Barham, T. 1998. Health and health expenditures in adjusting and non-adjusting countries. Social Science and Medicine, 46(8), 995–1009.

White, H. 1996. Adjustment in Africa. Development and Change, 27, 785–815.

WHO (World Health Organization). 2004. Maternal mortality in 2000: estimates developed by WHO, UNICEF and UNFPA. World Health Organization, Geneva, Switzerland. 39 pp.

World Bank. 2005. Health, Nutrition and Population Statistics (HNPStats), http://devdata.worldbank.org/hnpstats/

Yin, R.K. 1984. Case study research: design and methods. Sage Publications, Newbury Park, CA, USA. 160 pp.

CHAPTER 4

HEALTH SECTOR REFORM UNDER MACROECONOMIC ADJUSTMENT IN BURKINA FASO: LOST OPPORTUNITIES?

Adrien Nougtara, Slim Haddad, Jacques Guéda Ouédraogo,
Salimata Ky-Ouédraogo, Valéry Ridde, Pierre Fournier

COUNTRY PROFILE

Burkina Faso is country landlocked within West Africa. The majority of its 12 million inhabitants (83%) live in rural areas, and two-thirds of the urban population is concentrated in the two cities of Ouagadougou and Bobo-Dioulasso. The country is comprised of more than 60 ethnic groups, of which the Mossi are the most numerous. Muslims account for the majority of the population (52%); the rest are either animists (26%) or Christians (21%).

Burkina Faso is counted among the group of least advanced countries. In 2001, it ranked 159th out of 162 on the Human Development Index of the United Nations Development Programme (UNDP). Its per capita GDP in 2001 was 240 USD. Three out of four adults are illiterate. One out of every 10 households is headed by a woman. Nearly half the population live below the poverty line (45%) and 65% live on less than a dollar (USD) a day. Poverty is essentially rural (94% of the poor in 1998) and affects more than half the peasants. Rainfall is minimal and unevenly distributed, and the soil is poor. Nevertheless, the economy is mostly based on the primary sector (agriculture, livestock), which employs about 90% of the active population, according to the 1996 census. This sector, which accounts for

40% of GDP, is largely made up of small family enterprises using low-technology methods of cultivation and husbandry, except in the case of cotton farming. The informal sector is the country's second largest source of employment, in urban centres as well as in the countryside, in both the secondary sector and the service sector. Production units are generally small, diverse, and often headed by women.

Health needs are enormous and largely unsatisfied. Life expectancy is 46 years. Maternal mortality is exceedingly high, with estimates varying between 484 and 1 000 per 100 000 live births. Infant mortality is 104 per 1 000, and nearly one out of five children dies before the age of five. One out of every three children under the age of five is malnourished. Infectious diseases continue to be fearsome killers: diarrhea, malaria, measles, and acute respiratory infections being the principal causes of death among children (INSD 1998). The incidence of diseases for which there are vaccinations has diminished, but there continue to be cyclical epidemics of measles and meningitis. In 1986, 10 cases of AIDS were reported; by 2000, there were 1 951, a 20-fold increase. Problems related to water and sanitation continue unabated. Only 29% of the population have access to potable water and 30% of urban households have access to toilets.

Health policies have emulated major changes observed on the African continent. The 1980s were mainly characterized by implementation of primary care services, broader vaccination programs, and family planning policies, which had until then been prohibited under law dating back to colonial times. It was the era of major health campaigns including "commando vaccination" and "one village = one primary care post." Beginning in 1992, the country entered a period of reform inspired by the Bamako Initiative and by measures advocated by international development agencies.

The country has 53 health districts grouped within 11 health regions. Public health services are organized in a classic pyramidal structure. The base is made up of peripheral health structures—health and social development centres (*centre de santé et de promotion sociale – CSPS*), dispensaries, and maternity centres. The medical–surgical centres (*centre médical avancé – CMA*) are the first line of referral, followed by eight regional hospitals. At the summit are the two national hospitals of Bobo-Dioulasso and Ouagadougou. In addition to the public sector, there is the army's health services system, as well as a private health sector flourishing in urban centres, offering a patchwork of more or less qualified practitioners. As in other countries of this region, the private sector is largely made up of the private practice of professionals on the state's payroll, a practice that is technically illegal but tolerated.

STRUCTURAL ADJUSTMENT AND SECTORAL REFORMS

Burkina Faso underwent two periods of adjustment. The first, implemented between 1983 and 1987, was carried out without the support of international financial institutions. This was an austerity program designed to bring public finances back into equilibrium after the upheavals caused by the advent of Thomas Sankara's revolutionary regime. Then, in 1991, to make the transition from a state-dominated to a market-based economy, the government decided to implement a new structural adjustment program (SAP), this time with the aid of the International Monetary Fund (IMF) and the World Bank. This assisted-adjustment program involved stabilization measures and a set of structural and sectoral reforms. The structural reforms consisted of a series of measures aimed at reducing public spending; reforming domestic and foreign taxation structures; easing restrictions on the labour market, businesses, and prices; privatizing and rehabilitating public enterprises; and reforming the banking sector. However, the most significant measure was adjustment of the exchange rate, under which the CFA franc, indexed to the French franc, was sharply devalued to one-half its value, effective 11 January 1994.[1] These structural reforms were accompanied by sectoral reforms in agriculture, environment, transportation, human resources, and health. Health sector reform focused on decentralization and cost recovery and on the establishment of health districts; reforming the hospital sector; liberalizing health services with regard to the private sector; and ensuring the supply of essential medicines.

THE MAPHEALTH STUDY IN BURKINA FASO

The methodology used in Burkina Faso conformed closely to that proposed for the MAPHealth project overall. The study covered the years 1983–2000 to include both periods of macro-economic adjustment. The macro aspect of the study is based upon documents from national and international sources, a database of secondary socioeconomic data reconstructed by the study team, and interviews of 18 key informants working in upper management, health institutions, or development organizations. These inputs were complemented by a survey conducted in three regions selected as being representative of the diversity of environments and living conditions and therefore of the effects of the reforms in different geographical areas. The first was the city of Bobo-Dioulasso. The second-largest city in the country, with a population of about 400 000, Bobo-Dioulasso is relatively prosperous and serves as a major crossroads between Mali, the Ivory Coast, Ghana, and Burkina Faso. The second study site was the Bazega region, a rural truck-farming area about 50 kilometres from Ouagadougou, the capital. The third region was Nouna, in the west, a rural area devoted primarily to growing cotton. In Nouna and Bazega, the study covered both rural villages and towns that are considered, in Burkina Faso, to be semi-urban zones.

Altogether, the study covered 53 communities composed of either villages or districts (Table 1). The household survey included 1 604 families randomly selected from within the participating communities. In these households, 857 persons had presented with an illness during the four weeks preceding the interview. The health facilities study looked at 13 of the 32 existing primary care institutions (CSPS and maternity centres).

There were 121 respondents to the staff questionnaire, and in each region, approximately 50 patients of each institution participated in exit interviews.

TABLE 1. DESIGN AND SAMPLES OF REGIONAL STUDIES, BURKINA FASO

	Study sites			TOTAL
	Bobo-Dioulasso	Nouna	Bazega	
Communities included	18	21	14	53
Cities (urban)	1	-	-	1
Small cities (semi-urban)	-	1	1	2
Villages (rural)	-	17	10	27
Samples				
Household surveys				
Households	694	510	400	1 604
Individuals	5 353	4 182	3 251	12 786
Persons with illness	300	118	439	857
Institutional surveys				
Institutions	7	3	3	13
Representatives	38	38	45	121
Users	43	43	59	145

Source: MAPHealth study (2001).

IMPLEMENTATION OF THE REFORM

Editorial constraints require that we limit our examination of results in this chapter to the period covering the assisted adjustment and the health system reform. First we will look briefly at the evolution of the economic environment during the assisted adjustment period and of the implementation of decentralization and other elements of the health system reform. Then we will examine changes in resource allocation, access to treatment and primary care services, and utilization. The last section is devoted to an analysis of the economic burden of illness and the effects of illness on poverty.

The economic context during the assisted adjustment period

Implementation of structural adjustment

The macroeconomic adjustment program was implemented gradually, within an initially difficult political context, because at the time of the discussions with the Bretton Woods organizations, the country was under an exceptional regime. The currency devaluation provoked a strong public reaction and forced the government to raise the guaranteed minimum wage and the salaries of civil servants by 5–10%. Implementation of certain measures, such as privatizing and liquidating public enterprises, was difficult. Overall, however, the adjustment program was carried out without major obstacles and Burkina Faso was considered by the IMF to have been a good adjuster.

Economic growth

Between 1992 and 1994, the economy was slowing down and by the time of the currency devaluation in 1994, the country was in recession. In 1995, the trend began to reverse itself, and the average rate of GDP growth from 1995 to 2000 was 4.4%. This growth can be attributed to significant expansion of the agriculture sector, increased consumption, and recovery in the mining, construction, and retail industries. After devaluation, foreign commerce benefited from market increases in cotton and in gold, and from the expansion of agricultural exports.

Poverty

Poverty surveys show a small increase in the level of poverty between 1994 and 1998, going from 44.5% to 45.3% (Table 2). Poverty remained concentrated in rural regions, with little change, while there was greater impoverishment in the cities. There, 1 out of 10 households was poor in 1994; four years later, the figure was 1 out of 6. In 1994, less than 4% of poverty was concentrated in the cities; by 1998, it was 6.1%, a 60% increase. Overall, income in rural areas increased during the period in question, especially among those in the agricultural sector. However, persons on fixed incomes and particularly civil servants, artisans, and day workers—mostly concentrated in cities—saw their real incomes stagnate or decrease.

TABLE 2. EVOLUTION OF POVERTY IN BURKINA FASO, 1994–1998

	Incidence of poverty (%)			Contribution to total poverty (%)		
	1994	1998	Change (%)	1994	1998	Change (%)
Socioeconomic groups						
Public sector employees	2.2	5.9	168	0.2	0.5	150
Private sector employees	6.7	11.1	66	0.4	0.7	75
Craftsmen, merchants	9.8	12.7	30	1.4	1.6	14
Other workers	19.5	29.3	50	0.3	0.4	33
Production farmers	50.1	42.4	-15	11.8	15.7	33
Subsistence farmers	51.5	53.4	4	78.9	77.1	-2
Unemployed	41.5	38.7	-7	7.1	4.0	-44
Environment						
Urban	10.4	16.5	59	3.8	6.1	61
Rural	51.0	51.0	0	96.2	93.9	-2
National	44.5	45.3	2	100	100	0

Source: Ministère de l'économie et des finances, Burkina Faso (2000).

Prices

Over the course of the decade, prices remained relatively stable. Average inflation was 5.8%. Inflation went into two-digit levels only in 1994, when it peaked at 24.7%. After devaluation, prices of basic goods were generally contained. On the other hand, the prices of grain, rice, equipment, and manufactured imports were automatically affected by the parity changes of 1994.

Public finances

The government considers that many of the SAP objectives were achieved. Public revenues have increased, from 11–12% of GDP at the beginning of the decade, to 13–14% at the end. However, controlling expenditures has been more of a challenge, especially when the government was obliged, in 1993, to back down from certain unpopular measures and satisfy public demands. The balance of payments remained in deficit, despite the positive influx of transfers in the form of grants and foreign subsidies, both public and private. Public investment was significant. Current expenditures, which were near 80% in the 1980s, decreased to less than 50% in the last three years of the 1990s, with public funds going primarily to benefit the water, agriculture, and public works sectors (Figure 1). If grants are taken into account, the deficit was on average no more than 4.8%, a level compatible with the macroeconomic objectives. Foreign debt grew considerably during the first half of the decade, going from 298 billion CFAF in 1990 to 770 billion CFAF in 1995. This was primarily due to increases in loans from multilateral organizations, mostly for structural adjustment credits. Since 1996, the country has not gone into arrears on its foreign debt, and debt servicing has decreased over the past five years, representing 2.26% of GDP and 17% of current revenues in 1999. In the end, the foreign trade deficit remains high, even though agricultural exports have very much benefited from the currency devaluation and price increases.

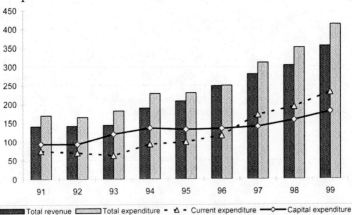

FIGURE 1. EVOLUTION OF PUBLIC FINANCES IN BURKINA FASO, 1991–1999, (CFAF BILLIONS).
Source: Ministère de la santé, Burkina Faso. Direction des études et de la planification.

The implementation of decentralization

To ensure decentralization, a number of laws and regulations were passed governing the functioning of the health districts and defining management structures and procedures. These gave public institutions a great deal of management autonomy and established the principle of cost recovery for operating expenses through setting fees for services, and particularly for essential drugs.

Decentralization began with the designation of 53 health districts in 1992. This was followed by the training of staff, construction and equipping of facilities, and the allocation—mainly through external partners—of financial resources to the districts. In 2000, six years after the beginning of decentralization, only two or three districts could be said to be operational, under the criteria set out in the reform.[2] Country-wide, fewer than five districts had the requisite number of physicians and only 17 of the 53 district hospitals had the capacity to do cesarean sections (Bodart et al. 2001). In the same year, in the Dédougou region, only 34% of health facilities had a dispensary, a maternity centre, and a depot for essential generic drugs (EGD), and barely half met the minimal staffing norms (GTZ 2000).

In many respects, decentralization was not accompanied by real transfer of power to the districts. A good example of this is in the critical area of human resources management, where recruitment of personnel is almost exclusively under the authority of the central management level, which keeps firm control over the movement and allocation of staff. Even though action plans are prepared, in most cases, by the districts, planning is more often based on available resources than on the needs of the population. Because of inadequate management capability, action plans are poorly justified, insufficiently resourced, and rarely executed as planned (the exceptions being districts with outside support). Districts complain particularly about urgent activities being parachuted onto them by the Ministry without warning, which take over their staff and budgets and interfere with planned programs.

Another source of problems is the devolution of financial resources and their availability to the districts. Officially, the decentralization was to have been accompanied by budget transfers to the districts. In fact, since 1996, the national budget has contained a line item showing the assignment of such funds. However, only a part of that amount actually devolves to the districts, and in any case, the amounts transferred constitute only a small fraction of public expenditure on health. Operating budgets continue to be concentrated and mostly managed at the level of the Ministry. In 1998, the budget allocated to the districts represented 14% of the Ministry's operating costs, excluding salaries, which was hardly more than the budget allocated to the two national hospitals. The central government continues to be responsible for a portion of expenses that should be assumed by the districts. According to a World Bank analysis of the 1998 law on finances, 70% of equipment and supplies for the districts and 52% of their staff expenditures were being handled by the central authorities. As of 2000, the districts and the regional boards of health still only managed about half of their material expenses (Government of Burkina Faso 2001).

Because of this, districts must rely heavily on cost-recovery revenues. However, this situation can have negative effects, as district management teams are motivated to hoard these revenues, and in fact to increase them, to ensure coverage of operating expenses. A GTZ study showed that between 1995 and 1999, in two regions, the contribution of sales revenues of EGD depots to district management operating budgets multiplied 50-fold (GTZ 2000). The current situation also reinforces inequities between districts depending on whether they have financial support from external partners. Since 1998, at least 20 districts receive financing either directly from the State or from its partners and are thereby advantaged in relation to other districts. There are also inequalities within these advantaged districts; some financing may be largely symbolic, whereas in other cases the financing in fact exceeds the capacity of the district to absorb it. This was the case in Kongoussi, where between 1995 and 1997 only 65% of funds received were able to be used (Aubel and Sobgo 1998).

Implementation of other elements of the health system reform

Easing of private sector restrictions

The private sector, which until then had been very constrained, was able to develop considerably during the 1990s. Legislation was revised and measures were introduced to promote and support the creation of laboratories, clinics, and private pharmacies. The result was a major expansion of the private sector, particularly in the cities. In 1996, nine out of 10 private health facilities and one out of four pharmacies were located in one or the other of the country's two largest cities. According to Ministry of Health statistics, between 1991 and 1996, the number of private health facilities went from 106 to 155, and the number of pharmacies from 40 to 69 (Bodart et al. 2001). There were 200 private pharmacies in operation in 2002, the vast majority (84%) being concentrated in the two cities of Ouagadougou and Bobo-Dioulasso (Ministère de la santé 2002). Nevertheless, there is general agreement that these figures are not very useful, as they do not take into account the number of undeclared providers, nor the widely practiced private services offered by public sector professionals.

The expansion has therefore been chaotic, with the State having left the sector to its own devices. In fact, neither the State nor the professional organizations exercise any form of effective regulation, and there seems to be no intention to control this activity, which led one of our key informants to confide that "actually, we are not engaged in private service, but rather in piracy." Laws regulating this sector are not applied, and there are no constraints on who may offer services on the market, nor on the quality or safety of their treatments. The fact that most establishments are not listed anywhere and that no one in authority has an up-to-date listing of providers in the private sector is a good indication of the extent to which the regulatory function has been abandoned and of the extreme disorganization of this sector.

The reform of the pharmaceutical sector

The pharmaceutical reform has focused primarily on rationalizing the supply and distribution of generic drugs at affordable prices. In 1992, a central buying office for essential generic drugs (*centrale d'achat en médicaments essentiels génériques* – *CAMEG*) was created, and a policy for essential drugs (*politique de médicaments essentiels* – PME) was implemented in 1994 (Ministère de la santé 1996). At the district level, this reform was carried out through community measures: setting up EGD depots to supply the health centres, training staff for prescribing and management, and creating community-based management committees. These committees set fees for treatments and medications charged to patients and are also responsible for public education.

The 1994 currency devaluation occurred just as the PME was being implemented. This had an immediate impact on the cost of imported drugs, prompting the authorities to accelerate the setting up of EGD depots, even though it also meant hurrying the process of setting up the committees and training staff and even by-passing certain measures. Government referred to this as the acceleration phase of the Bamako Initiative (Ministère de la santé 1999). The result was that by 1997, 85% of health facilities had already built and equipped EGD depots. One study carried out in Nouna showed that these expediencies had the effect of improving not only utilization but also acceptance of EGDs among the population.

Nevertheless, by the end of the 1990s, implementation in the districts was still not complete. For example, in Dédougou, 62% of health facilities still did not have an EGD depot (Krause et al. 1999). Moreover, early studies tended to show that, as elsewhere in the subregion, rationalization measures had a limited impact on inappropriate prescribing and use of medicines (Krause et al. 1999). Of greater concern, as we shall discuss later in this chapter, were the prices for essential drugs being supplied that were actually not as affordable as expected.

Hospital reform

The final element of health system reform was hospital reform, which focused on redefining the roles of each level in the hospital hierarchy, the governance of the institutions, and the improvement of operations. Interventions in this arena included efforts to upgrade the pool of equipment, strengthen human resources and the organization of care, and improve the quality of services. Hospital reform has been slower to get off the ground and so was not examined in depth in this study.

THE REFORM AND RESOURCE ALLOCATION

Financial resources

Public contribution

Public expenses in health have increased in both nominal and real value (Figure 2). The nominal budget was 7.7 billion CFAF in 1990 and reached 33 billion CFAF by 2000, representing a public expenditure of less than five dollars (USD) per capita. Setting aside the devaluation year, in which inflation went over 20%, real spending has been increasing steadily over the decade. The proportion of

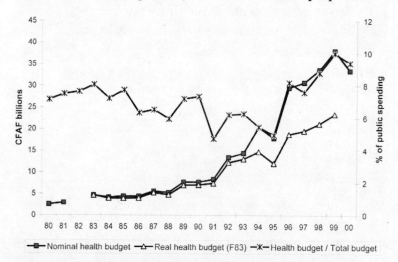

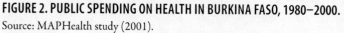

FIGURE 2. PUBLIC SPENDING ON HEALTH IN BURKINA FASO, 1980–2000.
Source: MAPHealth study (2001).

health expenditure within overall public expenditure increased by nearly five percentage points between 1995 and 2000, demonstrating the particular attention given to this sector by government. These amounts include contributions from external partners, who played a key role in the expansion of public contributions. From 3.6 billion CFAF in 1986, their commitments grew to 27 billion CFAF in 1997. Between 1992 and 1998, their contributions increased at an average rate of 31% annually. This being said, the actual total of the contribution is most certainly underestimated, as the only figures available are those in the State budget and some agencies fund NGOs directly.

Analysis of public expenditure by major line item (Table 3) shows important changes, particularly in the allocation of resources between salaries and investments. Before the SAP, the budget was primarily devoted to salaries, which accounted for 51% of the health budget between 1986 and 1991. With decentralization and the inclusion of a portion of salary expenses under the heading of current transfers, it became difficult to calculate the salary component in public expenditures, but we can reasonably estimate that, from then on, it was about 40%. One of the most striking aspects of the reform was that the SAP, with the commitments of external partners, greatly benefited capital investments.

TABLE 3. BUDGET ALLOCATIONS (%) IN BURKINA FASO BY MAJOR LINE ITEM, 1990–1999

Item	1990	1994	1997	2000
Staff	54	37	18	19
Supplies and equipment	12	12	7	12
Current transfers	3	19	22	27
Capital investment	31	32	53	42
Total	100	100	100	100

Source: Ministère de la santé, Burkina Faso. Direction des études et de la planification.

Nevertheless, the allocation of resources at different levels of the hierarchy is still unbalanced (Table 4). Health system reform has not resulted in any notable reallocation of public hospital funding to the primary care level, nor from the centre out to the periphery. Government is spending more on health but without much better result, and budgets have not been redeployed to improve service to a population that is still 80% rural.

TABLE 4. DISTRIBUTION OF THE PUBLIC HEALTH BUDGET IN BURKINA FASO, 1998

Item	%
Central hospitals	22
Central administration	29
Regional hospitals (9)	9
Regional administrations (11)	1
Health districts (53)	14
Other expenses (school of public health, national laboratory, training)	25
Total	**100**

Source: Bodart et al. (2001).

Private contribution

In the absence of any nation-wide study on consumption, it is difficult to estimate the proportion of private spending on health within total expenditure. For the period 1997–2003, UN agencies reported a value of 29.3% (World Bank 2003). Total private spending, at about 1 600 CFAF per capita, would therefore have been less than half as much as total public expenditure. These values are highly improbable—in a subregion where it is generally estimated that private spending on health care exceeds public spending, Burkina Faso would be exceptional. Studies by Peters et al. (1999) led them to estimate a value of 61% for private spending on health in sub-Saharan Africa.

Because the MAPHealth household surveys do not represent the entire country, we cannot use them to produce aggregate national estimates. Nevertheless, even in the most remote areas, the results of our observations grossly exceed the values of the WHO and the World Bank; average per capita spending, in all 53 participating communities, was never less than 3 000 CFAF (Table 5). It therefore seems reasonable to assume that, despite the best efforts of government and its partners, private spending on health in Burkina Faso probably exceeds public spending, in both rural and urban areas.

TABLE 5. PRIVATE EXPENDITURE (IN CFAF) ON HEALTH PER CAPITA IN BURKINA FASO, MAPHEALTH STUDY ESTIMATE

Environment	Average expenditure	Standard deviation	Minimum	Maximum
Urban areas	12 699	25 326	10 809	14 589
Semi-urban areas	12 818	46 504	7 307	18 328
Rural areas	4 226	13 412	3 180	5 272

Source: MAPHealth study (2001).

As we have seen, partial cost recovery has become a generalized practice in public establishments. Unfortunately, there are no national statistics to show the size of the communities' contributions to the financing of health facilities' services. A 1995 study in Bazega and Gourda concluded that the average monthly revenue of a CSPS was 137 633 CFAF; but the disparities are significant, and a similar study in the region of Bobo-Dioulasso reported monthly revenues of 476 800 CFAF (Nacoulma et al. 1995).

At first sight, the few studies done on EGD sales suggest that cost recovery works well, from the perspectives of the depots and the health facilities. Between July 1997 and June 1998, the health region of Kaya as a whole had EGD revenues of more than 27 million CFAF, coming entirely from user payments (Chabot et al. 1999). In the province of Gnagna, the depots had, on average, annual revenues of 3 million CFAF each. Thus, each EGD depot recovers most of its operating costs (Condamine et al. 1999). It is important, however, to put these results in perspective, as the cost recovery is only partial. The results do not take into account salaries, technical assistance, supervision, depreciation of equipment, or of any other items; taking these into consideration, it becomes evident that the recovery applies only to a small part of the real costs of the facilities. Simulations done in Mali have shown that, of 26 health facilities with positive financial results, only two would remain positive if depreciation were factored in (Blaise et al. 1997).

Human resources

In the case of Burkina Faso, the SAP entailed significant increases in health-care staff. Unlike other ministries, the Ministry of Health was able to embark upon an active recruitment process. Between the periods 1987–91 and 1992–1999, staffing in the public health sector increased 40%. Except for pharmacists (−25%), of whom many took advantage of the liberalization to move into the private sector, all other categories of public-service staff experienced significant increases in numbers: doctors (+37%), dental surgeons (+32%), midwives and state licensed nurses (+30%), childbirth aides (+112%), and field officers (+113%). The rate of increase in health-care staffing was greater than the rate of population growth, leading to an overall reduction in the population–health professionals ratio, as shown in Table 6.

TABLE 6. EVOLUTION OF DENSITY AND DISTRIBUTION OF PUBLIC SECTOR STAFF, BURKINA FASO

Category	Ratio per 100 000 population			Proportion of staff assigned to rural areas (%)			
	1990	1999	Change 1990–99 (%)	1988	1991	1998	Change 1988–98 (%)
Doctors	29.3	20.0	-32	55	51	48	-13
Pharmacists	80.8	90.1	12	-	-	-	-
Dental surgeons	484.8	327.1	-33	-	-	-	-
Midwives	28.3	23.7	-17	42	38	47	12
State licensed nurses	7.5	6.1	-19	74	68	59	-20
Registered nurses	7.5	7.4	-1	76	69	73	-4
Childbirth aides	15.3	11.1	-28	79	90	80	1
Auxiliary nurses	28.8	11.1	-62	-	-	-	-

Source: Ministère de la santé, Burkina Faso. Direction des études et de la planification.

It is difficult to know whether this effort was sufficient to meet the demand for human resources. First, even though progress has been made, the overall level of resources remains modest, well below the norms set by the WHO of one doctor per 10 000 inhabitants, and one pharmacist and one midwife per 20 000 inhabitants. Also, and more importantly, these recruitments have not rectified the imbalance in allocation of personnel. The increase in human resources has not been uniform across the country. Some zones, such as the urban areas and the central and western regions of the country, are better endowed with health professionals than are the northern and eastern regions.

The percentage of physicians working in rural areas decreased between 1988 and 1998 (Table 6); this is partly due to some moving into the private sector (including NGOs), which is largely concentrated in urban centres. But this is only part of the story, because during this period the Ministry was actively recruiting physicians. Country-wide studies on workload undertaken in 1998 demonstrated that there was 10 times more health-care personnel in Bobo-Dioulasso than in the other cities (Ouedraogo 1999). More than half of all physicians (57%) and midwives are concentrated in Ouagadougou and Bobo-Dioulasso, where 16% of the population resides (Bodart et al. 2001). In the rural areas covered in the MAPHealth study, there were twice as many inhabitants per nurse and four times as many inhabitants per midwife as in the urban centres (Table 7). This is not counting the fact that some of the personnel assigned to the interior never actually assume their positions and are incorrectly numbered among the resources working in rural areas. In semi-urban areas, the majority of specialized services in reference centres are provided by nurses. In Nouna, for example, one reference centre serves the entire population of the district and has only one physician.

TABLE 7. DENSITY OF PUBLIC SERVICE STAFF IN BURKINA FASO, IN THE REGIONS STUDIED, RATIO STAFF–POPULATION

	Urban	Semi-urban	Rural
Nurse	6.856	2.048	12.499
Midwife	21.057	11.473	87.483
Traditional birth attendant	7.19	7.17	12.497

Source: Ministère de la santé, Burkina Faso. Direction des études et de la planification.

The reticence of health professionals to work in the interior can be partly explained by the appeal of a lucrative parallel private practice in the city and the constraints of rural life. The management of human resources and, in particular, the allocation of personnel remain mostly centralized at the Ministry level. It is generally believed that these decisions are largely influenced by political factors and vote-seeking considerations, resulting in excessive centralization and a lack of policies on human resources and career planning.

As a consequence of this indifferent management of human resources, motivation among health-care workers in the public service is low and absenteeism high. Nearly 80% of the workers we interviewed were unhappy with their schedules and work-loads. Half of them said they were unmotivated. Fewer than half were satisfied with the training they had received on the job, and nearly 60% were dissatisfied with the way in which they were being supervised. Forty percent were content with their level of involvement in the management of the health centres. This was reflected in the arena of communications, as 39% of respondents felt they were being well informed on their centre's activities. The majority of workers were not satisfied with their salaries (79%) and bonuses (53%). More than half thought their lifestyles had deteriorated in recent years. Two-thirds felt that possibilities for advancement were unsatisfactory. The study of workload showed that, on average, 70 days per year per person were lost for a variety of reasons: training, participation in meetings, re-provisioning of equipment and medicines, etc. (Ouedraogo 1999). One study of seven health districts demonstrated 37% physician absenteeism (Bodart et al. 2001) and another reported 39% (GTZ 2000).

The health system reform did, in some measure, respond to a portion of overall human resources needs. However, the country unfortunately did not take full advantage of development opportunities, in that it did not adequately resolve major inefficiencies in resource use, nor the most glaring pre-existent inequities.

Facilities and services

Investment has been largely focused on increasing the number of primary care facilities. Consequently, there has been a significant increase in coverage (Figure 3) such that 80% of the population now live within five kilometres of a public primary care facility.

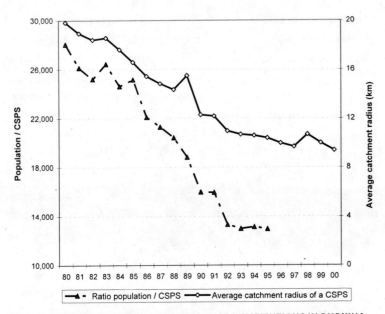

FIGURE 3. SERVICE COVERAGE BY PRIMARY CARE INSTITUTIONS IN BURKINA FASO, 1980–2000
Source: Ministère de la santé, Burkina Faso. Direction des études et de la planification.

But even there, disparities continue. In the north and east, the catchment areas of health centres and CSPSs are larger than in other regions of the country. Urban areas are also better endowed in infrastructure than rural areas. Our household surveys showed an overall satisfaction with the availability and accessibility of primary care services. In the cities, 12% of respondents were dissatisfied with the time required to get to a health centre and 8% held negative opinions about the hours of service (Table 8). The level of dissatisfaction remained low in semi-urban areas, most likely due to the proximity of functional reference centres. The greatest dissatisfaction was in rural areas. Hospital accessibility was felt to be insufficient, owing to the much smaller number of public facilities, particularly in the countryside. The government's master plan calls for the creation of nine regional hospital centres and two national hospitals with an average catchment radius of 89 kilometres, which would involve significant travel

time for users. For this reason, district medical centres were pro-
grammed to receive additional surgical satellites and the number
of planned emergency facilities was increased. However, these
facilities are not yet all operational.

**TABLE 8. UNFAVOURABLE OPINIONS REGARDING PHYSICAL ACCESSIBILITY OF
SERVICES, BURKINA FASO, (%)**

	Physical accessibility		
Institution	Travel time	Open hours	Waiting time
CSPS			
Urban	11.9	8.6	31.2
Semi-urban	5.7	4.6	21.4
Rural	20.1	7.3	10.2
Pharmacist			
Urban	8.0	3.1	9.2
Semi-urban	9.5	7.8	11.4
Rural	17.8	5.6	5.5
Public hospital			
Urban	18.7	12.4	49.9
Semi-urban	14.6	11.6	24.9
Rural	40.8	18.1	19.0

Source: MAPHealth study (2001).

Primary care facilities are expected to provide a standardized
range of health care, preventive, and health promotion services,
as defined in the minimum activities package. Visits to 14 of the
health facilities in our sample demonstrated that service continuity is not constant, but rather is subject to the uncertainties
of resource availability. Most health facilities have recurring
shortages of vaccine stocks that disrupt their activities and affect
vaccination coverage. The consequences are particularly serious
for populations looked after through outreach programs; stock
shortages at the time of wintering can make it impossible to reach
them for another year. DTC shortages were greater in rural areas
(60.5 days per year in the Nouna health district) than in urban
areas (35 days on average for Bobo-Dioulasso).

Eleven of the 14 centres provided effective nutritional monitoring of children in their catchment area. During the previous

year, two CSPSs had run out of oral contraceptives for a month, and one maternity centre ran out for two months. Two centres suffered serious shortages (30 days) of high-use medicines such as chloroquine, paracetamol, and salicylic acid. A study carried out by GTZ in Nouna found that 53% of the health facilities did not have an EGD depot, 67% offered at least one form of contraception, and 89% offered well-baby clinics daily.

It is generally agreed that significant progress has been made in the availability of basic services. Seventy percent of workers interviewed felt the availability of EGDs had improved in their centre, and 80% of user respondents thought the medicines were of good quality. Seventy percent of workers were satisfied with the quality of their equipment. Our own observations, further-more, showed that the condition of buildings, the level of equip-ment, and the quality of assigned personnel were satisfactory in the majority of cases. However, these marks of progress do not conceal the enormous problems posed by shortfalls in consum-able supplies that compromise the continuity of care and, more generally, by the shortcomings in service quality repeatedly pointed out by users, service providers, and health authorities.

The MAPHealth study did only a partial analysis of service quality. Nevertheless, as mentioned earlier, it did demonstrate the vulnerability of service activities to supply shortages. We have also discussed the lack of motivation and high levels of absenteeism among the staff, and we can assume these also have a significant effect on service quality. The study in the health facilities also revealed that more than half the appointed staff had not been trained to use the therapeutic guide provided to staff for guid-ance in diagnosis and treatment. Registers are not properly com-pleted, and supervision is more in the nature of follow-up than training. There are no formal mechanisms for quality assurance, and neither public nor private service providers are subject to any quality control measures, whether from professional organiza-tions or from the authorities. A study carried out in the Nouna region showed significant deficiencies in the quality of prescrip-

tion, with frequent dosage errors and with contraindicated medicines being prescribed to one-third of pregnant women (Krause
et al. 1999). A 1998 Ministry of Health opinion survey found
that 66% of users were not satisfied with their reception in health
service centres, particularly in cities (78%). Finally, our household survey showed that in the city of Bobo-Dioulasso, where
the existence of different types of service allows for comparative
analyses, private service providers are judged more favourably
than the different types of public health facilities (Table 9). The
private sector is preferred to public health centres for the five
elements explored, and in particular for the technical quality of
care, the quality of interpersonal relations, and accessibility.[3] As
for the public hospital, despite its status as the national hospital,
it was less favourably judged on three of the five criteria. These
findings are confirmed by an analysis of the maximum amount
that the households of Bobo-Dioulasso are willing to pay for services from existing providers. On average, this maximum amount
is 7 080 CFAF for services in public centres, 11 230 CFAF for
private services, and 10 070 CFAF for the national hospital.

**TABLE 9. PERCEIVED QUALITY OF SERVICE PROVIDERS IN URBAN AREAS,
BURKINA FASO: MEAN AND STANDARD DEVIATION (N=600)**

	Public hospital	CSPS	Private provider	Traditional provider	Religious centre
Technical quality	2.69	2.66	2.81	2.75	2.81
	(0.40)	(0.42)	(0.30)	(0.37)	(0.32)
Interpersonal quality	2.33	2.55	2.91	2.9	2.8
	(0.72)	(0.61)	(0.25)	(0.25)	(0.44)
Equipment and supplies	2.77	2.48	2.69	2.49	2.55
	(0.50)	(0.71)	(0.57)	(0.72)	(0.72)
Accessibility	2.03	2.28	2.31	2.69	2.47
	(0.51)	(0.49)	(0.44)	(0.37)	(0.48)
Cleanliness and hygiene of the facilities	2.75	2.8	2.94	2.6	2.92
	(0.53)	(0.45)	(0.24)	(0.64)	(0.31)
Total scores	2.53	2.56	2.75	2.71	2.72
	(0.35)	(0.37)	(0.21)	(0.32)	(0.30)

Source: MAPHealth study (2001).

In brief, everything points to the fact that even if it did serve to extend and consolidate public services, the health-care reform did not resolve the most glaring deficiencies in quality of care. The 1998 observation by a mission of experts, to the effect that the activities of the health districts were not results-oriented in terms of service offered to the population (World Bank 1998), seems unfortunately to be still true.

THE REFORM, PRICES, AND ECONOMIC BARRIERS TO ACCESSING BASIC SERVICES

As elsewhere, the liberalization of the private sector did not lead to a reduction in the price of services; between 1988 and 1999, fees for private consultations rose by 100–150% and for delivering a baby, 20–30% (Quinti et al. 1998). Costs for transferring patients for care outside the country have become so prohibitive that the government has greatly reduced the number of such medical evacuations. On the other hand, the currency devaluation in January 1994 had an immediate effect on prices. The costs of supplies and vaccines nearly doubled and the average price increase for drugs was 76% (Nyamba 1994).

What about drugs in the public sector, given that one of the central objectives of the reform was to guarantee access to essential drugs at affordable prices? As previously noted, the government's voluntarist policy had encouraged the rapid setting-up of a system of depots and EGD distribution covering most of the country. But high margins add to their costs, and Burkina Faso now has the reputation of being one of the countries in that region where drugs are the most expensive. Some drugs are even more expensive in the private sector than in the public one (Afogbe 1997).

In principle, the margins applied by wholesalers, warehouse distributors, and retailers are defined by the Ministry and the CAMEG. In practice, however, margins are higher. Although Ministry directives set the margins for warehouse distributors at 10%, they often go as high as 37% (Chabot et al. 1999). Our calculations estimate that a drug purchased for 100 CFAF by the

CAMEG would, in the end, be sold to the patient for 172 CFAF, or nearly double. The population also finds EGDs expensive. In our study, two out of five respondents were dissatisfied with the cost of medicines in the health centres, and one out of two in hospitals (Table 10). Of course, there are somewhat more who find medicines sold in pharmacies to be too expensive, but the difference is modest, and pharmacists are nevertheless very much appreciated, especially in the countryside. Notably, it is mainly in cities that medicines sold in pharmacies and hospitals are considered too costly. It would be interesting to explore the source of these differences further. Perhaps they are related to the selective deterioration of living conditions among that part of the urban population who became impoverished under the adjustment period.

TABLE 10. UNFAVOURABLE OPINIONS REGARDING FINANCIAL ACCESSIBILITY OF SERVICES, BURKINA FASO, (%)

Institution	Financial accessibility		
	Visits	Medicines	Payment options
CSPS			
Urban	25.7	37.7	53.6
Semi-urban	24.8	42.1	50.5
Rural	17.9	41.4	30.1
Pharmacist			
Urban	34.5	65.2	60.5
Semi-urban	20.3	52.2	46.1
Rural	17.7	44.9	31.0
Public hospital			
Urban	50.3	55.0	59.9
Semi-urban	30.4	51.4	52.3
Rural	22.0	40.7	27.7

Source: MAPHealth study (2001).

Medication represented 80% of the cost of an illness episode for those persons who visited a professional during their illness (Table 11). The consultations cost only one-sixth as much, which explains why respondents, whether in the city or the countryside, are more accepting of service fees than drug costs. In fact, a review of fees applied for services in the 14 health facilities reveals relatively modest prices. A consultation for an adult is, on average, billed at 120 CFAF, and for a child, 108 CFAF; the delivery of a baby, 808 CFAF; a prenatal consultation, 285 CFAF; and a family planning visit, 69 CFAF. In 12 of the 14 health facilities, vaccinations are free; two CSPSs charge 25 CFAF and 125 CFAF. Health workers and school children are exempted from these charges. Finally, people's perceptions of hospital costs are even more critical, particularly in Bobo-Dioulasso, where fees at the national hospital are considered excessive by more than half of respondents.

TABLE 11. AVERAGE EXPENDITURE PER ITEM DURING AN EPISODE OF ILLNESS, AMONG PERSONS HAVING CONSULTED A HEALTH-CARE PROFESSIONAL, BURKINA FASO, 2001

Item	N =	CFAF
Visits	236	1 054
Tests	313	717
Hospitalizations	49	1 607
Travel	420	310
Meals	420	165
Medicines	420	6 529
Total cost of episode	420	8 320

Source: MAPHealth study (2001).

We asked households to indicate whether they had, in recent years, had difficulty meeting any of their basic consumer needs—food, clothing, schooling of children, health, etc. They were asked to respond to 12 questions, three of which related to health. On average, they had experienced difficulties with five out of 12 needs (40%). Seventy percent of families reported having had difficulties meeting expenses for food, and the same proportion said they had had, at one time or another, difficulties coping with health-care expenses. Multiple regressions (Table 12) showed that poor households, those with an uneducated head of household, and those that live in the countryside far from any health centre encounter many more difficulties in dealing with their health-care needs.

TABLE 12. FACTORS ASSOCIATED WITH THE OCCURRENCE OF DIFFICULTIES IN MEETING BASIC NEEDS. MULTIVARIATE MULTILEVEL REGRESSION: ESTIMATES OF PARAMETERS, STANDARD DEVIATION, AND PROBABILITIES

| | Model 1 (bin.) | | | Model 2 (cont.) | | Model 3 (cont.) | |
| | Health care needs (yes–no) | | | Other needs (cont.) | | All needs (cont.) | |
	B	SE	OR	B	SE	B	SE
Intercept	0.92	0.19		2.77	0.21	4.56	0.30
Household size							
5–9	0.33	0.14	1.40	0.54	0.16	0.88	0.22
10+	0.59	0.16	1.80	1.00	0.17	1.51	0.24
Education							
None, or primary	-0.31	0.16	0.73	-0.10	0.18	-0.25	0.25
High school or university	-0.95	0.19	0.39	-0.57	0.22	-0.12	0.32
Independent study	-0.04	0.16	0.96	-0.42	0.17	-0.57	0.24
Employment							
Employed	-0.27	0.30	0.77	-0.49	0.37	-0.64	0.52
Merchant, tradesman	-0.82	0.20	0.44	-0.93	0.24	-1.42	0.34
Environment							
Urban	-0.06	0.18	0.94	0.87	0.18	0.85	0.27
Random effects	Variance	SE		Variance	SE	Variance	SE
Level 1 (communities)	0.19	0.07		0.10	0.06	0.35	0.15
Level 2 (households)	1.00	0.00		6.09	0.20	12.16	0.36

Source: MAPHealth study (2001).

* bold: p<0

bin.: binomial dependent variable – logistical modeling

cont.: continuous dependent variable – linear modeling

B: beta; SE: standard error; OR: odds ratio

The country is poor and living conditions are hard. One out of two heads of families (53%) reported having encountered new difficulties during the previous five years, and one out of three (35%) had encountered new difficulties during the previous year. When the question is specifically focused on new difficulties in meeting health expenses, these proportions become, respectively, 30% and 20%. Nine percent of households said they had not been able to provide care for a child during the previous five years, and just as many said they had had to delve into their savings to care for a family member (Table 13).

TABLE 13. NEW DIFFICULTIES ENCOUNTERED BY HOUSEHOLDS IN THE PREVIOUS FIVE YEARS, BURKINA FASO

Proportion (%) of households who:	Environment		
	Urban	Semi-urban	Rural
Withdrew a son from school	8.3	8.7	2.4
Withdrew a daughter from school	5.3	6.5	1.9
Gave up land or cattle	4.7	27.2	35.2
Reduced their assistance to relatives	21.2	13.8	5.4
Sought help from relatives	16.0	15.9	14.2
Sold agricultural stocks	1.3	12.7	21.6
Pawned some of their belongings	2.7	1.4	1.1
Borrowed from relatives	11.2	11.2	6.9
Gave up caring for children	8.7	10.1	9.8
Drew upon savings to pay for health care	5.9	12.0	6.8
Gave up land to treat a sick person	0.3	0.4	0.6

Source: MAPHealth study (2001).

The study showed that consumption of health care is strongly constrained by households' ability to pay. Seventy percent of those who had been ill in the previous four weeks believed they would have been better able to care for themselves if they had had more money, and 60% felt they had not received good care for the same reason. These constraints have an important influence on families' readiness to pay for health services and allow us to describe better the effects of price and fee structures on access to care. One-quarter of all survey respondents declared themselves unwilling to spend anything, on any service, provided in any setting at all. For 75% of households, the maximum amount they were willing to pay for a moderately serious health problem was 2 000 CFAF. The 75th percentile was poised at 5 000 CFAF for a serious illness in an adult, 5 000 CFAF for serious illness in a child, 4 500 CFAF for delivering a baby, and 1 250 CFAF for treatment of a malaria attack. In other words, 5 000 CFAF, or approximately 8 USD, was the maximum price that three-quarters of households were prepared to pay for treating one of their members. Given existing prices, this amount was modest and probably constraining. In any case, it was much inferior to the average cost incurred during one episode of illness or one visit that, as mentioned earlier, was more than 8 000 CFAF.

In this context, the cost of illness in general, and the fee structure for services in the public sector in particular, become sources of inequality and exclusion. Inequality is naturally expressed in the consumption of care and services, as is seen in the curve of health consumption as a function of income and of availability of primary care services (Figure 4). The demand is income elastic and, unfortunately, income elasticity is more pronounced at the point where there is already a confluence of opportunity deficits, i.e., in rural areas where poverty is concentrated and where primary care services are much less available. Inequality is also

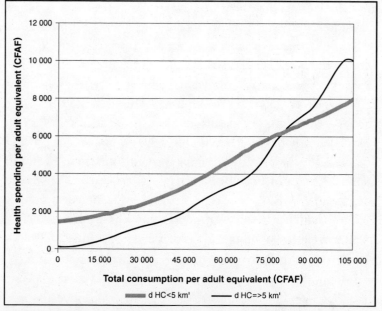

FIGURE 4. HEALTH SPENDING IN BURKINA FASO AS A FUNCTION OF HOUSEHOLD INCOME (TOTAL CONSUMPTION PER ADULT EQUIVALENT) AND DISTANCE TO NEAREST HEALTH CENTRE

Legend:
d HC < 5km: distance to health centre less than 5km
d HC => 5km: distance to health centre 5km or more
Source: MAPHealth study (2001).

expressed as the families' capacity to overcome economic barriers to access. Among families in the lowest income quintile, fewer than a quarter of persons had gone to a health centre by the seventh day of illness. In families of intermediate income, 35% had gone for care, and among persons from the highest income stratum, more than half had visited a centre before the end of the first week of illness (Figure 5a). The poorer people are, the less they use public services, and usually later. Women use services less often and later than men (Figure 5b). Finally, for the two rural areas in the study, and likely for the rest of the country as well, living in the countryside and being far from a health centre are serious obstacles to accessing care (Figures 5c and 5d).

Although some simply postpone using the services, others are excluded. Among those who experienced an episode of illness during the preceding four weeks and did not see a professional, 35% stated that it was because they did not have the money. Moreover, two earlier studies have shown that utilization of public services decreased significantly after cost-recovery fees were instituted, which corroborates the findings of numerous other studies showing the regressive nature of such strategies (Yoder 1989; Haddad and Fournier 1995; Gilson 1997; Watkins 1997; Wood 1997). After these fees were implemented, utilization of health facilities for treatment in the Kaya region decreased by 17% (Sakho and Yonli 1997). Over a three-year period, utilization decreased by 15% in health centres that introduced the fees, while it increased by 30% in centres of other regions that had not (Ridde 2003).

Certainly, the reform has removed physical barriers to access, and essential services such as generic drugs are now more available than they were before. These results nevertheless conceal significant territorial inequities; improvement in resource availability has not removed existing obstacles. Economic barriers persist for those whose social condition, gender, or location of residence result in a concentration of opportunity deficits, i.e., those whom these reform policies were originally intended to serve.

FIGURE 5. LIVING CONDITIONS, OPPORTUNITY DEFICITS, AND INEQUITIES IN ACCESS TO CARE IN BURKINA FASO. CUMULATIVE PROBABILITIES OF USING PUBLIC HEALTH CARE SERVICES, AS A FUNCTION OF INCOME, GENDER, GEOGRAPHICAL LOCATION, AND AVAILABILITY OF HEALTH RESOURCES

Source: MAPHealth study (2001).

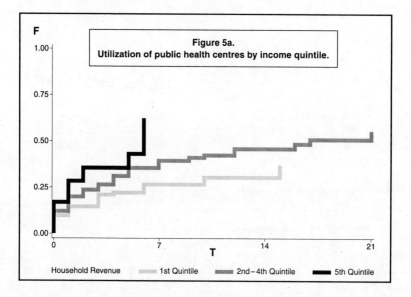

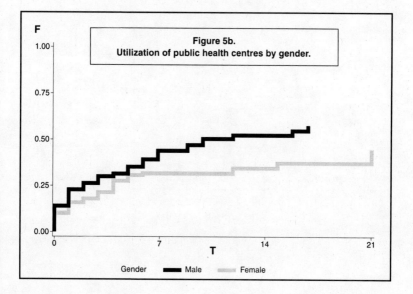

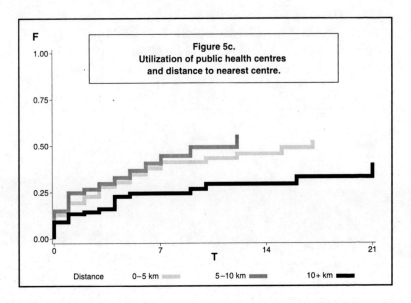

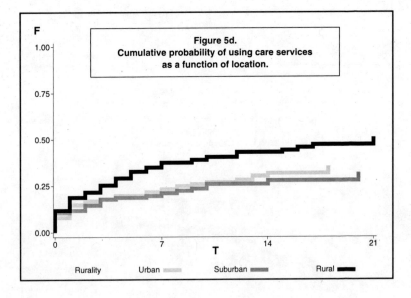

THE REFORM AND THE UTILIZATION OF PUBLIC HEALTH SERVICES

The government's specific objective was to create a new dynamic that would increase attendance at public primary care health facilities. Unfortunately, the results have been disappointing. None of the strategies adopted—investment in additional facilities, institutional changes, making EGDs more available and improving their use, and efforts to involve communities more in governance and management of facilities—has led to an increase in the level of utilization of public health facilities, which is still among the lowest in West Africa. For many people, access to public services remains a privilege (Figure 6). Given the Ministry's ineffectiveness in meeting the very real challenges of allocative deficiency, poor service quality, concentrations of opportunity deficits, and economic barriers for much of the population, the health system reform is, in this respect, a bitter failure.

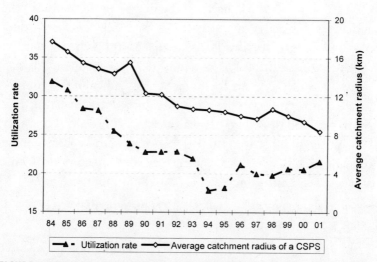

FIGURE 6. UTILIZATION OF PRIMARY CARE PUBLIC SERVICES IN BURKINA FASO, 1984–2001

Source: Ministère de la santé, Burkina Faso. Direction des études et de la planification.

THE REFORM AND THE ECONOMIC BURDEN OF ILLNESS

More than two-thirds of families stated that their health expenses had increased in the previous two years. Among the 802 persons who had been ill in the four weeks before being surveyed, one out of 20 had to sell food products to cover health expenses, one out of 15 had taken out a loan, one out of 15 had taken money from savings, and 14 had to pawn a household belonging. In cities, there is more recourse (9.9%) to taking out loans, whereas in rural and semi-urban areas, people are more likely to sell their food supplies (8% rural, 5.8% semi-urban) or take money from savings (2% urban, 11.6% semi-urban, 6.4% rural). These results are evidence of adaptive behaviors linked to the local economic context and available resources. Urban density and the more common use of money in transactions make recourse to loans easier in cities, whereas the same level of poverty among peasants is more likely to incite them to use savings or sell food stocks.

As with utilization, an analysis of households' consumption of health services sheds light on the overall performance of the system, as this consumption is also, to some extent, the product of many factors that can facilitate or constrain the capacity to receive care. In the prior 12 months, 73% of households had incurred health expenses for at least one member. In this country where families must devote most of their income to meeting their needs for food, spending on health care is constrained to a very modest level (Table 14). These statistics must be kept in context, remembering that health spending is elastic in relation to income and is largely constrained by the household's ability to pay.

TABLE 14. ALLOCATION OF ANNUAL CONSUMPTION OF HOUSEHOLDS IN THE STUDY, BURKINA FASO (IN CFAF)

Item	Environment		
	Urban	Semi-urban	Rural
Health	103 920	85 807	42 767
Food	467 625	27 897	255 083
Education	93 642	33 342	13 001
Total	1 100 520	605 062	394 244

Source: MAPHealth study (2001).

Multivariate regressions help to refine these observations. The model presented in Table 15 aims to identify, simultaneously, factors associated with the incidence of health expenses and with the amounts paid out by the households concerned. It can be seen that income determines both the propensity to spend and the amounts. Looking at propensity to spend in very poor households, i.e., those whose income was less than half the poverty limit established in 1998 of 72 690 CFAF (110 USD) per adult equivalent, the results are gratifying. All other things being equal, their propensity to spend is twice as low as other poor households (those between the half-way mark and the poverty limit), four times less than those whose income is one or two times the poverty limit, and six times less than those families whose income is more than double that limit. At equal income levels, those with secure incomes use more services, most certainly because they are less exposed to seasonal risks. All things being equal, larger households consume more, and more often, than smaller ones, which may be due to having more needs. Households in remote villages, too far from health centres, will consume half as much; this would seem to be a function of poor geographical access and of the difficulties of satisfying health-care needs in that context. Finally, given equal individual capacity, it is in the city of Bobo-Dioulasso that spending is the lowest. To the extent that the model takes into account the effects of income and other individual characteristics, this finding probably illustrates a price effect: the diversity and proximity of service providers and drug retailers, in both the formal and informal sectors, would result in lower prices than are seen in smaller towns and villages.

The economic burden of health care is thus unevenly distributed. Furthermore, analysis of Lorenz curves and coefficients demonstrates that inequality in households' health consumption is more pronounced in cities, where the offer—public as well as private—is more dense and income more unevenly distributed. The Gini coefficient, which measures the extent of inequalities in households' out-of-pocket spending for health care, is 0.49

TABLE 15. FACTORS ASSOCIATED WITH HOUSEHOLDS' CONSUMPTION OF HEALTH CARE. MULTIVARIATE CONDITIONAL REGRESSIONS: CONDITIONAL PARAMETERS AND PROBABILITIES

	Model 1 (binominal) Incidence of expenditure (yes–no)			Model 2 (continuous) Amounts spent*	
Fixed effects	B	SE	OD	B	SE
Intercept	-0.68	0.23	0.51	-4 171	3 174
Revenue (Y)					
0.5PL<Y<1PL	0.80	0.20	2.23	2 262	3 091
1PL<Y<2PL	1.32	0.20	3.74	6 943	3 085
2PL<Y	1.76	0.22	5.81	28 602	3 356
Household size					
1-4				4 271	2 014
5-9	0.78	0.15	2.18		
10+	1.36	0.17	3.90		
Profession of head of household					
Employed in private sector				5 940	2 930
Employed in public sector				15 820	3 533
Environment					
Small cities (semi-urban)				8 504	2 516
Rural				3 648	2 194
Distance from CSPS					
d > 5 km	-0.54	0.19	0.58		
Random effects	*Variance*	*SE*		*Variance*	*SE*
Level 2	0.27	0.09		0.00	0.00
Level 1	1.00	0.00		1 161 334	41 004 770
Covariance	*0.00*	*0.00*		*6 699*	*844*

Source: MAPHealth study (2001).

* Health expenditure per adult equivalent

B: beta; SE: standard error; OR: odds ratio; PL: poverty line

All associations presented are statistically significant to within 5%.

at Bobo-Dioulasso and 0.54 and 0.46 in the semi-urban areas of Nouna and Bazega, respectively. In rural areas, it is no more than 0.39 and 0.33. In the city, the inequality in health spending mirrors that of income, and the Kakwani index of redistribution is not significantly different from zero. However, in outlying villages, where primary care services are less accessible and relative prices higher, health expenditures are significantly more unevenly distributed than income (Figure 7). This is to a large extent due

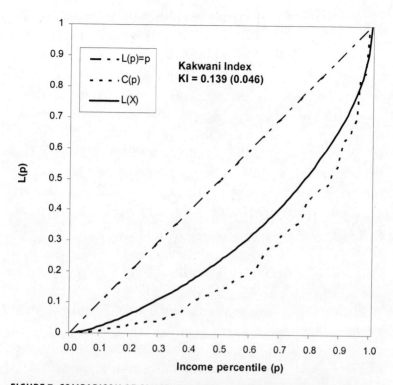

FIGURE 7. COMPARISON OF CONCENTRATION OF INCOME AND OUT-OF-POCKET SPENDING FOR HEALTH IN BURKINA FASO IN VILLAGES MORE THAN 5 KM FROM A CSPS

Legend:

L(p) = Lorenz curve of income inequality (total consumption per equivalent adult)

C(p) = Concentration curve of out-of-pocket spending per equivalent adult

Source: MAPHealth study (2001).

to the financial barriers to access experienced by poorer households and the high income elasticity of demand.

What is the impact of illness and health-care spending on households? This has not been easy to evaluate, because it depends on the extent to which the illness has drawn upon the family's resources and on the loss of income that may be incurred in the short, medium, or long term. Unfortunately, the information available does not allow us to analyze the impact of illness on productivity and household outputs. We have nevertheless estimated some of these impacts, focusing on the monetary impoverishment of households. The evaluation rests on the hypothesis, reasonable in this context, that health expenses reduce the capacity to satisfy essential needs. The available income is reduced by the amount spent on health care. Because the poverty line is defined on the basis of satisfying basic nutritional needs, we can assume that: (i) poor households will become poorer by an amount corresponding to what they have spent on health; (ii) households that were originally not poor but whose residual incomes are below the poverty line, become newly poor; and (iii) monetary impoverishment[4] attributable to direct health-care expenses can be measured as follows:

$$\Delta(PI) = [PI(z)_2 - PI(z)_1] \, / \, PI(z)_2$$

$\Delta(PI)$ is the impoverishment attributable to direct health-care expenses measured in terms of incidence, z is the poverty line, and $PI(z)_1$ and $PI(z)_2$ are the incidence levels of poverty before and after accounting for the deduction of health expenses.

$$\Delta(PG) = PG(z)_2 - PG(z)_1$$

$\Delta(PG)$ is the impoverishment measured in terms of the intensity of poverty, z is the poverty line, and $DI(z)_1$ and $DI(z)_2$ are the poverty gaps before and after accounting for the deduction of health expenses from household income. $\Delta(PG)$ is also the poverty gap attributable to direct health-care expenses and has the advantage of being expressed in monetary units. It corresponds to the per capita minimum cost of a financial protection strategy in poor households (Ravaillon 1992). It can also be broken down to estimate the relative contribution of different opportunity deficits to overall impoverishment tied to health expenses. Finally, as measures of poverty are sensitive to the level of the poverty line, this parameter is used for sensitivity analysis.

The analysis demonstrates that illness is manifestly a factor of monetary impoverishment. Health expenses contribute to poverty, creating newly poor households and further impoverishing those already poor. They bring the greatest poverty to outlying rural regions where opportunity deficits are concentrated. In these areas, we find economic poverty, isolation, insufficient local solidarity mechanisms to help families in need, poor availability of public infrastructures, and relatively high health-care costs. Veritable poverty traps, where opportunity deficits converge, these areas are where the economic damages of illness are the greatest and where the need for financial protection of households against the risks of illness is most pronounced.

What strategies should the authorities implement to protect these households? Responses to this question are still to be found, as the issues are complex and the situations are specific. Nevertheless, our analysis suggests that part of the impoverishment observed was among families originally living above the poverty threshold. So, it is not enough to develop strategies that target only the poor.

The unpredictable nature of illness and its associated costs suggest the need for financial protection of households via interventions targeting barriers to access and opportunity deficits, rather than focusing on households that have been defined from the start as poor. A variety of strategies could be considered to overcome access barriers and protect families against the financial risks of illness. Some, like support to micro-insurance and mutual benefit societies, primarily target demand. Others target the supply side and might involve improving physical accessibility of public services or reducing prices. Our simulations suggest that targeting poverty traps by ensuring adequate geographical access to public health resources could reduce the poverty deficit attributable to households' direct health-care expenses by 20%. Another 20% of the marginal poverty deficit could be saved if the population were at least minimally covered by health insurance, which could be co-financed by the state and individuals, where the fees would be comparable to those already in place locally, on a smaller scale. The combination of approaches, one focused on supply (geographical access) and the other on demand (health insurance) could reduce impoverishment caused by illness by about half.

CONCLUSION

The Burkinabé reform was originally full of promise. It could certainly have become a model for others, as it brought together many favourable conditions, including the rare combination of a benevolent Minister of Health and an adjustment that aligned sectoral reform and expansion of public resources with a manda-tory macroeconomic adjustment exercise. Burkina Faso's health-care reform brought together several convincing strategies aimed at improving the efficiency of the health sector, rectifying existing inequalities of resource allocation, reinforcing the governances of the health districts, and, of course, removing barriers and provid-ing access to services of quality.

However, the result has been disappointing, and, to para-phrase Bodart et al., the health-care system itself is a patient still in need of treatment. More has been spent, much more, but not better. Illness continues to impoverish the poor and even the less poor, access to services of good quality evades the majority of the population, regulation and governance leave much to be desired, community participation is reduced almost exclusively to fundraising; resource allocation is still very inefficient, national experts are leaving the country, attendance at publicly funded health centres is hopelessly low, and the overall system—deci-sion-makers, contributors, managers, and those working in the field—continues to evade accountability.

Does this reform represent a lost opportunity? It may be so, as it is difficult to imagine those in charge being able to assemble, again, so many favourable conditions. Of course, they, and par-ticularly the Minister of Health, have this responsibility. But responsibility lies also with development agencies, multilateral and bilateral, that have supported a reform that has not gone far enough in achieving a governance that is more efficient, equitable, and democratic.

Notes

1. The currency of Burkina Faso is the *CFA franc BCEAO (Banque Centrale des États de l'Afrique de l'Ouest)*, currency code XOF, symbol CFAF. All references to this currency in this chapter are given as CFAF.
2. The typical district covers a population of 150 000–300 000 and is organized around a network of CSPSs within a radius of 10–12 km, with an appropriate level of administrative and community support.
3. For more detail on the composition, construction, and validation of the quality scores, the reader is invited to consult Haddad et al. (1998).
4. Of course it must be recognized that measuring poverty in this way, i.e., considering only direct, short-term monetary impacts, accounts only for the minimum impoverishment of the household. It does not take into account other losses of productivity and long-term effects on monetary and non-monetary elements of the household's well-being.

References

Afogbe, K. 1997. Rapport de l'étude sur l'utilisation des médicaments essentiels génériques (MEG). Ministère de la santé, Ouagadougou, Burkina Faso, BASP'96. 72 pp.

Aubel, J.; Sobgo, G. 1998. Étude de cas: un partenariat entre l'ONG Save the Children Pays-Bas et le district sanitaire de Kongoussi au Burkina Faso. Ministère de la santé, Ouagadougou, Burkina Faso. 38 pp.

Blaise, P.; Kegels, G.; Van Lerberghe, W.; Diakité, B.D.; Touré, G. 1997. Coûts et financement du système de santé de cercle au Mali. ITG Press, Antwerp, Belgium. 130 pp.

Bodart, C.; Servais, G.; Lamine, Y.M.; Schmidt-Ehry, B. 2001. The influence of health sector reform and external assistance in Burkina Faso. Health Policy and Planning, 16(1), 74–86.

Chabot, J.; Conombo, S.C.; Meuwissen, L.; Yonli, L. 1999. Rapport de l'évaluation finale du programme d'appui aux soins de santé primaires dans la région de Kaya (PASSPK). Ouagadougou, Ministère de la santé and Save the Children Pays Bas (SCPB). 86 pp.

Condamine, J.-L.; Artigues S.; Midol, S.; Buisset, K.; Burkina, K.B. 1999. Programme de soutien à la mise en place de l'Initiative de Bamako : analyse de la création de huit aires de santé, province de la Gnagna. Cahier Santé, 9(5), 305–311.

Gilson, L. 1997. The lessons of user fee experience in Africa. Health Policy and Planning, 12(4), 273–285.

Government of Burkina Faso. 2001. Rapport du conseil des ministres du 7 février 2001. Ouagadougou, Burkina Faso.

GTZ (Deutsche Gesellschaft für Technische Zusammenarbeit, GmbH). 2000. Étude sur la mise en place des médicaments essentiels et génériques dans les régions sanitaires de Gaoua et de Dédougou. GTZ, Dédougou, Burkina Faso.

Haddad, S.; Fournier, P. 1995. Quality, cost and utilization of health services in developing countries: a longitudinal study in Zaïre. Social Science and Medicine, 40(6), 743–753.

Haddad, S.; Fournier, P.; Potvin, L. 1998. Measuring community perceptions of the quality of primary health care services in developing countries. Validation of a 20-item scale. International Journal for Quality in Health Care, 10(2), 93–104.

INSD (Institut National de la Statistique et de la Démographie); Macro International Inc. 2000. Enquête démographique et de santé, Burkina Faso 1998–1999. Macro International Inc., Calverton, MD, USA.

Krause, G.; Borchert, M.; Benzler, J.; Heinmüller, R.; Kaba, I.; Savadogo, M.; Siho, N.; Diesfeld, H.J. 1999. Rationality of drug prescriptions in the rural health centres in Burkina Faso. Health Policy and Planning, 14(3), 291–298.

Ministère de la santé. 1996. Document cadre de politique pharmaceutique nationale. Ouagadougou, Burkina Faso. 17 pp.

_____ 1999. Revue de la mise en oeuvre de l'initiative de Bamako au Burkina Faso. Ouagadougou, Burkina Faso. 15 pp.

_____ 2002. Annuaire statistique 2002. Direction des études et de la planification. Ouagadougou, Burkina Faso. 165 pp.

Ministère de l'économie et des finances. 2000. Burkina Faso: cadre stratégique de lutte contre la pauvreté. Ouagadougou, Burkina Faso. 65 pp.

Nacoulma, D.; Petitjean, F.; Sanou, A.; Some, M. et al. 1995. Une expérience de mutuelle en zone rurale au Burkina Faso. Paper presented at the IVe Journées des Sciences de la Santé de Bobo-Dioulasso, 1995. 15 pp.

Nyamba, A. 1994. Un an après la dévaluation du Franc CFA : la réponse des consommateurs. Ouagadougou, Burkina Faso.

Ouédraogo, G.J. 1999. Étude sur la charge de travail dans les formations sanitaires. Rapport final. Ministère de la santé, Direction des études et de la planification. Ouagadougou, Burkina Faso.

Peters, D.H.; Kandola, K.; Elmendorf, A.E.; Chelleraj, G. 1999. Health expenditures, services, and outcomes in Africa: basic data and cross-national comparisons, 1990–1996. Report no. 19578. Health, Nutrition, and Population Series. World Bank, Washington, DC, USA. 55 pp.

Quinti G. et al. 1998. Etude de faisabilité d'un projet de santé au Burkina Faso dans le cadre du 8e FED (Fonds européen de développement). Rapport de faisabilité définitif. CERFE, Rome, Italy.

Ravaillon, M. 1992. Poverty comparisons: a guide to concepts and methods. Living standards measurement study. Report no. LSM88. World Bank, Washington, DC, USA. 138 pp.

Ridde, V. 2003. Fees-for-services, cost recovery, and equity in a district of Burkina Faso operating the Bamako Initiative. Bulletin of the World Health Organization (WHO): the International Journal of Public Health, 87(7), 532–538.

Sakho, M.; Yonli, L. 1997. Rapport de backstopping sur le recouvrement des coûts dans la région de Kaya. Ministère de la santé, Ouagadougou, Burkina Faso.

Watkins, K. 1997. Cost-recovery and equity in the health sector: issues for developing countries. Paper presented at World Institute for Development Economics Research (WIDER) Project on Provision and Financing of Public Goods in Developing Countries, 27 February 1997, London, UK. Oxfam, Oxford, UK, and Ireland Policy Department. 31 pp.

Wood, A. 1997. Annotated bibliography on user charges in developing countries. Discussion paper prepared for the ODA Research Work Programme "Improved care of diseases of childhood". Centre for International Child Health (CICH), Institute of Child Health, London, UK. 50 pp.

World Bank. 1998. Annexe de l'aide mémoire. Mission de supervision du PDSN (Plan de développement sanitaire national), 1–29 March 1998. Ouagadougou, Burkina Faso.

Yoder, R.A. 1989. Are people willing and able to pay for health services? Social Science and Medicine, 29(1), 35–42.

CHAPTER 5

AIMING FOR EQUITY IN COLOMBIA'S HEALTH SYSTEM REFORM: ACHIEVEMENTS AND CONTINUING CHALLENGES

Francisco José Yepes, Manuel Ramírez, María Gloria Cano,
Rodrigo Bustamante

INTRODUCTION

Health system reforms have been a regular occurrence in countries around the world for several decades. Many have been aimed primarily at controlling health expenditures and making health systems more efficient. Others have been driven by political agendas promoting universal coverage, solidarity, equity, and social participation. Most, however, have been both politically and economically motivated. During the 1990s, the pace of reforms accelerated. In some countries, this occurred in response to internal political changes, but in many others it was caused by external pressures from international organizations. A common thread has been the search for universality and efficiency, with most health reforms of the 1990s being market-oriented. Decentralization has also been a strategy of many reforms, being seen as effective in stimulating service delivery, better allocating resources according to needs, and involving communities in decisions on priorities, so as to reduce inequities.

In this chapter, we examine the equity effects of health sector reforms in Colombia resulting from macroeconomic adjustment policies introduced over the course of a 20-year period (1980–2000), focusing on changes introduced in the health-care system during the latter half of that period. We document increases in public social expenditure and particularly in health expenditure (public and private) as well the effects on equity in terms of financing, targeting of subsidies, health insurance coverage, and access to health services in an economy under profound recession.

STUDY METHODS

This was a retrospective time series study with several points of observation, using secondary data from government sources in health and economics, as well as from several household surveys carried out by different institutions over almost two decades. Additionally, in two selected regions—one with the highest and one with the lowest level of development—specific data collection was done through a survey of health facilities (hospitals, health centres, and health posts[1]), individual interviews, and focus groups with executives at municipal levels, as well as through content analysis of documentation about national health and economic policies.

The results presented in this chapter are based on both government and cross-sectional secondary data. Macroeconomic analysis used secondary data from the Central Bank (*Banco de la República*), the National Planning Department (*Departamento Nacional de Planeación – DNP*) and the Statistics Department (*Departamento Administrativo Nacional de Estadística – DANE*). Cross-sectional data were taken from 1993 and 1997 Quality of Life Surveys carried out by DANE.

COUNTRY PROFILE

Located at the northwest extreme of South America, Colombia is a lower-middle-income country with a per capita GNI of 1 810 USD in 2002 (World Bank 2003a) and an estimated population of 44 583 577 in 2003, 49.4% males and 50.6% females. Population growth rate in 2003 was 2% (World Bank 2003b) and demographic density was 32.4 inhabitants per km², with 71% of the country's inhabitants living in urban areas. Indigenous population represents 1.7% of all inhabitants and blacks, 1.6%. In general, the demographic indicators showed steady improvement between 1970–1975 and 1990–1995. On average, life expectancy has increased and both infant mortality and the overall fertility rate have decreased. However, there are still significant regional and socioeconomic differences.

Until 1997, economic growth of about 4.5% per year in the previous four decades, combined with a decrease in the population growth rate to 2.05% per year, led to substantial improvements in social conditions. Since 1997, with the slowdown of economic activity, economic growth (around zero between 1998 and 2002) has been smaller than population growth, with decreases in per capita income and social conditions. The Gini coefficient worsened in the last years and was .57 in 2000 (Ministerio de Salud et al. 2002).

Life expectancy at birth in 2002 was 71.8 years (World Bank 2003b), up more than 21% compared with 1965, when it was 59 years. Primary school enrolment was close to 90% in 1998, and the literacy rate was 97.2% (World Bank 2003b). Nonetheless, poverty remains a critical problem. It was estimated that, in 1992, more than six million Colombians, 19% of the population at that time, had incomes below a commonly accepted subsistence level, with three out of four of these living in rural areas.

During earlier decades, Colombia had made substantial progress in improving the living standards of its population, with poverty declining steadily from an estimated 50% in 1964 to 19% in 1992; but by 2002, poverty had increased again to levels near 30%.

Some 6.7% of children under age five are malnourished, 19% of the population have no access to health services, and about 30% lack access to safe water (1998). Sharp regional disparities in quality of life contribute to social disintegration in large areas of the country. Coverage for basic services at home increased significantly between 1985 and 1993, from 70.5% to 82% for water supply and from 59.4% to 69.9% for sewerage connections. Nevertheless, there are still 6 million persons without water supply and 10 million without sewerage. The situation is more critical in rural areas, where between 5 and 8 million people lack at least one of these services. The gaps are even greater when it comes to water quality. The ratio of the population living in abject poverty (presence of two or more indicators of unmet basic needs) in rural areas relative to those in the municipal seats increased from 2.2 to 5.0 between 1985 and 1993, reflecting improvement in urban areas that did not correspond to the situation observed in rural areas.

Estimated infant mortality in 2002 was 25.6 per 1 000 live births, and maternal mortality was 67.7 per 100 000 live births, with 93% of deliveries being institutional, 91.3% by a physician and 1.7% by nurses or auxiliary nurses (Ministerio de Salud et al. 2002). In 2001, immunization coverage in children under one year old was 77.6% for diphtheria, pertussis, and tetanus, 80.5% for polio, and 87.7% for prenatal tetanus vaccine.

The four greatest causes of mortality (1999) were cardiovascular diseases (121.1 per 100 000 inhabitants), homicides and suicides (67.5), cancer (64.8), and perinatal causes (19.4). Morbidity due to communicable diseases continues to be important. The incidence rate (per 100 000 inhabitants) for malaria was 766.5; for dengue, 180.1; for tuberculosis, 26.2; and for AIDS, 2.3.

MACROECONOMIC CONTEXT

Between 1980 and 2000, Colombia had two severe periods of adjustment, the first during the early 1980s with an IMF advisory and the second from 1999 to date. From 1980 to 1995, average GNP growth was 3.8% per year. Between 1995 and 2002, GNP stagnated; whereas growth averaged about 3% per year from 1995 to 1997, there was no economic growth between 1997 and 2002.

Four periods can be distinguished during these 20 years. The first corresponds to the debt crisis of the early 1980s, with a marked decrease in economic growth. The second, from 1985 to 1989 when the first, but incomplete, macroeconomic adjustment policies were implemented, was characterized by partial recuperation of economic activity. The third occurred in the early 1990s, with major structural reforms and rapid GNP growth after a semi-recession in 1991. The fourth, from 1995 to the present, has resulted in the greatest recession in Colombia in the 20th century.

Two main political reforms took place during this 20-year period. The first was the political, fiscal, and administrative decentralization of the State that started in the early 1980s, with substantial transference of autonomy, resources, and responsibilities to the municipal level. This decentralization had very important consequences for the health sector. The second was the formulation of a new Constitution (1991) replacing that of 1886. Under this new Constitution, the Central Bank was given autonomy from government action, transfers from central to local governments were increased (from 4.3% of GNP in 1990 to 7.7% in 1997), and, as a consequence, there was an unprecedented increase in public social expenditure (Figure 1). A labour reform law (Law 50, 1991) changed the labour regime to reduce rigidities and facilitate industrial restructuring. In June 1993, Congress passed legislation to further develop the ongoing decentralization in Colombia and, in December 1993, introduced profound social security reform in both the financial and health sectors.

There are important differences of opinion over the economic consequences of the reforms. There is consensus that the new Constitution increased social expenditure and introduced serious rigidities. It is also generally recognized that regional transfers increased local expenditure without diminishing central expenditure. The reforms did not create new income sources, hence contributing jointly with other internal and external factors to the deep fiscal crisis of the end of the century.

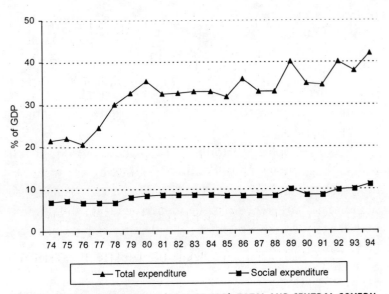

FIGURE 1. PUBLIC EXPENDITURE (AS % OF GDP), TOTAL AND CENTRAL GOVERN-MENT, COLOMBIA, 1974–1994

Source: DNP and DANE. Estimates of the Social Mission.

THE HEALTH SYSTEM IN COLOMBIA BEFORE 1991

The Colombian health system was reformed several times during the 20th century, in accordance with prevailing conceptions of the State and with the influence of international organizations (Quevedo 1990). In the second half of the 1970s, the National Health System (*Sistema Nacional de Salud*) was created, with a highly centralized structure headed by a powerful Ministry of Health. This system, which existed up until the most recent reforms, was three-tiered: (i) a private sector, serving mainly but not exclusively the affluent; (ii) a social security sector, which never reached beyond 23% coverage and which was mainly concentrated in the largest urban areas and among workers of the formal sector; and (iii) a public sector, with hospitals, health centres, and health posts serving the poor and uninsured (Diagram 1). Government accepted that 20% of the population was not reached by any sector. Traditionally, the national budget financed health centres, hospitals, and other public health programs. The private sector offered services through insurance or direct payment. The social security institutions financed themselves through their members' payments.

This health system was both inequitable and inefficient: inequitable because real access to health services privileged those with least need, and inefficient because Colombia was already spending 7.4% of its GNP on health with poor results, compared to other countries with similar or lower levels of spending, such as Costa Rica (Yepes 1990).

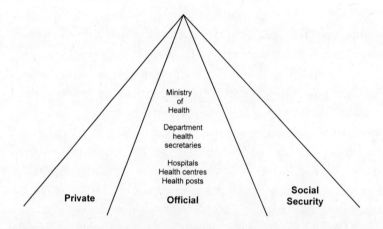

DIAGRAM 1.   HEALTH SECTOR STRUCTURE IN COLOMBIA BEFORE 1993 REFORM

REFORMS AFFECTING THE HEALTH-CARE SYSTEM

Since the late 1980s, there have been two main sets of reforms, decentralization and reforms to the social security system, both of which changed profoundly the functioning and configuration of the health-care system.

Decentralization

During the period 1986–1990, the health system was decentralized to the municipal levels as part of a general political, administrative, and financial decentralization of the State. Department governors and municipal mayors were elected by popular vote, and administrative competencies were transferred to the municipalities along with the financial resources required to support them. Through decentralization (Law 10, 1990) municipalities assumed major responsibility for the health of their communities, which they had not had before, and a significant number of new local health actors came into the sector (Yepes et al. 1999). Mayors became the heads of municipal health systems, with the duty of developing local health plans integrated into the municipal plans. Municipalities' responsibilities included defining local health policies, health planning, constructing and maintaining health facilities, and providing first-level health services to their communities either directly or by contracting with public or private providers, as well as by developing public health activities.

Decentralization entailed important power shifts among the various governments involved (national, departmental, municipal). The national level was freed of the actual provision of services, allowing it to concentrate on policy formulation and technical assistance. Municipalities assumed control over local health decisions, and departments' control over municipal decisions was reduced. Social participation in health was strengthened by regulating the Local Health Committees (*Comités de Participación Comunitaria – COPACOS*) and by including the community in boards of directors of public hospitals (one-third representation).

However, the decentralization process has not been easy. Many interests at the national and departmental levels have opposed it in one form or another with some success. In several departments, such as in Cundinamarca, it was systematically opposed and impeded by the departmental governments. This has led to an uneven process, such that decentralization is very advanced in some regions while almost non-existent in others. Recent changes in national legislation (Law 715, 2001) have created even more obstacles to the decentralization process. In fact, this law halted the process in municipalities that had not yet been decentralized by the time it was enacted.

Social security reform

Under the new Constitution of 1991, health and social security became rights. The social security reform introduced a concrete system to attain those rights based on five guiding principles: efficiency, universality, solidarity, comprehensiveness, and social participation. It significantly transformed the health sector and introduced new actors and practices into the system (Diagram 2).

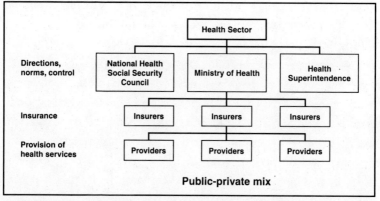

DIAGRAM 2. HEALTH SECTOR STRUCTURE IN COLOMBIA AFTER 1993 REFORM

The health sector reform enacted by Law 100 in 1993 and implemented after January 1995 was extremely ambitious, aiming to integrate the social security and public health sectors and to create universal access to the system, while bringing market pressures to bear on institutions to improve their efficiency. In pursuit of universal access, Law 100 set the framework for a national health insurance system, with the goal of increasing insurance coverage from 20% to 100% by 2001 and ensuring entitlement to a basic package of services (*Paquete obligatorio de servicios – POS*) for all. By 2003, health insurance coverage was at 53% (up from 23% before the reform, although still far from 100%).[2]

Under the reform, a new General System of Social Security in Health (*Sistema General de Seguridad Social en Salud – SGSSS*) was created with two regimes: the *contributive* for those who can afford to pay and the *subsidized* for the poor. Anyone with a labour contract or an income above two minimum salaries (if working independently) must be affiliated to the contribituve regime and pay 12% of their declared income. The poor must apply to their municipality and undergo a means test. If they are under a certain level of income, they qualify and are authorized to become affiliated. The number of poor affiliates authorized in each municipality depends upon the resources available. Those with no insurance coverage, either because they do not have a labour contract or are not poor enough to be subsidized under currently available resources, receive care in public hospitals for as long as there are enough resources to universalize insurance.

New entities were also created. The contributive regime insurers (*Entidad promotora de servicios – EPS*) were wholly new to the system, as were the Compensation Fund and the National Health Social Security Council (*Consejo Nacional de Seguridad Social en Salud*). The Compensation Fund is a fiduciary account that manages all income from the EPSs, which must report their affiliates and premiums received every month. In this process, called *compensación*, they either compensate the Fund with the surplus collected, if the average premium collection exceeds the capitation, or are compensated by the Fund for any negative difference between the collected premiums and the corresponding capitation. The National Health Social Security Council is a collective body with representation from all system actors (government, employers, workers, professionals, pensioners, insurers, providers, and rural community). This Council makes the most important decisions in the day-to-day functioning of the system, such as defining the content of the POS and the amount of the capitation unit to be recognized to the insurers.

The Ministry of Health and the Health Superintendence (*Superintendencia de Salud*) were significantly restructured to adapt to the new circumstances, and a large body of regulations was enacted. Since the beginning of the reform, the Ministry of Health has put aside the direct provision of services and has undertaken a continuous process of adaptation to strengthen its normative and regulatory capacity. At the same time, the Health Superintendence was strengthened to increase its capacity to inspect and control public and private insurers and providers. However, it is generally acknowledged that it is overwhelmed by the magnitude of this task.

Public hospitals became autonomous entities called State Social Enterprises (*Empresas Sociales del Estado – ESE*) and were progressively moved from supply financing (historic state budgets) to demand financing (selling services in the market). Old institutions changed roles, as in the case of the Ministry of Health, now concentrating on sector stewardship while leaving service provision in the hands of the departments and municipalities and of public and private providers. The Health Superintendence became a major actor in the system, responsible for supervision and control. The private sector enhanced its participation as insurer and provider, and the public sector was forced to modernize and become efficient and competitive. Previous social security institutions were either closed or transformed into EPSs. Social participation was reinforced by the creation of consumer alliances.

With the Ministry of Health at the top and the Health Superintendence in charge of control, the system operates with two layers of competition, one at the level of insurers and another at the level of providers.

At the level of insurers

Insurers compete in both the contributive and the subsidized regimes within narrow limits. All must offer the same package of services set by the Ministry of Health, and all receive the same capitation unit (*Unidad de pago por capitación – UPC*). Competition rests on quality of services and profits depend on efficiency. Although, by law, all insurers must accept any person asking to be affiliated, to avoid cream skimming, in practice it nevertheless occurs by subtle means.

As of 2003, there were 35 insurers (EPSs) in the contributive regime, eight public and 27 private. In the subsidized regime, there were 33 insurers, nine of them serving the indigenous population.

At the level of providers

Updated information on providers is very limited, but it is estimated (2003) that there are approximately 55 000 hospital beds in the country, 60% public and 40% private. All public and private hospitals, as well as health professionals, compete in the market to contract with insurers to provide health services to the insured population.

Between 1994 and 1998, human resources regulations were issued to address such matters as integration and organization of consultative commissions, the salary regime of territorial public health employees, salary increases for health employees in public institutions, and requirements and functions of ESEs. The regulation process was also reinforced. For example, the National Health Institute internal structure and functions were modified (it being assigned the control and vigilance of communicable diseases and public health laboratories). Regulations were also issued related to the new health and social security systems, such as the content of POSs that all insurers must offer to the affiliated population, the operational norms for EPSs, and regulations governing the functioning of ESEs, among others.

Public health

The public health component of the reforms had several aspects. Law 100 contemplated that promotion and prevention should be a part of the POS to be offered by insurers. It set a proportion of the UPC specifically for their financing. The law also stipulated that a Basic Care Plan (*Plan de atención básica – PAB*) including public health activities should be offered free of charge by the territorial authorities.

The functioning of institutions dedicated to extraction, processing, preservation, and transportation of total blood or its derivatives was also regulated, and both the Network and the Council of National Blood Banks were created.

Finally, measures were formulated to prevent people's displacement and to look after, protect, consolidate, and stabilize people who had been socioeconomically displaced by war in Colombia.

Financing

The system is financed by a mix of employer–employee contributions and general taxes. The contributive system is financed exclusively by 12% of the declared income contribution, two-thirds paid by the employer and one-third by the employee. Independent workers must pay 100% of the corresponding contribution.

The subsidized system is financed by general taxes collected by the national government and transferred to the municipalities. These resources are reinforced by departmental and municipal contributions plus the transfer of 8.33% of total collections from the contributive system.

Solidarity

There are solidarity mechanisms both within the contributive system and between it and the subsidized system. Within the contributive, paying a fixed percentage over declared income creates solidarity between those earning more and those earning less, and through the use of capitation, the sick are subsidized by the healthy. Between the contributive (richer and with employment) and the subsidized (poorer) systems there is a cross-solidarity, because 8.33% of the collected funds in the contributive system go to the subsidized. Finally, all taxpayers contribute to the financing of the subsidized insurance for the poor.

REGIONAL ANALYSIS

An in-depth analysis was carried out using two geographical, cultural, and socioeconomic regions deliberately selected to maximize socioeconomic differences. The richer of these (Antioquia) was a subregion of the Antioquia department, corresponding to the municipalities of the Aburra valley, an urban, mostly developed region. The other (Pacifico) was a subregion of the Pacific coast, mostly rural and underdeveloped, with small urban centres.

Analysis was carried out using the 1997 Quality of Life Survey. For our analysis, we defined the following general model to include all variables we thought might explain coverage:

Coverage = f (ability to pay[3]; income; characteristics[4] of the head of household; individual characteristics). For the national level, the model included dummies for zone and strata.

Before proceeding to interpretation of the models, the following comments on the variables should be noted:

— Income and ability to pay presented the expected differences between regions, where Antioquia's mean was higher than the national average and Pacifico's was lower.

— Gender differences were not evident. Over 70% of individuals lived in households headed by a male.

— Age profiles also did not differ between the two regions. For more than 70% of individuals, their household head was aged between 25 and 59 years.

— Education level was higher in Antioquia. Household head education level had the same profile as the individual distribution. More than 70% of individuals lived in households in which the head worked. Regarding other characteristics, there was a higher proportion of pensioner household heads in Antioquia compared with Pacifico and with the national average.

— Differences in economic position were more evident. In Antioquia, household heads worked mainly as private workers or freelancers, whereas in Pacifico freelance, farm, and day workers were very prevalent.

— Antioquia's insurance coverage was 1.35 times that of Pacifico, although Pacifico's was near the national average (55% vs. 57%). The most important cause given for not being affiliated was lack of money, although in Antioquia, lack of employment was also significant.

Because the model gave contradictory results for ability to pay and household income, separate models were run with each of these. The results were statistically significant in all cases.

Logit models were used to estimate the probability of a household having the characteristic studied (health coverage) as a function of a group of explanatory variables.

Logistic regression models allow for modeling the probability of a yes/no outcome as a function of a set of independent variables (such as household income or ability to pay). We used Categorical Data Modeling (CATMOD) in SAS to estimate the effects of individual variables as well as to identify the most predictive model.

To interpret results, we used estimated equations to compute predictions of individual social security coverage, controlling for income or ability to pay (ATP), for persons with different individual and household characteristics, with the following results:

Coverage controlled by ability to pay

The probability of being covered was higher for those of working age (16–59), those with heads of household 25–59 years old, public workers, and pensioned household heads. There was also a positive relationship between the probability of being covered and the individual and household head level of education. There were no differences of coverage probability by gender, even by household head gender. The probability of being covered grew with household ATP. Regionally, the independent variables and coverage profiles were the same as at the national level, although there were differences between regions:

— The probabilities of being covered in Antioquia were over 90% for almost all the cases. The internal differences were not significant.

— By contrast, in Pacifico the differences in ATP were much more significant and affected the probability of being covered. For example, the probability of being covered with a female head of household grew from 55% to 83% as ATP increased, whereas in Antioquia this same probability decreased from 88% to 80%.

— In the Pacifico region the differences of coverage related to ATP were much more significant, and the standard deviation in all cases was much higher than in Antioquia and nationally.

The most important differences are seen in education level and in economic position of household head. The probability of being covered increased with increasing household income and with each additional educational level achieved by the head of the household. In terms of economic position, individuals with household heads who were public employees had a very high probability of being covered regardless of their income, whereas freelancers, employers, and domestic employees had 50% less probability of being covered. As was the case for ATP, household income levels had less effect on the probability of being covered in Antioquia than in Pacifico. For example, the probability of being covered with a household head with no education in Pacifico grew from 55% to 90% as household income increased, whereas in Antioquia it went from 80% to 94%.

Quality

The household quality of life survey used in this analysis measures health services quality through two variables: perception of timeliness of response when care is requested and the degree of satisfaction with the received services. Over 78% classified the service as good, although there was less satisfaction among those covered by the Institute of Social Security in the contributive regime. More than 78% answered that the service was timely although those covered by the Institute of Social Security in the contributive regime reported more service delay. The regional analysis presented similar tendencies in terms of quality and timeliness although the Pacifico region had lower service quality and longer delays in relation to Antioquia.

The survey also evaluated reasons given by the covered population for not using health services. The principal reason overall was "lack of money" followed by "the illness was not serious." In Pacifico, the principal reason given was "lack of money," and in Antioquia it was that "the illness was not serious."

POSITIVE RESULTS OF THE REFORMS

The main positive results of the social security reform have been the increased resources, both public and private, devoted to health; increased coverage; improved equity in financing and insurance coverage; and people's satisfaction with the system.

Increased health financing and improved equity in health financing

Public expenditure on basic health activities increased from 0.53% of GNP in 1980 to 1.41% in 1996. Private health expenditure also rose after 1990 because of the prepaid medicine system, going from 2–2.5% of GDP before the 1990s to 3.7% in 1995 (Vargas and Sarmiento 1997). Meanwhile, per capita expenditure more than doubled in a period of eight years (1987–1995) going from 24.7 USD to 58.7 USD, while expenditures per person among the poor tripled, going from 58.5 USD to 192.4 USD.

Increased insurance coverage

The main impact of the reform was on insurance coverage. Before the mid-1990s, the rate of affiliation was around 23%; it reached 57% by 1997 but then decreased to 53% in 2003, as mentioned earlier. By comparison, in the 1980s the rate of coverage had increased very slowly, from 10.3% in 1980 to 11.9% in 1986. Health sector reform not only increased global coverage but made it more equitable across income levels, age, and education. A very important portion of the observed increase in coverage comes from the coverage extended to the worker's family and to the poorest sectors of the population.

Improved equity in insurance coverage and access

In 1993, subsidies for people affiliated to the social security system constituted 1.21% of GNP, with lower-income families receiving 0.04% of GNP, quintiles 3–4 receiving 0.7% (60% of the subsidy), and the higher-income group receiving 0.27% of GNP (22.3% of the subsidy).

By 1997, subsidized regime subsidies had reached 3.2% of GNP, with 66% going to the poorest 40%, while those with higher income received only 2%. In the contributive regime, subsidies reached 0.63% of GNP, with 0.9% going to quintiles 2–4. The participation of the richest group was negative, i.e., they had to pay instead of being subsidized. Adding both systems, 62% of the subsidies went to the 40% poorest population, and the highest quintile had a negative subsidy of –5.3%.

As can be seen in Figure 2, health system reform reduced the subsidies of the richest segment of the population. Between 1993 and 1997, subsidies for the fourth quintile went from 0.61% to 0.51% of GNP, and for the fifth quintile, from 0.38% to –0.20%.

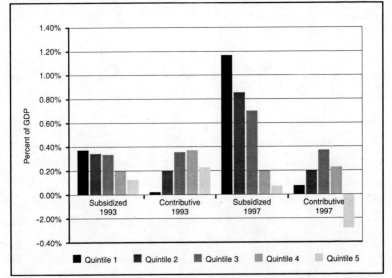

FIGURE 2. HEALTH SECTOR NET SUBSIDIES BY INCOME QUINTILES AND AFFILIA-TION REGIMES (AS % OF GDP), COLOMBIA, 1993 AND 1997

Source: CASEN Survey (2000). Quality of Life Surveys (1993, 1997)

Institutional changes entailed not only a significant increase in net health expenditure, from 2.57% to 3.82% of GNP, but also a significant effort of focalization, as the total increase of the expenditure was destined to the 40% poorest population. As Figure 3 shows, by 1997, health system subsidies represented 45% of households' total income for the first quintile, compared with 12% in 1993. Health subsidies implied a better income distribution, reflected in the reduction of the Gini coefficient from 0.535 to 0.52 in 1993, and from 0.565 to 0.523 in 1997, when the Gini was recalculated after subsidies.

In the following figures, the expansion of coverage for the family is evident. Figures 4 and 5 show coverage expansion by age groups and education level. Figure 6 shows the evolution of social security coverage by income deciles; it can be seen that social security coverage after 1994 is more equitable. In Figure 7, we can see that health system reform reduced the strong relation between

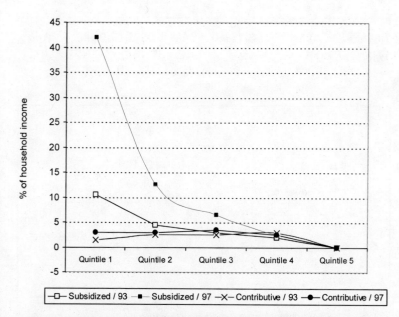

FIGURE 3. INCOME INCREMENT CAUSED BY HEALTH SECTOR SUBSIDIES, BY QUINTILES AND REGIMES, COLOMBIA, 1993 AND 1997.
Source: CASEN Survey (2000). Quality of Life Surveys (1993, 1997).

income and coverage. In 1980, coverage of the 10th income decile was 31 times higher than in the first decile; by 1986 it was just 13 times higher, and by 1997 that factor had been reduced to only 1.86.

The levels of expenditure and coverage increased dramatically, but even more important was the effect of health system

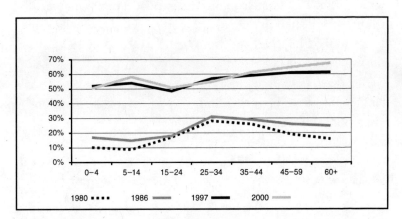

FIGURE 4. SOCIAL SECURITY COVERAGE BY AGE GROUPS, COLOMBIA, 1980, 1986, 1997, 2000

Sources: National Health Surveys 1980, 1986; Quality of Life Surveys 1993, 1997; Demography and Health Survey 2000.

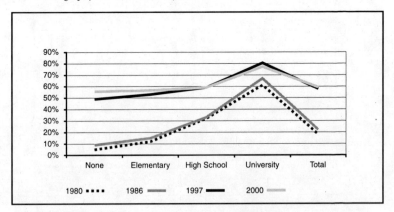

FIGURE 5. SOCIAL SECURITY COVERAGE BY EDUCATION LEVEL, COLOMBIA, 1980, 1986, 1997, 2000

Sources: National Health Surveys 1980, 1986; Quality of Life Surveys 1993, 1997; Demography and Health Survey 2000.

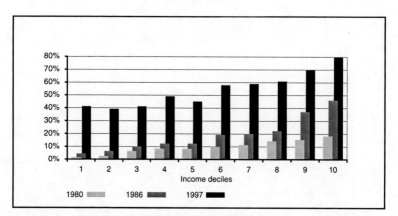

FIGURE 6. SOCIAL SECURITY COVERAGE BY INCOME DECILES, COLOMBIA, 1980, 1986, 1997

Sources: National Health Surveys 1980, 1986; Quality of Life Surveys 1993, 1997.

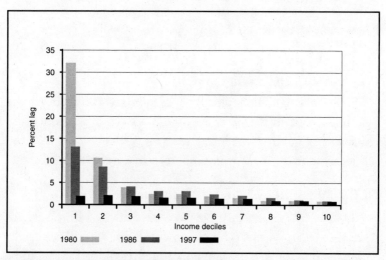

FIGURE 7. LAG FROM EACH INCOME DECILE WITH RESPECT TO THE HIGHEST INCOME DECILE, COLOMBIA, 1980, 1986, 1997

Sources: National Health Surveys 1980, 1986; Quality of Life Surveys 1993, 1997.

reform on the gap between social sectors and geographical zones. Figure 8 shows the gap between rural and urban coverage. It is evident that although urban zone coverage in the 1980s was almost four times the rural coverage, by 1997 it had decreased to only 1.25 times.

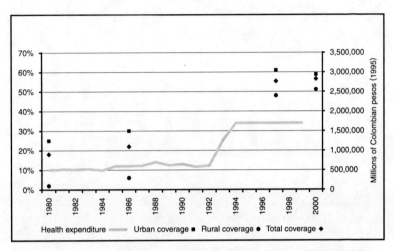

FIGURE 8. SOCIAL SECURITY COVERAGE BY ZONE AND PUBLIC HEALTH EXPEN-DITURE (PRICES OF 1995), COLOMBIA

Sources: health expenditure – DNP, Misión social; health coverage – National Health Surveys 1980, 1986; Quality of Life Surveys 1993, 1997; Demography and Health Survey 2000.

People's satisfaction with the system

In several national studies, population satisfaction with the health-care system has been rated high. Over 78% classified the treatment as good, and more than 78% also answered that the service was timely.[5] Similar findings have been reported elsewhere.

NEGATIVE RESULTS OF THE REFORMS

Despite the many positive outcomes of the reforms, there were also negative aspects whose repercussions are still being felt. These include the detrimental consequences of inadequate transition measures and the high costs of monitoring and controlling the system.

Detrimental effects on public health services

Public health programs and activities were adversely affected, first by decentralization and then by social security reform. Decentralization transferred public health responsibilities to the municipalities without the required training, technical assistance, and supervision by the Ministry of Health or the Department Health Secretaries. Immunization levels decreased, and the epidemiologic surveillance system went into disarray, leading to a series of outbreaks of communicable diseases (dengue, measles, and yellow fever).

With social security reform, the Ministry of Health became immersed in organizational changes and the new insurance system, relegating public health responsibilities to second place. Although the reform contemplated delegating responsibilities for health promotion and disease prevention to the territorial levels (national, departmental, municipal), as well as to insurers and providers, the Ministry of Health was very slow in regulating them. It was only in 1996, with the PAB, that the Ministry regulated the public health responsibilities of the territorial levels and, only in 2000, the health promotion and disease prevention activities of insurers and providers.

Although the reform law specifically contemplated promotion, prevention, and public health in the PAB, it took several years to regulate them (Resolutions 412 and 3384 of 2000). Even today, there is no adequate information as to how public health responsibilities are being carried out by the different municipalities.

Inadequate transition support for public insurers and providers

Before the reform, public insurers and public hospitals operated within protected environments. Public insurers had been working under monopoly conditions (the respective workers did not have any choice), which made them extremely inefficient. They also had very strong unions that, through the years, had attained very considerable and expensive labour conditions. Public hospitals were also inefficient because of high fixed costs, due to excessive personnel, and likewise had expensive labour conditions imposed by labour unions. The situation was further aggravated by the fact that both public insurers and public hospitals had been under politicized managements.

Although the reform was intended to correct this state of affairs by bringing competition to both insurers and hospitals, thereby forcing them to become efficient, it unfortunately failed to address the conditions of public institutions comprehensively. The reasons for this were both political (incapability or lack of decisiveness in dealing with labour unions) and economic (lack of funds to pay laid-off personnel).

In the case of public insurers, the reform did not provide adequate transition conditions to protect them from the very unequal competition of new insurers, who had very low fixed cost structures and, in many instances, practiced cream skimming against the public insurers. This combination of inadequate transition planning, lack of political will to make the required changes on time, and unequal competition led to serious trouble for both public insurers and hospitals. Several of them now face bankruptcy.

Higher system costs for checks and controls

The model adopted by the Colombian reform is complex and cumbersome, difficult to understand, and lacking in transparency. Dealing with this complexity and lack of transparency requires multiple checks and controls, resulting in system costs that could otherwise have been avoided. Among these are:

— The poor must prove their condition to get into the subsidized regime. The State incurs the expense of applying a means test, which must be repeated periodically because the condition of poverty may change.

— The State must verify that the level of income declared by those in the contributive regime corresponds to reality. Otherwise, people tend to under-declare in order to lower their contribution. It has been estimated that evasion, which includes both under-declaring and not becoming affiliated at all, is around 35% (Econometría S.A. et al. 2002).

— The insurers, paid by capitation, must document the names of their affiliates every month. The State has to check that persons reported by the insurer are really their affiliates and do not appear in the lists of other insurers or in the subsidized regime.

— Persons who become unemployed and do not have means to pay their contributive insurance must move to the subsidized insurance. However, this transit from one regime to the other is not automatic, being subject to the application of the means test and the availability of openings.

CONCLUSION

One of the main achievements of the Colombian health system reform has been an overall increase in health insurance coverage, resulting in improved equity, with significantly lower urban–rural and socioeconomic differentials and better targeting of subsidies to the poor. The coverage increase is even more significant if we take into account the deep economic recession the country has been through since 1995. However, there is still much room for improvement, as the regional analysis demonstrates, given the persistence of a positive association of coverage with income and education and the more important effect of these variables in the poorer region.

After nine years of implementation, the reforms had not attained their target of universal coverage, and in fact the level of coverage was stalled at the same position for nearly seven years. This raises many questions about the feasibility of achieving universal coverage, the strategies employed thus far, and the conditions necessary to make it work.

There are also many questions to be explored related to the funding and costs associated with the current system. Is it possible to reduce the transaction costs associated with controlling and monitoring the system? How can evasion and misreporting be eliminated or significantly reduced? Are there more effective models for the mix of private–public insurers and providers? What are the best strategies to ensure their survival and healthy competition? Can the overall system be made more efficient?

Another issue that needs attention is the inequality between the packages of services offered in the contributive and subsidized systems. What conditions would be required to align these more closely and achieve more equity? Is this really feasible, politically and economically, and if so, what strategies would be most appropriate?

Available information, although scarce, shows evidence of improved equity in access to health services. There is not yet any information on equity in quality. Additional research would be required to look at the effects of the reform on access and equity in quality.

Notes

1. Health centres and health posts are both ambulatory facilities. Health centres vary in size and complexity but always have at least an MD. Health posts do not have a permanent MD and are staffed by auxiliary personnel.
2. By 1997 the official coverage reported was 57%. However, this figure later decreased due to corrections of double counting and to decreased contributive insurance because of higher unemployment after 1999.
3. Ability to pay was estimated using as a parameter the household's availability of domestic appliances.
4. Gender, age, education level, main occupational activity, whether in the formal or informal employment sector.
5. From our own analysis of DANE 1997 Quality of Life Survey.

References

Econometría S.A.; Ministerio de Salud Pública; Banco Interamericano de Desarrollo. 2002. Evaluación y reestructuración de los procesos, estrategias y organismos públicos y privados encargados de afiliación, pago y recaudo de aportes al Sistema General de Seguridad Social de Salud en Colombia, SGSSS. Technical report presented to the Ministerio de Salud Pública.

Ministerio de Salud; Instituto Nacional de Salud; OPS (Pan-American Health Organization). 2002. Situación de salud en Colombia: indicadores básicos 2002.

Quevedo, E. 1990. Análisis socio histórico. *In* Yepes, F.J., ed., La salud en Colombia. Estudio Sectorial de Salud. Departamento Nacional de Planeación, Ministerio de Salud. Editorial Presencia, Bogotá, Colombia. 105 pp.

Vargas, J.E.; Sarmiento, A. 1997. La descentralización de los servicios de salud en Colombia. Economic Commission for Latin America and the Caribbean. Public Policy Reforms Series, no. 51, Santiago, Chile. 82 pp.

World Bank. 2003a. World development indicators database, August 2003 (Atlas method). http://devdata.worldbank.org/data-query/
_____ 2003b. World development indicators database, August 2003. http://devdata.worldbank.org/data-query/, cited June 2004.

Yepes, F.J. 1990. La salud en Colombia. Estudio Sectorial de Salud. Departamento Nacional de Planeación, Ministerio de Salud. Editorial Presencia, Bogotá, Colombia. 1124 pp.

Yepes, F.J.; Sánchez, L.H.; Cantor, B. 1999. La descentralización de la salud: el caso de tres municipios colombianos. Investigaciones en Salud Pública. Documentos Técnicos, no. 14, May 1999. OPS/OMS (Pan-American Health Organization / World Health Organization), Washington, DC, USA. 21 pp.

CHAPTER 6

ADJUSTMENT AND HEALTH SECTOR REFORMS: THE SOLUTION TO LOW PUBLIC SPENDING ON HEALTH CARE IN INDIA?

Delampady Narayana

INTRODUCTION

India, a country of continental proportions, holding almost one-sixth of the world's population in about one-fiftieth of the world's geographical area, is one of the poorest in the world, with a poor record of improving the living conditions of its population. India accounts for more than half the total population of the 52 countries of the world where elementary deprivation is concentrated. The country reports an extremely low level of life expectancy (LE) at birth, low literacy levels, and a high infant mortality rate (IMR). However, within this large country of 28 states[1] and a number of union territories, there are important variations in living conditions. At one end of the spectrum lies the state of Kerala, comparable to the developed countries in LE, IMR, and total fertility rate. At the other end are the states of Bihar, Madhya Pradesh, Orissa and Uttar Pradesh, where living conditions are not very different from those prevailing at the lower end of the 52 deprived countries.

After its independence from British rule in 1947, India followed a strategy of planned economic development, with a strong import substitution orientation, for the next four decades. The country has had a precarious foreign exchange reserve position since the

1960s. Despite the rising oil prices and import bill beginning in the mid-1970s, India did not face a balance of payments (BOP) crisis, owing to the Gulf boom and large worker remittances. However, in the 1980s, the complacent Indian economy moved into an import-dependent growth strategy. The rising import bill, slack in the foreign exchange inflow, and heavy external commercial borrowing in the late 1980s developed into a BOP crisis following the Gulf War in 1991. India was compelled to approach the IMF for a loan, and thus began the Adjustment era.

Since then, the overall thrust of macroeconomic adjustment policies (MAPs) has been toward less government and more private enterprise, the reasoning behind which has been that in many sectors private enterprise could do as well, if not better, than government, ushering in rapid economic growth. It has, however, been recognized that less government may not be the best idea in social sectors characterized by market failures and large externalities. This was especially so in India in the beginning of the 1990s, where:

> India's social indicators at the start of the reforms in 1991 lagged behind the levels achieved in southeast Asia 20 years earlier, ... The gap in social sector development needed to be closed, not only to improve the welfare of the poor ... but also to create the preconditions for rapid economic growth. While the logic of economic reforms required a withdrawal of the state from the areas..., it also required an expansion of public sector support for social sector development (Ahluwalia 2002, p. 85).

The need for increased public spending on health was even greater. While total spending on health care in India in the 1990s was over 5% of GDP, public spending, at less than 1% of GDP, was one of the lowest in the world.

> In India's economy—allegedly committed to 'social-ism'—the share of public expenditure in total health expenditure is only around 15%, compared with 75% in Western Europe's 'market economies', rising to 84% in Thatcherism-ravaged Britain. In fact, the share of public expenditure in total health expendi-ture is lower in India than in any other major region of the world (Dreze and Sen 2002, pp. 203–4).

In the Indian Constitution, health is a state responsibil-ity. During Adjustment, many state governments in India had recourse to Health Systems Development Project loans from the World Bank for carrying out health sector reforms (HSR), of which one of the key policies has been to raise public spending on health care from the abysmally low levels seen up to then.

In this chapter, we analyze three issues:

i)   whether the health sector budget has been protected in India during the Adjustment years;

ii)   whether states implementing HSR have enhanced public spending on health; and

iii) in one state with a high burden of communicable diseases, how disease control programs are affected when HSR does not succeed in raising health budgets.

The first two issues are discussed in the general context of health spending on the part of the central and state governments, and the third is presented in the specific context of Orissa, one of the poorest states in India, with a very high burden of communicable diseases.

The first issue is analyzed using data on public spending across the states over the period between 1980/81 and 1997/98, and the second, using data from 1994/95 to 2002/03.[2] Such a division of time periods is called for, as the states began implementing HSR from 1995/96 (e.g. Andhra Pradesh from 1995/96, Karnataka and Punjab from 1997/98, West Bengal from 1998/99, etc.). Therefore, analysis of the first issue was done up to 1997/98, as after that point the effects of HSR would begin to complicate the results.

Our approach has been to compare states pre- and post-Adjustment, with and without HSR. We have concentrated our analysis on 18 states representing approximately 96% of the country's population. The data have been taken from the supplement on state finances of the Reserve Bank of India Bulletin. The proportions needed for the analysis of both issues have been computed using expenditure data at current prices. For the first issue, expenditure data have been converted to constant price series using the implicit deflator of the state domestic product. For the second, two constant-price series have been computed, one using the Wholesale Price Index and another using the Drug and Medicine Price Index.

The chapter is organized in seven sections, beginning with this Introduction. The following section provides, as background, a brief account of India's vast diversity in terms of health status and health systems development within the states and in the patterns of financing health expenditure. The third section briefly presents the salient features of MAPs and Health Systems Development Projects implemented in some of the Indian states since 1994. Government health-care spending in the overall context of government spending up to the mid-1990s is analyzed in the fourth section. The fifth section takes up the analysis of health-care spending by the states from 1994/95 to 2002/03, with the objective of seeing whether HSR has led to enhanced budget allocation to the health sector in the reforming states. The sixth section analyzes the impact of HSR on disease control programs under fiscal pressure in Orissa. The final section presents some conclusions and outstanding issues.

HEALTH STATUS AND HEALTH-CARE ENVIRONMENT IN INDIA

The 20th century has seen a dramatic decline in the crude death rate in all developing countries. In India, the crude death rate (per 1 000 persons) declined from 22.4 in 1931 to 10.2 in 1991. Although in itself the decline is quite significant, given that India has a much larger proportion of the younger age population than other developed countries, a crude death rate of 10.2 nevertheless suggests a poor record in bringing down mortality.

The aggregate mortality rate of a country of India's continental size could conceal marked differentials across the states. As is seen in Table 1, the crude death rate varies from 6.2 to 11.0. Kerala stands apart, reporting a crude death rate of 6.2, which is even lower than that of many developed countries. One group of eight states—Andhra Pradesh, Gujarat, Haryana, Karnataka, Maharastra, Punjab, Tamil Nadu, and West Bengal—report crude death rates within a narrow range of 7.3 to 8.3. Another group of four states—Bihar, Madhya Pradesh, Orissa, and Uttar Pradesh—report crude death rates of above 10.0. A further striking feature across these groups of states is the differentials in crude death rates between male and female. In Kerala, the crude death rate for females is 2.3 points lower than that for males. The group of eight states shows slightly lower crude death rates for females than for males. In the group of four states, however, crude death rates for females are significantly higher than those for males. Thus, not only do the levels of crude death rates vary across the groups of states, but also the differentials between male and female rates show entirely different patterns.

The IMR presents a pattern similar to that of overall death rates across the states of India (Table 1). Compared to the all-India average of 71 for 1997, the variation ranges from 12 for Kerala to 96 for Orissa. Karnataka, Maharastra, Punjab, Tamil Nadu, and West Bengal report IMRs within a narrow range of 47 to 55. At the upper end, the states of Orissa, Madhya Pradesh, Rajasthan, and Uttar Pradesh report IMRs over 85.

The pattern is similar in the death rate of the ages 0–4 group. Kerala reports an extremely low rate of 3.8 deaths per 1 000 population. Karnataka, Maharastra, Punjab, and Tamil Nadu report rates between 12.6 and 16.6, and Orissa, Madhya Pradesh,

TABLE 1. DEATH RATES OF THE YOUNG IN THE INDIAN STATES, 1971–1997

State	Crude death rate		Infant mortality rate		Death rate 0–4 years		Death rate 5–9 years	
	1971	1997	1971	1997	1971	1996	1971	1996
Andhra Pradesh	14.6	8.3	106	63	44.9	17.8	4.7	1.6
Assam	17.8	9.9	139	76	45.7	24.0	7.2	3.5
Bihar	13.9*	10.0	118*	71	42.5*	27.9	5.3*	3.9
Gujarat	16.4	7.6	144	62	64.9	23.3	4.1	1.3
Haryana	9.9	8.0	72	68	32.5	23.4	3.0	1.9
Karnataka	12.1	7.6	95	53	37.5	16.6	4.3	0.9
Kerala	9.0	6.2	58	12	24.5	3.8	2.3	0.9
Madhya Pradesh	15.6	11.0	135	94	49.8	33.5	5.0	3.0
Maharastra	12.3	7.3	105	47	44.6	13.1	3.2	1.0
Orissa	15.4	10.9	127	96	54.2	30.6	5.4	2.9
Punjab	10.4	7.4	102	51	38.9	15.2	1.6	1.2
Rajasthan	16.8	8.9	123	85	55.9	31.4	5.3	2.0
Tamil Nadu	14.4	8.0	113	53	40.7	12.6	4.6	0.6
Uttar Pradesh	20.1	10.3	167	85	83.7	31.4	5.4	3.0
West Bengal	11.0*	7.7	91*	55	33.5*	18.1	2.6*	1.6
All India	**14.9**	**8.9**	**129**	**71**	**51.9**	**23.9**	**4.7**	**2.3**

Source: Registrar General of India (1999).

Note 1: *1981 data; earliest data available within this source for these states.

Note 2: All-India total includes all states and union territories.

Rajasthan, and Uttar Pradesh report rates above 30.5. Thus, with regard to overall mortality, infant mortality, and child mortality, Kerala is far ahead of the rest of the states of India and is comparable to many developed nations, but four states report very high mortality rates that are closer to those in many poorer developing countries. The rest of the states are at various points along the spectrum in between.

The striking differences observed across the states with regard to infant and child mortality rates are not seen in mortality rates for ages above four years. For the ages 5–9 group, the death rate for Kerala is no lower than for some other states. Karnataka, Kerala, Maharastra, and Tamil Nadu report death rates below 1.0. Assam, Bihar, Madhya Pradesh, Orissa, and Uttar Pradesh report death rates above 3.0. The rest of the states report rates in between. The reduction further narrows when groups above age 55 are considered. Only Haryana and Punjab report death rates significantly lower than the all-India average, and Kerala reports death rates closer to the all-India average in those age groups (for detailed discussion, see Narayana 2001).

On the whole, the striking differences observed with regard to crude death rates across the Indian states are largely owing to differences in infant and child mortality rates rather than to differences in mortality rates at higher age groups. Thus, the unique achievement of Kerala and better performance of some other states can be attributed to having lowered the death rates of the younger (ages 0–4) population.

Turning now to the Indian health-care environment, we observe wide variations in the density of medical institutions, their composition, and ownership patterns. The most striking example of inequality in the distribution of medical institutions is the concentration of 45% of all institutions in only three states—Gujarat, Kerala, and Maharastra—accounting for just 18% of the Indian population (Table 2). Five states—Bihar, Madhya Pradesh, Rajasthan, Uttar Pradesh, and West Bengal—account for almost 50% of the Indian population but have only 25% of the total medical institutions. This inequality in distribution of medical institutions is reflected in the variation in population served per institution: over 25 000 per institution in Bihar, Madhya Pradesh, and West Bengal; fewer than 10 000 in Goa, Gujarat, Kerala, Maharastra, and Punjab; between 10 000 and 25 000 in the rest of the states. Behind the fairly low population per institution lies another type of inequality, that between rural and urban areas. In Goa, Gujarat, and Maharastra, over 50% of the institutions are located in urban areas, whereas such an imbalance is not to be seen in Kerala and Punjab.

The composition of medical institutions varies enormously across the states. In Andhra Pradesh, Assam, Gujarat, Kerala, Madhya Pradesh, and Maharastra, over 20% of the institutions are hospitals. In these states, where institutions are concentrated

TABLE 2. DISTRIBUTION OF MEDICAL INSTITUTIONS IN INDIA BY STATES, 1993

State	TMI	Population per institution	Share of urban in TMI	Share in TMI (%) Hospitals	PHC/ CHC	Share of private in TMI (%)
Andhra Pradesh	3 495	19 029	34.65	53.20	38.03	55.05
Assam	1 261	17 764	11.45	21.25	52.93	6.98
Bihar	3 112	27 763	7.84	10.54	75.74	2.89
Goa	769	1 560	50.72	14.82	3.38	90.38
Gujarat	10 724	3 851	65.36	22.10	10.31	82.57
Haryana	748	22 059	33.02	10.43	60.56	8.16
Himachal Pradesh	500	10 400	11.80	11.40	49.80	1.80
Jammu & Kashmir	1 009	7 631	2.87	6.64	32.90	--
Karnataka	2 628	17 123	19.10	11.15	57.27	2.55
Kerala	4 953	5 875	22.39	41.20	19.42	76.64
Madhya Pradesh	1 992	33 233	12.25	30.45	68.93	--
Maharastra	13 237	5 975	78.84	23.53	14.95	74.75
Orissa	1 664	19 050	14.30	17.07	68.99	2.70
Punjab	2 255	9 002	17.16	9.62	25.54	2.26
Rajasthan	2 145	20 513	22.00	10.16	76.64	--
Tamil Nadu	2 428	23 023	28.17	16.80	62.11	6.10
Uttar Pradesh	6 470	21 499	16.75	11.36	61.59	3.52
West Bengal	2 576	26 436	16.38	15.22	63.39	7.41
All India	**64 393**	**13 143**	**39.92**	**21.26**	**36.18**	**40.97**

Source: Government of India, Ministry of Health and Family Welfare (1993).

Note 1: TMI = Total number of medical institutions; includes hospitals, dispensaries and PHC/CHCs.

Note 2: All-India total includes all states and union territories

in urban areas and hospitals account for a larger share, primary health centres (PHCs) and community health centres (CHCs) make up a small proportion of the total institutions. In the rest of the states, over 60% of the institutions are PHCs and CHCs.

The distribution of hospital beds is as unequal as that of medical institutions. The three states of Gujarat, Kerala, and Maharastra account for 37% of the total beds, whereas the five states of Bihar, Madhya Pradesh, Rajasthan, Uttar Pradesh, and West Bengal account for 28% (Table 3). The inequality in the population per bed follows from the inequality of bed distribution across the states. However, there is one important difference in the distribution of beds, in that over 80% of the beds in the

TABLE 3. DISTRIBUTION OF HOSPITAL BEDS IN INDIA BY STATES, 1993

State	Total beds	Share of urban (%)	Population per bed	Share of private (%)
Andhra Pradesh	26 972	64.67	2 466	90.53
Assam	12 703	68.63	1 763	16.01
Bihar	29 186	89.66	2 960	29.19
Goa	3 644	63.09	329	48.38
Gujarat	69 359	86.81	595	61.52
Haryana	7 430	92.45	2 221	30.04
Himachal Pradesh	4 035	83.77	1 289	4.81
Jammu & Kashmir	8 202	1.71	939	1.71
Karnataka	38 838	90.78	1 159	25.76
Kerala	77 362	42.87	376	63.56
Madhya Pradesh	18 143	65.93	3 649	--
Maharastra	80 542	87.01	980	47.85
Orissa	14 629	76.06	2 167	9.37
Punjab	20 142	64.36	1 008	18.84
Rajasthan	20 605	94.90	2 135	--
Tamil Nadu	49 058	91.09	1 139	21.33
Uttar Pradesh	53 007	85.43	2 624	22.83
West Bengal	54 767	86.33	1 243	12.62
All India	**621 376**	**78.26**	**1 362**	**35.66**

Source: Government of India, Ministry of Health and Family Welfare (1993).
Note: All-India total includes all states and union territories.

states are located in urban areas. Only Kerala has about 60% of its hospital beds in rural areas.

States reporting a higher density of hospital beds, especially states with one bed for every 1 000 population or less, have a high proportion of beds in the private health-care sector—close to 50% in Goa and Maharastra, and over 60% in Gujarat and Kerala. Only Andhra Pradesh has a higher private share, combined with a lower density of beds.

The states present striking differences in population covered per institution. Low-density states owe their achievements to the efforts of the public sector in expanding PHCs and CHCs, providing a rural spread. With regard to the density of beds, the story is similar. The share of the private sector is low in the low-density states. However, unlike the medical institutions in the public sector, which are largely in the rural areas, the private-sector beds are largely in the urban areas.

The major Indian states have been categorized by the World Bank according to variations in mortality, fertility, immunization, and the capacity of the public health sector (Table 4). The differences in health transition status mean that while a state like Kerala, at one end, faces the burden of dealing with the high per-episode cost of health care, states like Madhya Pradesh and Orissa, at the other end, face the more urgent need to focus on pre-transition (i.e., predominantly communicable) diseases by implementing public control programs (World Bank 2001). Hence, states in each category face different challenges.

TABLE 4. CATEGORIZATION OF MAJOR INDIAN STATES BY CHARACTERISTICS INFLUENCING FUNDAMENTAL HEALTH SYSTEM CHOICES

Characteristics	States	% of India's population
A. Middle to late transition, moderate to high capacity	Kerala Tamil Nadu	9.1
B. Early to middle transition, low to moderate capacity	Andhra Pradesh Gujarat Haryana Karnataka Maharastra Punjab West Bengal	39.1
C. Very early transition, very low to low capacity	Madhya Pradesh Orissa Rajasthan Uttar Pradesh	33.1
D. Special cases of instability, high to very high mortality, civil conflict, very poor governance	Assam Bihar	13.3

Source: World Bank (2001), Report no. 22304, Table 3.2.

Note: Major states (>15 million population) were ranked according to Infant Mortality, Child Mortality, Total Fertility, and Full Immunization Coverage rates. The estimates included the major states before bifurcation, so the state of Bihar includes Jharkhand, and Madhya Pradesh includes Chattisgarh, but Uttar Pradesh does not include Uttaranchal.

MACROECONOMIC ADJUSTMENT POLICIES AND HEALTH SYSTEM REFORM IN INDIA

Provision of health care in India is a responsibility shared by state, central, and local governments. Health care delivery is actually a responsibility of state governments. The central government is responsible for health care in Union Territories without legislature. It is also responsible for developing and monitoring national standards and regulations; providing the link between state governments and international and bilateral agencies; and sponsoring numerous programs, through the provision of financial and other inputs, for implementation throughout the states. Within the overall ambit of national policies, there is scope for each state to formulate its own health policy and administer health programs in conformity with local conditions.

The contribution of the central and state governments to overall public spending on health may be seen in Table 5. The states mainly finance primary health-care facilities, hospitals, and insurance. Of the two departments at the centre, the Department of Health allocates over 45% of its budget to the central teaching hospitals and research institutions, about 15% to the Central Government Health Scheme benefiting its own employees, and about 35% to disease control programs. The Department

TABLE 5. CENTRE AND STATE SHARES IN DIFFERENT COMPONENTS OF THE GOVERNMENT HEALTH BUDGET IN INDIA, 1991/92

	Centre (%)	States (%)
Hospitals	3.1	96.9
Public health	0.0	100.0
Primary care (disease control)	99.7	0.3
Family welfare	22.6	77.4
Insurance (CGHS, ESIS)	18.2	81.8
Medical education & Other	41.7	58.3
Administration & Other	11.0	89.0
Capital investment	49.7	50.3

Source: World Bank (1995), Report no. 13402-IN.

Note: CGHS = Central government health scheme; ESIS = Employees' state insurance scheme.

of Family Welfare allocates about 85% of its budget to family planning and 15% to maternal and child health and universal immunization. Local governments have no significant financial authority in India except in large cities.

The first and most important MAP targets are the amount and the distribution of government expenditure. Setting these targets consitutes a key policy objective as well as a policy tool in shaping other sectors of the economy. In the Indian context, in the initial years of Adjustment, one way in which reduced public expenditure affected state spending on health care was a decrease in direct spending on health care by the central government. Another was in loans advanced by the central government to finance health expenditure in the states, because in the Indian context the primary lender to the states is the central government.

Since 1992, the Government of India and the World Bank have been engaged in a dialogue on health sector development. The focus of that dialogue has been on addressing the most burdensome diseases cost-effectively and moving toward efficient and effective health systems. Development projects in seven states were begun at different times and were of different durations. Andhra Pradesh was the first to begin in 1994 and completed its project in 2002. Karnataka and Punjab began their projects a year later and were completed in 2004. West Bengal began in 1997 and finished in 2004. The projects in Maharastra and Orissa started in 1998; the former was concluded in 2005 and the latter in March 2006. Uttar Pradesh (including Uttaranchal) began in 2000 and will continue until December 2006. As mentioned, health is a state responsibility, and MAPs have not led to HSR in all the Indian states. We therefore differentiate states, in this discussion, as being with HSR and without HSR.

There is some uniformity in the development objectives of HSR across the seven states. The Health Systems Development Project seeks to develop strategic management capacity; strengthen performance, accountability, and efficiency; and build implementation capacity. Further, it seeks to improve clinical service quality by renovating and expanding district, subdistrict, and community hospitals and improving access to services. In all seven reforming states, around 15% of the total project cost is borne by the state governments.

All the project documents note the low levels of funding for secondary hospitals in the reforming states. This is attributed to the small share of overall public spending allotted to health, the limited portion of total health spending going to hospitals, and, within this, a skewed distribution of funds in favour of the tertiary hospitals. After analysis of the problems of the health sector, the governments of the reforming states have agreed—using terminology ranging from "assurances" to "commitments"—to several undertakings. These are: (i) to enhance the overall size of the health budget; (ii) to redress imbalances in public expenditure between secondary and tertiary care levels; (iii) to safeguard the operations and maintenance components of current expenditure allocations for the secondary health-care sector; (iv) to charge user fees for selected services; and (v) to address workforce issues.

Even though the reform is focused on community, area, and district hospitals—or first-referral hospitals—in all the reforming states, there is variation both in the number of hospitals designated for renovation and expansion and in the specific geographical areas and population groups targeted. In Andhra Pradesh, 21 district hospitals, 49 area hospitals, and 80 community hospitals are slated to be renovated and expanded, with an expected addition of around 5 000 beds. In Punjab, 13 district hospitals, 46 subdivisional hospitals, and 74 community hospitals will receive financing, with a relatively larger share of the investment targeted in the upper Bari Doab and rural Southern Malwa regions, where poverty is concentrated. The expected addition of beds in the secondary sector is only around 2 000. Although 15 district hospitals, 60 subdivisional hospitals, and 95 rural hospitals are to be renovated in West Bengal, no beds are to be added. However, 28 primary health centres and 8 subdistrict primary health centres will be upgraded in the Sunderban area, where the poorest in the state are concentrated. As Sunderban has a large number of widely distributed small islands, three floating medical units will also be set up. In Uttar Pradesh, 152 hospitals of various sizes are targeted for renovation, largely in the poorest three regions of the state: Bundel Khand, Uttar Khand, and eastern Uttar Pradesh. In none of the states is construction of new hospitals being financed; the focus is entirely on renovation, expansion, and addition of clinical specialties in existing rural hospitals.

There is considerable variation in the size and geographical focus of the various projects and in the population groups targeted. Nevertheless, the Health Systems Development Projects being implemented in the seven states are quite similar in their development objectives and key policy reforms. It is this similarity in project objectives, approaches, and components that allows us to consider the HSRs in all these states together as one HSR.

ADJUSTMENT PROGRAM AND GOVERNMENT EXPENDITURE

Expenditure trends of the central government

As in all other adjustment programs, the Indian program began with central government bringing down the gross fiscal deficit (GFD) as a percentage of GDP. A decrease of about two and a half percentage points was achieved by cutting total expenditure by over two percentage points in the initial burst in 1991/92. Since then, both the GFD and the total expenditure have come down slowly, reaching 4% and 14.14%, respectively, by 1996/97 (Table 6). The total expenditure of the central government consists of revenue expenditure and capital disbursements; cuts have fallen more heavily on the latter and the decline continues. The reduction in capital disbursements is more acute when viewed in the context of a persistent decline since the mid-1980s. Capital disbursements fall under two headings: capital expenditure by the central government, and loans and advances to state governments and union territories. The two had equal shares in total capital disbursements throughout the late 1980s. Then the year 1990/91 saw a sharp drop in capital expenditure followed by a steady decline, reaching 1.12% of GDP in 1996/97, with only marginal increase since then. Loans and advances had shown a slower decline, reaching 1.72% of GDP in 1996/97, then a pause in the following two years. Thus, the reduction in the central government's total expenditure has translated into cuts in loans advanced to state governments and in capital expenditure by the central government, with capital expenditure bearing it more heavily in the initial years.

TABLE 6. EXPENDITURE (% GDP) OF THE CENTRAL GOVERNMENT, INDIA, 1986/87–1998/99

Year	Government expenditure		Capital expenditure		Revenue expenditure	
	Total	DE	Total	SS	Total	SS
1986/87	20.30	17.15	3.16	0.13	13.96	0.95
1987/88	19.23	15.86	2.79	0.08	13.86	1.02
1988/89	18.83	15.14	2.59	0.09	13.67	0.96
1989/90	19.25	15.35	2.58	0.07	14.06	0.87
1990/91	18.60	14.59	1.77	0.05	14.23	0.78
1991/92	16.62	12.31	1.36	0.04	13.36	0.83
1992/93	16.26	11.84	1.66	0.04	13.19	0.80
1993/94	16.94	12.36	1.65	0.04	13.51	0.89
1994/95	16.66	12.05	1.41	0.08	13.28	0.87
1995/96	15.97	11.41	1.42	0.05	12.74	0.96
1996/97	14.14	9.51	1.12	0.05	11.30	0.89
1997/98	14.86	10.21	1.30	0.04	11.58	0.92
1998/99	15.96	11.58	1.41	0.05	12.22	1.15

Source: Government of India, budget documents, various years.

Note: DE = Discretionary expenditure; SS = Social services.

The total capital expenditure of the central government may be viewed as a sum of capital expenditures on defense, social service sectors, and sectors providing economic services (Table 6). Capital expenditure on defense declined somewhat, mostly between 1993/94 and 1998/99. In contrast, after a declining trend seen earlier (1986/87 to 1991/92) in the social sectors, this area stagnated at around .05% of GDP during the Adjustment years. The largest cut was imposed on economic services, beginning in the late 1980s (2.45% of GDP in 1986/87) and continuing with greater intensity during the Adjustment years (0.73% of GDP in 1998/99). Thus, the cut in capital expenditure has largely been borne by economic services, of which the major headings include agriculture, industry, transport and communications, and irrigation and power.

Two headings of expenditure that had not experienced any systematic cuts before 1990/91 and were subjected to cuts during Adjustment are subsidies and grants-in-aid to states. Subsidies, which had increased to 2.29% of GDP by 1989/90, declined steadily to 1.16% of GDP by 1996/97. Grants-in-aid to states continued to increase until 1993/94, then fell by 1.23% of GDP by 1998/99. Social services show a reversal of the trend; expenditure increased mildly after 1993/94, with a significant increase in 1998/99. However, during that period the share allotted to health and family welfare decreased from 29.7% to 21.85%. Expenditure in economic services has been cut, going from about 4.4% of GDP in 1990/91 to 2.81% in 1998/99. Thus, overall, the sharp decrease in discretionary spending by the central government has fallen on subsidies, grants to state governments, and spending on economic services, whereas social sector spending by the central government has been protected during Adjustment.

Like all other adjustment programs, the Indian program has not been able to cut total expenditure to any significant extent since Adjustment began in 1991. As experienced the world over, the burden has fallen largely on economic services and not on defense or public services. In that respect, the Indian adjustment experience is no different from that elsewhere. However, the social sector has been protected. The distinctly Indian attribute of the constraint on spending is its translation into a contraction of capital disbursements and grants-in-aid to the states.

Expenditure trends in the states

The states in India enjoy considerable autonomy and are not bound by the central government's undue concern for cutting the fiscal deficit under Adjustment. However, the central government is the source of financing for the states' deficits, and close to 50% of the states' debt is to the central government. The early 1980s witnessed unlimited overdrafts on the Reserve Bank of India (the central bank) by the states. Various control measures were imposed beginning in the mid-1980s, such as not allowing overdrafts for more than seven continuous working days. Since then, the gross fiscal deficit of all states has remained at around 3%.

The total expenditure of the state governments as a percentage of net state domestic product (NSDP) had shown significant increase throughout the 1980s. At the level of all-states, total expenditure increased from 20% to 22% between 1981/82 and 1987/88. Most of the individual states showed similar increases, with the exception of Bihar, Orissa, Tamil Nadu, and West Bengal, where there was no increase or only a marginal increase. Total expenditure dipped during the next four years in most of the states, except Bihar, Orissa, Tamil Nadu, and Uttar Pradesh. Of these exceptions, all but Uttar Pradesh had also shown no increase in total expenditure during most of the 1980s. The increase in total expenditure came in these states only between 1987/88 and 1991/92. The 1990s saw stagnation in total expenditure for almost all the states, except Bihar, Goa, Haryana, Himachal Pradesh, and Kerala.

A freeze on total expenditure often leads to pressure on capital expenditure, as various components of revenue expenditure, such as salaries and interest payments, are not amenable to contraction. The Indian states have had a similar experience since the late 1980s. Revenue expenditure as a proportion of NSDP had shown a significant increase of over three percentage points between 1981/82 and 1987/88 at the level of all-states. The exceptions were Bihar, Orissa, Tamil Nadu, and West Bengal, where the increase was of a smaller order and where there was no increase in total expenditure during this period. However, the period from 1987/88 to 1991/92 showed a reversal, with revenue expenditure coming down. Again Bihar, Orissa, Punjab, Tamil Nadu, Uttar Pradesh, and West Bengal were the exceptions. The 1990s saw increases in revenue expenditure in all the states except Gujarat, Maharashtra, and Tamil Nadu, where total expenditure stagnated.

As seen above, the 1980s were a period of significant increases in total expenditure. However, revenue expenditure was increasing in most of the states, and capital expenditure was decreasing in all the states except Jammu and Kashmir well into the 1990s. Between 1981/82 and 1997/98, there was a decline in capital expenditure of 2.5 percentage points at the level of all-states.

One component of total expenditure that drives revenue expenditure during Adjustment is higher interest payment on past debt. Already by the early 1980s, interest payments were over 1% of NSDP for all the states except Maharastra and rose steadily throughout the 1980s and 1990s. By the end of 1980s, they had reached close to 2% of NSDP and, by the end of 1990s, more than 3%. Meanwhile, discretionary expenditure at the level of all-states has shown a mild decline since 1987/88, except in Bihar, Goa, Himachal Pradesh, and Kerala. When total expenditure is frozen and interest payment increases, fewer resources are available for discretionary expenditure by the states.

Medical and public health (MPH) expenditure by the states

The share of medical and public health (MPH), including water supply and sanitation (WSS), in total government expenditure increased in the 1980s. Although the total increase was only on the order of half a percentage point, almost all states showed an increase between 1981/82 and 1987/88. The next four years reversed this trend, and both MPH and WSS lost the gains of the 1980s. The exceptions were Bihar, Goa, and Himachal Pradesh, which showed gains in both these components during this period. The decline continued through the 1990s in

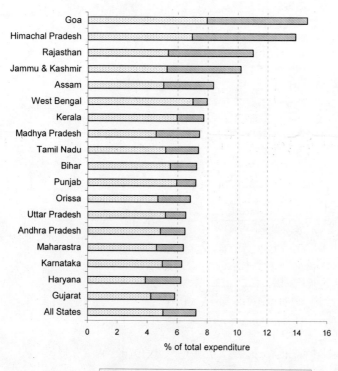

FIGURE 1A. TOTAL (REVENUE AND CAPITAL) EXPENDITURE ON MEDICAL AND PUBLIC HEALTH, WITH WATER SUPPLY AND SANITATION, AS % OF TOTAL EXPENDITURE, INDIA, 1991/92

Source: Reserve Bank of India, RBI Bulletin, various issues.

almost all the states, except Gujarat, Karnataka, Rajasthan, and Tamil Nadu (Figures 1a, 1b).

It is possible that while the share of a sector within total expenditure does not show much of an increase, the per capita spending does. Turning to per capita expenditure (in constant 1980/81 prices) on MPH, it may be seen that the 1980s were a period of significant increase in per capita expenditure in MPH, including WSS, in all the Indian states (Figures 2a, 2b). At the all-state level, the increase was about 40% in six years, with increases of comparable magnitude recorded by most of the major states. The next four years (1987/88 to 1991/92) showed no increase

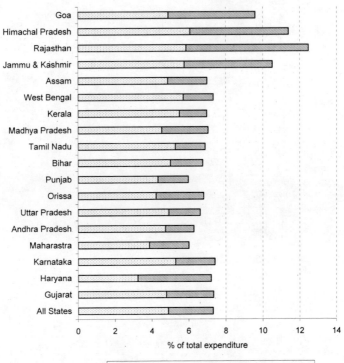

FIGURE 1B. TOTAL (REVENUE AND CAPITAL) EXPENDITURE ON MEDICAL AND PUBLIC HEALTH, WITH WATER SUPPLY AND SANITATION, AS % OF TOTAL EXPENDITURE, INDIA, 1997/98

Source: Reserve Bank of India, RBI Bulletin, various issues.

in per capita expenditure at the all-state level, with most major states also showing no increase in expenditure. Tamil Nadu was an exception, in that it continued to increase. At the other end, Andhra Pradesh, Gujarat, Madhya Pradesh, and Maharastra experienced a decline in expenditure of about 15%. The initial years of Adjustment (1991/92 to 1995/96) showed a mild increase in per capita expenditure at the all-state level, although the pattern across states varied widely. All the southern states and Gujarat, Haryana, Himachal Pradesh, and Rajasthan showed increases, while Assam, Bihar, Punjab, and Uttar Pradesh showed decreases in per capita expenditure. Especially striking were the decreases

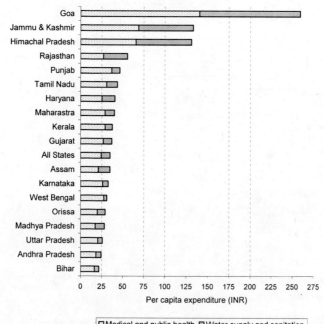

FIGURE 2A. PER CAPITA EXPENDITURE (IN INR) ON MEDICAL AND PUBLIC HEALTH, WITH WATER SUPPLY AND SANITATION, INDIA, 1991/92

Source: Reserve Bank of India, RBI Bulletin, various issues.

in Assam, Bihar, and Uttar Pradesh, where per capita expenditures are the lowest.

Per capita expenditure on MPH, with WSS, varies enormously across the states. In 1981/82, within an all-state average of 25.26 INR, expenditure varied from 13.82 INR in Bihar to 91.54 INR in Himachal Pradesh.[3] At the lowest end, in the per capita expenditure class of below 25 INR, were the states of Andhra Pradesh, Assam, Bihar, Karnataka, Madhya Pradesh, Orissa, and Uttar Pradesh (Table 7). At the highest end, Himachal Pradesh and Jammu and Kashmir spent over 80 INR per capita. The 1980s saw a clear upward movement in almost all states. Only Bihar and Uttar Pradesh remained at the bottom class. Four more states were added to the top expenditure class of above 45 INR per capita. During the period 1987/88 to

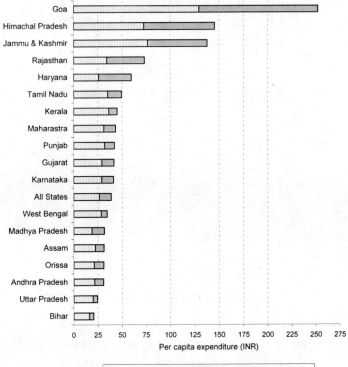

FIGURE 2B. PER CAPITA EXPENDITURE (IN INR) ON MEDICAL AND PUBLIC HEALTH, WITH WATER SUPPLY AND SANITATION, INDIA, 1995/96

Source: Reserve Bank of India, RBI Bulletin, various issues.

1991/92, while Bihar remained at the bottom class of less than 25 INR and Andhra Pradesh dropped to that class, five states at the top class maintained their position.

Because the inclusion of water supply and sanitation creates a data series that is not amenable to the analysis of MPH, we also looked at MPH alone. No significant increase in per capita expenditure was seen between 1987/88 and 1991/92, and in most states the expenditure had stagnated. The exceptions were Bihar, Goa, Himachal Pradesh, Jammu and Kashmir, Rajasthan, and Tamil Nadu. This trend continued in most states throughout the Adjustment years, with fewer exceptions. Among the six exceptional states of the previous period, two—Bihar and Goa—

TABLE 7. DISTRIBUTION OF INDIAN STATES BY PER CAPITA EXPENDITURE ON MEDICAL AND PUBLIC HEALTH (INCLUDING WATER SUPPLY AND SANITATION)

	1981/82	1987/88	1991/92	1995/96
Below INR 25	Andhra Pradesh	Bihar	Andhra Pradesh	Bihar
	Assam	Uttar Pradesh	Bihar	Uttar Pradesh
	Bihar			
	Karnataka			
	Madhya Pradesh			
	Orissa			
	Uttar Pradesh			
INR 25–34	Gujarat	Andhra Pradesh	Assam	Andhra Pradesh
	Haryana	Assam	**Karnataka**	Assam
	Kerala	**Karnataka**	Madhya Pradesh	Madhya Pradesh
	Maharastra	Madhya Pradesh	Orissa	Orissa
	Punjab	Orissa	Uttar Pradesh	West Bengal
	Tamil Nadu	West Bengal	West Bengal	
	West Bengal			
INR 35–44	Rajasthan	Gujarat	Gujarat	Gujarat
		Haryana	**Haryana**	Kerala
		Kerala	Kerala	**Karnataka**
		Tamil Nadu	Maharastra	Maharastra
			Tamil Nadu	Punjab
INR 45 and above	Himachal Pradesh	Goa	Goa	Goa
	Jammu & Kashmir	Himachal Pradesh	Himachal Pradesh	**Haryana**
		Jammu & Kashmir	Jammu Kashmir	Himachal Pradesh
		Maharastra	Punjab	Jammu & Kashmir
		Punjab	Rajasthan	Rajasthan
		Rajasthan		**Tamil Nadu**

Source: Reserve Bank of India, RBI Bulletin, various issues.

Note: States in bold are those that made the most progress.

dropped out, and Karnataka and Kerala came in. Overall, there was hardly any improvement in per capita expenditure on MPH after 1987/88 in the Indian states. Eleven of the 18 states analyzed were spending amounts in the mid-1990s that equaled the amount they had been spending in the late 1980s. Many of these poorer states were spending 30% less than the all-states average.

Summary

On the whole, Adjustment has led the central government to cut total expenditure to bring down the fiscal deficit. The cut has fallen more heavily on capital disbursements, i.e., capital expenditure and loans and advances to the states. Central government expenditure on the social sector has been left untouched. The total expenditure of the states, which increased in the 1980s, became stagnant in the 1990s following Adjustment. At the same time, interest payments rose, leaving less for discretionary spending.

The share of MPH, including WSS, within total spending of the states showed a mild increase in the 1980s, which was reversed in the late 1980s, with Adjustment further accentuating that downward trend. The increase in the share allotted to MPH in the 1980s translated into a significant increase in per capita expenditure, which then stagnated under Adjustment and the consequent contraction. The extremely low spenders, namely Andhra Pradesh, Assam, Madhya Pradesh, Orissa, Uttar Pradesh, and West Bengal, have remained at that level for a long time. It is therefore not surprising that many of them have availed themselves of the World Bank loan for health sector reforms.

HEALTH SECTOR REFORMS AND PUBLIC SPENDING

HSRs undertaken by the states in India have sought to enhance health sector spending. However, projects funded by the World Bank in India have generally been characterized by 60% to 75% of total funding being earmarked for capital spending on upgrading hospital buildings and purchasing equipment. Hence, it is pertinent to analyze trends in capital spending during the HSR era in India.

Capital spending on health care

Capital expenditure on MPH, excluding WSS, as a percentage of total capital expenditure has shown a declining trend in all the Indian states since the early 1980s, with few exceptions (Table 8). The exceptions were mostly smaller states with special status, such as Assam, Goa, Himachal Pradesh, and Jammu and Kashmir, with only Tamil Nadu and Uttar Pradesh being the real exceptions among the larger states. The picture in the mid-1990s, just before some of the states decided to go for the World Bank-funded Second Health Systems Development Project, stood as shown in the second column of Table 8. Nearly one-quarter of the states were spending less than 1% of total capital expenditure on the health-care sector, one-third were spending 1–2%, and another one-third, 3–5%. Only two states were spending more than 5% on the health-care sector.

The dominant trends in capital spending on health care during the next 10 years (HSR era) were either of the health sector share steadily falling or of it being maintained at an already low level. The distinction of maintaining capital spending at a relatively high level goes to only one state, Kerala. The states showing a sharp increase from extremely low levels of capital spending were all states that had gone for HSR, the exception being Himachal Pradesh, which increased its capital spending without World Bank funding. Andhra Pradesh and Punjab, despite implementing World Bank-funded HSR, do not show significant improvement in their status because in both states, resources are received by parastatals and their expenditures are not shown in government budgets.[4] The increase in capital spending seen in Andhra Pradesh as of 1998/99 must also be interpreted with caution, as that state had managed to get another World Bank project by then, called the Andhra Pradesh Reconstruction Project, of which 24% of the loan amount—around Rupees 300 crores (approximately 66.7 million USD)—was earmarked for primary health centres. Discounting that amount, there has been no

TABLE 8. DISTRIBUTION OF INDIAN STATES BY CAPITAL EXPENDITURE ON MEDICAL AND PUBLIC HEALTH (AS % OF TOTAL EXPENDITURE)

	1994/95 to 1996/97	1997/98 to 1999/00	2000/01 to 2002/03
Less than 1 percent	Andhra Pradesh Bihar Gujarat Maharastra* Punjab **West Bengal***	Assam Bihar Maharastra* Punjab	Gujarat Haryana Punjab
1 to 3 percent	Himachal Pradesh* **Karnataka*** Madhya Pradesh Orissa* Rajasthan	Andhra Pradesh Gujarat Haryana Madhya Pradesh Orissa* Rajasthan	Andhra Pradesh Assam Bihar Goa Jammu & Kashmir Madhya Pradesh Maharastra* Rajasthan Tamil Nadu Uttar Pradesh
3 to 5 percent	Assam Haryana Jammu & Kashmir Kerala Tamil Nadu	Goa Himachal Pradesh* Jammu & Kashmir Kerala Uttar Pradesh **West Bengal***	Himachal Pradesh* **Karnataka*** Kerala Orissa*
Above 5 percent	Goa Uttar Pradesh	**Karnataka*** Tamil Nadu	**West Bengal***

Source: Reserve Bank of India, RBI Bulletin, various issues.

Note 1: * States with HSR.

Note 2: States in bold are those that made the most progress.

capital spending from the regular budget by the Andhra Pradesh government on the health-care sector.

The steady decline in capital spending by a large number of states, combined with the boost in spending by the reforming states due to HSR, has resulted in the clustering of 10 of the 18 states into the 1–3% expenditure group at the end of the period. Of the five states in the above-3% expenditure category, three have risen to that level owing to the World Bank loan, and it is almost certain that once the project is implemented they will quickly fall into the below-1% expenditure group. This is already the case for Punjab and, if the 2002/03 data are any indication, for Karnataka as well.

Current spending on health care

We begin our analysis looking at the share of health-care sector revenue expenditure within discretionary expenditure (defined as total revenue expenditure minus interest payment). The non-reforming states, as a group, show a decline in the share of the health sector within total current spending after accounting for non-discretionary spending (Figure 3a). The share, which ranged from 6% to 10% in 1994/95, had fallen to between 4% and 8% by 2002/03. The two exceptions to this trend are Jammu and Kashmir and Haryana, the former still showing a share of over 8%, and the latter going from 2% in the mid-1990s to 5% by 2002/03. With the exception of West Bengal, the reforming states as a group, which were spending less than 8% of discretionary expenditure in the mid-1990s, have shown a mild decline in expenditure (Figure 3b). Nevertheless, their spending levels are still only around that of non-reforming states, reflecting their poorer record from the start. Thus, in a small way, HSR has helped moderate the fall in the share of health-care sector within total expenditure.

The above conclusion, however, requires an important amendment, because HSR has also introduced the policy of charging user fees, thereby raising the revenue receipts of the

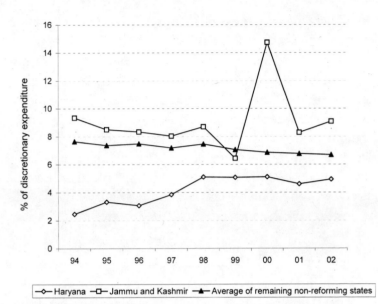

FIGURE 3A. REVENUE EXPENDITURE ON MPH, AS % OF DISCRETIONARY EXPENDITURE: NON-REFORMING STATES, INDIA, 1994–2002

Source: World Bank (1995), Report no. 13402-IN.

Note: Remaining non-reforming states: Assam, Bihar, Goa, Gujarat, Himachal Pradesh, Kerala, Madhya Pradesh, Rajasthan, and Tamil Nadu.

government to some extent. Part of the collection—the proportion varies across the states—is retained at the level of the health facility and, to the extent that it is spent on equipment maintenance, drugs, and consumables, constitutes an addition to the health budget. The rest flows into the state treasury as a revenue receipt. The revenue expenditure on the health sector, minus the revenue receipts, is then the allocation from the total discretionary expenditure to the health sector. When this allocation is analyzed, the reforming states show a slightly sharper fall over the period. The share tends to lie between 5% and 7%, except for West Bengal, which reports closer to 8%. These proportions look no different from those reported for the non-reforming states, thus suggesting that HSR has not helped to maintain the share of health sector budgets at levels prevailing in the mid-1990s.

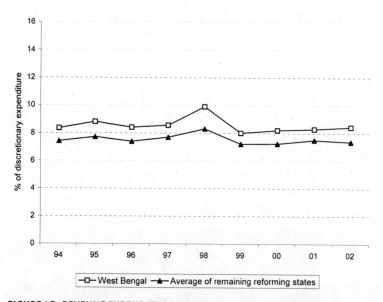

FIGURE 3B. REVENUE EXPENDITURE ON MPH, AS % OF DISCRETIONARY EXPENDITURE: REFORMING STATES, INDIA, 1994–2002

Source: World Bank (1995), Report no. 13402-IN.

Note: Remaining reforming states: Andra Pradesh, Karnataka, Maharastra, Orissa, Punjab, and Uttar Pradesh.

The share of the health-care budget within the government's total expenditure is one indicator of the priority accorded to health care by the state. Another is the per capita expenditure. To do a trend analysis on this aspect, we converted the expenditure at current prices to constant prices and built two series using the wholesale price index and the drug and medicine price index. The per capita expenditure in the mid-1990s ranged from 50 to 100 INR among the reforming states and 40 to100 INR among the non-reforming states (Figures 4a, 4b). After nine years, when some states had already completed the World Bank project and others were midway through it, the per capita expenditure of the reforming states had risen to between 75 and 120 INR, except for Punjab, where it had reached close to 180 INR, while the expenditure of the non-reforming states had risen to between

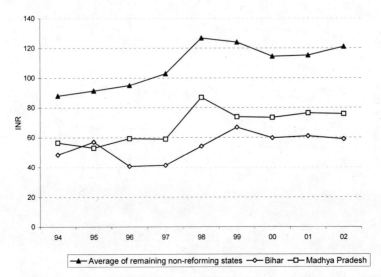

FIGURE 4A. PER CAPITA REVENUE EXPENDITURE ON MPH, 1993/94 PRICES, USING WHOLESALE PRICE INDEX (WPI): NON-REFORMING STATES, INDIA, 1994–2002

Source: World Bank (1995), Report no. 13402-IN.

Note: Remaining non-reforming states: Haryana, Gujarat, Kerala, Rajasthan, Tamil Nadu, and Assam.

60 and 140 INR, suggesting that the non-reforming states have done better than the reforming states. In both groups, there are two poorly-performing states pulling the group down—Orissa and Uttar Pradesh among the reforming states, and Bihar and Madhya Pradesh among the non-reforming states.

When deflated by the drug and medicine price index, the per capita expenditure shows a lower rate of increase than when deflated by the wholesale price index. The per capita expenditure of the reforming states showed a mild increase; the expenditure ranges between 45 and 80 INR toward the end of the period, with many states reporting closer to 80 INR. Among the reforming states, Punjab has shown the sharpest increase, spending about 120 INR as of 2002/03. The non-reforming states began within a range of expenditure of 60 to 90 INR in the mid-1990s and continued within that range at the end of the period, with two excep-

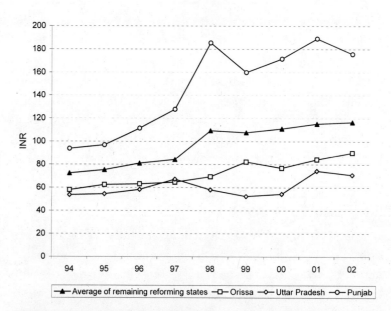

FIGURE 4B. PER CAPITA REVENUE EXPENDITURE ON MPH, 1993/94 PRICES, USING WHOLESALE PRICE INDEX (WPI): REFORMING STATES, INDIA, 1994–2002

Source: World Bank (1995), Report no. 13402-IN.

Note: Remaining reforming states: Andra Pradesh, Karnataka, Maharastra, and West Bengal.

tions. These are Bihar and Madhya Pradesh, which were spending less than 60 INR in the mid-1990s and continue at the same level with hardly any increase. Among the reforming states as well there are two exceptions, Orissa and Uttar Pradesh, that continue to spend less than 60 INR per capita in constant prices.

Main trends in public spending with HSR

Capital expenditure in the Indian health-care sector shows a general decline since the early 1980s. The World Bank loan for Health Sector Development boosted capital spending in states with HSR during the period of the project, and the general falling tendency was arrested. The share of MPH in total revenue spending in the states also shows a decline, but milder for the reforming states. Despite the availability of the World Bank loan for capital spending, the reforming states have not enhanced the share of the health-care sector in their total spending.

Unlike the declining tendency of the share of health sector capital and revenue spending, the per capita spending—whether deflated by wholesale price index or by the drug and medicine price index—shows a mild increasing tendency. However, it cannot be said that the performance of the reforming states is better than that of the non-reforming states.

HEALTH SECTOR REFORM AND DISEASE CONTROL PROGRAMS IN ORISSA

Orissa is one of the poorest states in India, with a population of over 30 million. In terms of infant mortality and maternal mortality, Orissa ranks lowest among the Indian states, with levels comparable to, or just above, levels reported by Bangladesh, Djibouti, Nepal, or Yemen. In 1996, intestinal, infectious, and parasitic diseases caused one out of every five deaths in Orissa, and more than one in 10 deaths were caused by conditions originating in the perinatal period. Over 30% of outpatient visits and inpatient admissions to hospital are for intestinal, infectious, and parasitic diseases (Narayana 2003). Orissa also ranks highest in the prevalence of certain major diseases, such as malaria and tuberculosis, with no perceptible decline over the past 20 years (Gupta 2002).

In 1993, Orissa reported a number of cases of vaccine-preventable diseases. The number of cases of diphtheria and measles had declined somewhat by 1993, but there was no perceptible decline in whooping cough and polio, and cases of tetanus and tuberculosis had, in fact, increased significantly.

The communicable disease situation in Orissa may be summarized in terms of disability-adjusted life years (DALYs). Communicable diseases account for over 60% of total DALYs lost. Perinatal conditions, diarrheal diseases, tuberculosis, and tetanus are the major causes of DALYs lost for both males and females (Padhi and Mishra 2000). In terms of Omran's epidemiological transition model, Orissa may be categorized as falling in the very early transition model, as has been done by the World Bank (see Table 4).

Nowhere in the Orissa Health Services Development Project (OHSDP) appraisal document could we find a systematic treatment of disease control, nor even a mention of it. The project document is completely silent on the issue of integrating disease control programs into the development of the health system in the state. The background document had, however, emphasized that the basic package of health services should address communicable diseases: "A basic health care package should take into account these state level variations in epidemiology and burden of disease. The package of services would consist of *communicable disease prevention and treatment*; limited clinical services; essential and emergency obstetric and pediatric care" (World Bank 1997, pp. 5–6; italics added). In the transition from the background document to the project document, communicable disease prevention seems to have been left behind. This leads us to examine the situation in Orissa under HSR with regard to disease control programs.

Epidemiological surveillance has improved in Orissa following the setting up of a surveillance system in 1999, under which Department of Public Health staff regularly transmit information on 10 epidemic-prone diseases.[5] The initiative was introduced in 12 cyclone-affected districts and was expanded to the entire state a year later. The available evidence suggests the system has been working well. One recent example was the detection of a measles outbreak that prompted the government to institute a mass measles campaign to reduce the number of susceptible children (Gupta 2002).

The introduction of the externally funded Revised National Tuberculosis Control Programme (RNTCP) in Orissa has virtually divided the state in two. The 10 districts where RNTCP has been introduced report sufficient quantities of drugs and chemicals and adequate numbers of trained staff. The program follows the directly observed treatment, short course (DOTS) strategy with regular program monitoring. In the rest of the districts, where the national TB control program is running, the regular treatment regimen of 18 months' duration is available. The national program, in which the state government is supposed to share the drug cost on an equal basis, has not seen any allocation for drugs by the state government since 1999, the year in which OHSDP was initiated. Many of the newly formed districts[6] do not have TB centres, and the posts of retired staff have not been filled. Neither of the control programs—RNTCP or NTP (National Tuberculosis Program)—has succeeded in establishing links with private providers who treat TB patients. The net result is that only 40–60% of the expected number of cases are detected in the state (Gupta 2002).

The World Bank-assisted Enhanced Malaria Control Program, which operates in about half of the state's 314 administrative blocks, is one of the largest such programs in India. The program suffers from delays in smear collection and reporting; poor availability of chloroquine tablets in remote hamlets; lack of awareness of presumptive radical treatment (PRT) among the staff in most areas; shortages of slides, lancets, and stains; and delays in reading blood smears collected and in sending the information back to the community. Going by the department's own evaluation, the project, which has been running for three years, has shown no significant development (Gupta 2002).

In situations of fiscal pressure, projects such as OHSDP serve the purpose of levering in external assistance. It is well-known that such assistance entails a commitment to fund part of the expenditure from domestic resources. However, as domestic resources are scarce—which is the original reason for levering in external assistance—diverting funds to such projects leaves other activities, whether of national priority or not, poorly funded (Narayana 1999). The NTP falls exactly into this category. The commitment to "strengthen and thereafter maintain a Policy and Strategic Planning Unit with adequate powers, functions and staff and resources satisfactory to the Administrator" (World Bank 1998, p. 14) leads to diverting personnel from other programs. Existing programs do not receive adequate attention, and their management suffers. This could well be the case of the malaria program.

SUMMARY AND RECOMMENDATIONS

India is one of the poorest countries in the world where elementary deprivation is concentrated. The country reports low levels of life expectancy and literacy and high levels of both general and infant mortality. Its record in the sphere of human development is also one of the poorest. India reports one of the lowest levels of public spending on health care, and there is increasing recognition among policymakers that public spending on social sectors needs to be enhanced. The persisting high burden of communicable diseases is an added reason for increased public spending.

India, with 28 states, many of which are larger than many countries of the world, has a federal structure wherein health care is a responsibility of the state governments. The central government confines itself to funding medical research and national disease control programs implemented through the state departments of health. By the end of 1980s, public spending on health (capital and current) was in decline, at the level of both the central and many state governments.

Following a BOP crisis in 1991, India initiated macroeconomic adjustment policies. As the Indian Adjustment came after UNICEF's advocacy of "adjustment with a human face," and as the need to safeguard social sectors was recognized, public spending on social services has largely been protected. However, because Adjustment has largely been a concern of the central government, the protection of social spending has occurred at that level, while state governments have followed their own policy directions. Many state governments, under fiscal pressure since the late 1980s, have been cutting both capital and current spending on health care. Some have obtained health systems development loans from the World Bank with the ostensible purpose of reforming the health sector.

The Health Systems Development Project initiated in the seven states recognizes the need for enhanced public spending on health and identifies it as the foremost policy reform to be pursued. Nevertheless, such assurances and conditions have not succeeded in enhancing health sector budgets in states implementing HSR. Worse, HSR has not been able to arrest the decline in the share of health spending within total government spending. The project has been used, rather, by reforming states as a tool for leveraging external financing.

That this external financing comes with its own cost is demonstrated by the case of Orissa. The International Development Association's assistance for the OHSDP is conditional upon the state government contributing about 15% of the total project cost. The funds-starved state has diverted resources from the TB and malaria programs to meet this condition, jeopardizing the disease control programs. This cost can be extremely high, as is shown by the repeated failure of control programs and the fact that disease incidence in the state is barely declining.

The findings of this study raise two fundamental questions regarding HSR in India. First, how is it possible to ensure a certain minimum public spending on health care? Second, is the uniform strategy of focusing on the secondary health sector across all states, irrespective of their health status and health systems development, the right one to pursue?

The Indian system is especially complicated, as the larger tax resources are controlled by the central government but the major responsibility for health-care spending is bestowed on the states. Even though the Constitution has provided for the Planning Commission and the Finance Commission for devolving capital and current resources respectively to the states, there is nothing in the Constitution to ensure that a certain minimum percentage of the total resources is spent on health care. If Colombia and Thailand, under conditions of high or low economic growth, could ensure such spending following amendments to the Constitution, then a similar approach could well be a solution for India with its rapid economic growth.

States in search of external funding often submit the most promising proposals with built-in assurances—all of which look similarly attractive across the states—that they are hardly in a position to fulfill. Surely the dominant funder, the World Bank, with all the technical expertise at its command, bears some responsibility for incorporating the specificity of the state into the project so that disease control programs do not suffer and current spending on health is enhanced?

What may be a good health sector reform strategy for infrastructure-rich, developed southern states, or for Punjab, may not be a good strategy for infrastructure-poor eastern states such as Orissa or West Bengal. The relative roles of access, cost, and quality in the utilization of health-care services are different in these two settings, and this factor must necessarily be incorporated into the HSD project design.

Notes

1. Although there are 28 states in India after the formation of Chattisgarh, Jharkhand, and Uttaranchal, the discussion carried out here is in terms of the erstwhile Bihar, Madhya Pradesh, and Uttar Pradesh, of which these newly formed states were part. This is largely necessitated by the non-availability of comparable data for the newly-formed states.
2. The Indian financial year is from April to March.
3. Currency: Indian Rupee, INR. Currently, 1 USD = approximately 40 INR. One lakh = 100 000 rupees, and one crore = 100 lakhs, or 10 million rupees.
4. This is a major lacuna in the analysis of public expenditure in India, as many externally funded projects do not get included in government budgetary accounts, and there is no easy way to get information on the total spending on such projects.

5. On 29 October 1999, a severe cyclone hit coastal Orissa, causing severe loss of life and property. Contaminated water and poor availability of food and shelter led to the spread of epidemics, which necessitated a surveillance system.

6. The districts were divided into smaller ones in the late 1990s and the total number of districts increased from 13 to 30.

References

Ahluwalia, M.S. 2002. Economic reforms in India since 1991: has gradualism worked? Journal of Economic Perspectives, 16(3), 67–88.

Dreze, J.; Sen, A. 1995. India: economic development and social opportunity. Oxford University Press, Delhi, India. 306 pp.

_____ 2002. India: development and participation. Oxford University Press, Delhi, India. 540 pp.

Gupta, M. 2002. State health systems: Orissa. Working paper no. 89. Indian Council for Research on International Economic Relations, New Delhi, India. 37 pp.

Ministry of Finance. 1993. Economic survey 1992–93. Government of India, New Delhi, India. 218 pp. + 115 pp. appendices.

Ministry of Health and Family Welfare. 1993. Health information of India. Government of India, New Delhi, India.

Narayana, D. 1999. Public expenditure reform without policy change: infrastructure investment and health care provision under fiscal squeeze in Kerala. In Mackintosh, M.; Roy, R., ed., Economic decentralization and public management reform. Edward Elgar, Cheltenham, UK. 296 pp.

Narayana, D. 2001. Macroeconomic adjustment policies, health sector reform and access to health care in India. Centre for Development Studies, Trivandrum, Kerala, India. 92 pp.

Narayana, D. 2003. Disease control programs and health sector reform in India: the non-intersecting paths? Paper presented at the International Workshop on Health Care Reform: The Missing Jigsaw, 26–28 February 2003, Phuket, Thailand. 11 pp.

Padhi, S.; Mishra, S. 2000. Premature mortality, health status and public health care facilities in Orissa. Nabakrushna Choudhury Centre for Development Studies, Bhubaneswar, Orissa, India. 210 pp.

Registrar General of India. 1999. Compendium of India's fertility and mortality indicators 1971–97. New Delhi, India.

World Bank. 1994. India – Andhra Pradesh first referral health system project. Staff appraisal report. 2 November 1994, Report no. 13402-IN. South Asia Country Department II. Population and Human Resources Operations Division, New Delhi, India. 259 pp.

_____ 1995. India – Policy and finance strategies for strengthening primary health care services. Sector report. 15 May 1995, Report no. 13042-IN. South Asia Country Department II, Population and Human Resources Division, New Delhi, India. 252 pp.

_____ 1996. India – Second state health systems development project. Staff appraisal report. 20 February 1996, Report no. 15106-IN. South Asia Country Department II. Population and Human Resources Operations Division, New Delhi, India. 276 pp.

_____ 1997. India – New directions in health sector development at the state level: an operational perspective. Sector report. 11 February 1997, Report no. 15753-IN. South Asia Country Department II. Population and Human Resources Division, New Delhi, India. 222 pp.

_____ 1998a. India – Orissa health systems development project. Project appraisal document. 4 May 1998, Report No. 17653-IN. Health, Nutrition and Population Sector Unit, South Asia Region, New Delhi, India. 68 pp.

_____ 1998b. India – Maharastra health systems development project. Project appraisal document. 5 November 1998, Report no. 18403-IN. Health, Nutrition and Population Sector Unit, South Asia Region, New Delhi, India. 73 pp.

_____ 2000. India – Uttar Pradesh health systems development project. Project appraisal document. 30 March 2000, Report no. 19570-IN. Health, Nutrition and Population Sector Unit, South Asia Region, New Delhi, India. 75 pp.

_____ 2001. India – Raising the sights: better health systems for India's poor. 28 May 2001, Report no. 22304. Health, Nutrition and Population Sector Unit, South Asia Region. Washington, DC, USA. 187 pp.

CHAPTER 7

HIGH HEALTH ACHIEVEMENTS AND GOOD ACCESS TO HEALTH CARE AT GREAT COST: THE EMERGING KERALA SITUATION

Delampady Narayana

INTRODUCTION

Kerala is well-known the world over for its achievements in reducing levels of both fertility and mortality. This small Indian state is often compared with Sri Lanka, Costa Rica, and China for having attained high measures of human development despite low levels of per capita income. The processes underlying such achievements are thought to be "public action promoting a range of social opportunities relating *inter alia* to elementary education, land reforms, role of women in society, and wide-spread and equitable provision of health care and other public services" (Dreze and Sen 1995, pp. 52–3). The rapid decline in mortality and fertility have been attributed to both health care and other factors. However, among the health-care factors, public health-care services alone have been credited with "breakthrough periods" in declining mortality for "taking advantage of the opportunity for reorganizing the health approach to pregnancy, birth and the very young" (Caldwell 1986, p. 182). There is no mention of the size and role of the private health-care sector.

The perspective wherein health-care services are largely seen as government entities is part of a dominant thinking that "is proving more and more difficult to sustain in the face of growing evidence that governments are often minority, or even minor providers of health care in many countries and that they are becoming more so" (Berman 1998, p. 1464). This is especially so in India, which has a highly pluralistic health-care system, and where the private sector is a major provider of health care. It is possible that "the government has never been a major source of care for ambulatory illness care for much of India, although it has been the major provider of personal preventive services and population based public health interventions" (Berman 1998, p. 1465). Kerala is no exception to this Indian phenomenon of a large proportion of health care being provided in the private sector. Increasingly, people in Kerala have been turning to private health-care services and paying out-of-pocket. Two questions arise in this context: why do people turn to private care in a situation of so-called equitable provision of health care, and what implication does recourse to private care have for household incomes? In this chapter, we argue that one of the main reasons people turn to private care is the perceived poor quality of the public service, and that the high utilization of private service is a heavy burden on the poorer segments of Kerala's population.

A study of Kerala's health-care experience is highly relevant for three reasons. First, Kerala is known the world over as a case of public-action driven, policy-assisted development, supposedly characterized by equitable provision of health and other public services. Second, high utilization of health care is generally attributed to provision of insurance, but Kerala shows high utilization in a situation of out-of-pocket expenditure, contrary to what would be expected. Third, income elasticity of health care demand is supposed to be high, but Kerala shows a pattern different from other areas, in that health expenditure is high and not related to income.

In this chapter, after a brief introduction, we begin by presenting some distinct characteristics of Kerala, as background. Then we summarize briefly the dominant explanations of the mortality reduction in Kerala. One explanation most often put forward for the gains in life expectancy in Kerala is the higher utilization of health-care services, and the equitable provision of public services is often taken as the major reason for this high utilization. What is not so evident is that Kerala has a large and growing private health-care sector spread over the rural and urban areas. We describe Kerala's health-care environment and show that the utilization of private services is very high. One reason for this is the perceived poor quality of public service. We then present measures of perceived quality of public and private services in two districts of Kerala. The utilization of private services without insurance means out-of-pocket spending by households. We offer an analysis of their health expenditure that shows how high a burden this is for the poorer segments of population in Kerala. Finally, we draw conclusions and raise concerns about future directions.

THE STATE OF KERALA

Kerala, situated at the southwestern corner of the subcontinent, is one of India's smaller states. It is a narrow strip of land, bounded by the Arabian sea on the west and high mountains on the east, and extending over 600 kilometres from north to south. Kerala accounts for a population of 32 million, within the overall Indian population of slightly over one billion. As per the 2001 census, Kerala's population density is 819 persons/km². Kerala has the third-highest population density among the Indian states, after West Bengal and Bihar. The population is distributed over 14 districts, among which Alappuzha has the highest density, at 1 489 persons/km², and Idukki the lowest, at 252 persons/km².

The steep decline in death rate and fertility in Kerala over the last 30 years has resulted in a rapidly aging population. India has the second largest number of elderly persons (age 60 or older) after China. In 1981, the elderly represented 6.5% of the population; in 1991, 6.7%; and by 2016, the proportion is expected to reach around 9%. By comparison, the proportion of elderly in Kerala was 6.2% in 1971, 7.5% in 1981, and 10.6% in 1991. By 2001, it was estimated to be around 15% (Economic Review 2002).

Despite having achieved high levels of life expectancy and low mortality rates, in particular infant mortality, at fairly low levels of income, Kerala reports one of the highest levels of morbidity. The morbidity rate is twice the all-India average in the rural areas and over 50% higher than the Indian average in the urban areas. In 1995/96, the number (per 1 000 population) of persons reporting an illness during the previous 15 days in Kerala's rural areas was 118, compared to the all-India average of 55, and in the urban areas 88, compared to 54 at the all-India level. Acute morbidity in Kerala is 80 in rural areas and 61 in urban areas, compared to 42 and 41, respectively, in rural and urban India. Chronic morbidity rates in rural and urban Kerala are 38 and 27, respectively, compared to 13 and 14 in rural and urban areas of India. The rural morbidity rate is over 40% higher than the urban morbidity rate; such a differential is not to be found in any of the major Indian states (NSSO 1998).

Kerala has a unique position with regard to gender ratio, with 1 058 females per 1 000 males in 2001, whereas the Indian average is only 933. The ratio in the two richest states is low: 861 in Haryana and 874 in Punjab. Kerala reports high levels of literacy—94% among males and 88% among females in 2001—compared to the all-India average of 76% and 54%, respectively. The exceptionally high level of female literacy and the low gender gap in literacy in Kerala are noteworthy, as these generally lead to lower infant mortality rate (IMR) and fertility. Kerala reports comparatively low IMR (16 per 1 000 live births in the mid-1990s) and total fertility rate (TFR) (1.8 live births expected per woman in her reproductive years). In terms of IMR, a half-dozen Indian states currently are where Kerala was in the early 1970s, while the others are worse off, and the Indian average TFR is almost twice Kerala's.

Thus, Kerala is more developed than the other Indian states, whichever aspect of human development is considered. Literacy levels, especially among females, are exceptionally high and mortality reduction in the last 50 years is one of the most rapid among all the states. At the same time, the fertility rate has fallen almost below replacement level. What explains such remarkable gains in Kerala?

THE PUBLIC PROVISION EXPLANATION

In the mid-1970s, a group of researchers at the Centre for Development Studies, Trivandrum, concluded that Kerala, "a relatively poor state," had made "fairly impressive advances in health and education." Their study postulated that the sharp decline in birth rates in Kerala resulted from "societal changes in attitude to family size resulting from longer life expectation, reduction in infant and child mortality and female education" (United Nations 1975, p. 153). The societal changes in attitude, in turn, had been spurred by substantial government investment in health and education.

Kerala has devoted the bulk of public funds to infrastructure and social services, particularly in education and health (World Development Report 2004). Investment in health is guided by three objectives: (i) a public medical institution in every panchayat (see below); (ii) government funded medical education, to ensure an adequate supply of medical personnel; and (iii) encouragement of traditional medical systems. Gradual implementation of this strategy led to most districts having one medical institution (allopathy) per 20 000 population by 1990. The expansion of facilities under the Indian system of medicine—which includes ayurveda, homeopathy, and others—has also progressed as per the accepted policy. The emphasis on publicly funded medical education has led to an increase in the share of medical education in the total health expenditure from around 10% in 1977/78 to over 17% by 1991/92. (For detailed treatment of these issues, see Narayana 1999.) The strategy has seen two changes in recent years, namely, decentralization in the early 1990s and permitting of private medical educational institutes in the early 2000s.

India has a long history of experimenting with decentralization. The 73rd and 74th amendments to the Indian Constitution adopted in 1993 introduced a third tier of government, called panchayat, below the union and states and required states to delegate some administrative functions and taxation powers to local bodies. These amendments constituted a watershed, in that they left no room for the successive state legislatures to change the local self-government institution (LSGI) according to their whims and fancies. They brought about a uniform three-tiered structure of local governance—district, block/taluk, and village—in the rural areas. Only for small states with populations under two million was the intermediate tier optional. The amendments also introduced the concept of township for smaller urban centres, that is, rural areas in the process of urbanization.

Among the states, Kerala was in the forefront of decentralization of powers. The large public health-care sector in Kerala was also affected by the decentralization. As per the government order dated 18 September 1995, following the Panchayatiraj Act, the primary health centres (PHCs) and government dispensaries were transferred to the village panchayats; block PHCs, community health centres (CHCs), taluk headquarters hospitals, and government hospitals, to block panchayats; and CHCs, government hospitals, and taluk headquarters hospitals in corporation and municipal areas, to the corporation councils and municipal councils. In 1999, the district hospitals were brought under the control of district panchayats. Similar transfers of institutions and staff have taken place in the cases of ayurveda and homeopathy as well. Thus, in Kerala, except for medical colleges and a few general hospitals, all health institutions are managed by the local governments.

Following decentralization, the personnel of these institutions are under the supervision and disciplinary authority of the local bodies during their tenure with them, but their service conditions remain undisturbed. Further, the government continues to pay salaries, allowances, and other dues to the employees and officers transferred to the local bodies from the central government. Thus, the new system envisages dual control over the staff (Narayana and Hari Kurup 2001).

The smooth functioning of the institutions is to be ensured by the constitution of certain committees. There are supposed to be standing committees for health and sanitation at the level of the municipal council and municipal corporation in the urban areas, and at the block panchayat and district panchayat in the rural areas. These standing committees are to deal with matters relating to public health and health service, sanitation, environment, dangerous and offensive trades, education, arts and culture, and sports. At the district panchayat level, a management committee must be constituted for every public health institution transferred to it by the government.

In Kerala, public medical institutions have been brought under the administrative control of the LSGIs, which receive intergovernmental transfers, the criteria being population size, area, and the proportion of SC/ST[1] population. The taluk hospitals and district hospitals also have duly constituted hospital development committees (HDCs), which collect user charges on some services and carry out some regular maintenance, cleaning, and repair.

The achievements of Kerala in the field of mortality and fertility were attributed to widespread health coverage. Although it was recognized that coverage was not lower in many other states, what distinguished Kerala was the extremely high utilization ratio, thought to have been enhanced by better physical accessibility (Krishnan 1975). Panikar (1979) added a new dimension by postulating that the progress of literacy and education had not only increased the rural population's awareness of the need to use health facilities, but also made it aware of its rights to demand and use them. Nag (1983, 1989) marshaled evidence to show that a high degree of political awareness in rural Kerala contributed to easier accessibility and better utilization of health facilities. In a comparative exercise with West Bengal, Nag (1985) brought out the aspect of higher utilization of public health facilities in Kerala. In terms of number of health facilities and medical personnel, the differences between the two states were not significant, but utilization of medical facilities—both preventive and curative—was distinctly higher in Kerala. The higher utilization was then explained in terms of accessibility, better transportation, and better literacy, especially female literacy:

> Higher female literacy in Kerala has contributed significantly toward higher utilization of maternal and child health services by the women of the state. They are also less inhibited regarding physical examinations and more open to traveling to the health centres without male escorts. Indirectly higher literacy has contributed to a higher level of political participation of the rural poor, which, in turn, has forced the state government in the post-independence era to cater to their health needs along with other needs (Nag 1985, p. 68).

The *need* and *right* have been variously reformulated. Sen (1992, p. 254) speaks of "people participating along with governments, in defining needs, in making choices appropriate to these needs, and in enforcing accountability." Making governments and local functionaries accountable depends upon the political mobilization and awareness of local communities, groups, and people generally. In this case, the unusual position of women in society and the surge of social and religious reform movements are at the root of Kerala's success.

The long-term decline of IMR in Kerala is characterized by three phases: 1956–1966, 1967–1976, and beyond 1976 (Krishnan 1985). The decline in the first phase was on the order of 50 per 1 000 live births; in the second phase, about 10; and in the third phase (up to 1990) it was 39. The first and last phases are called breakthrough periods. The 1956–66 breakthrough was explained partly by the expanded provision of health services in Malabar (the northern six districts of Kerala) and the strong emphasis on the immunization of children: "The first phase of decline in Kerala's infant mortality can be attributed largely to the expansion in vaccination programs against smallpox and other infectious diseases and possibly an expansion of health facilities in the northern region" (Krishnan 1985, p. 43). Then, between 1976 and 1988, neonatal mortality declined from 22 to 10 and post-neonatal mortality from 34 to 18, and by the early 1990s the IMR in Kerala was around 17 per 1 000 live births.

The decline in mortality beyond 1976 could be attributed to two sets of factors. The epidemiological data seemed to indicate that already by 1980 there was a decline in the proportion of children treated for diphtheria, whooping cough, measles, and enteric fever in southern Kerala. The immunization programs launched by Kerala in the late 1970s seem to have played a role in this development. It may also be noted that, in Kerala, maternal and child health programs were initiated a decade earlier than the WHO-sponsored Universal Immunization Program launched in 1985 at the all-India level. Tetanus toxoid (TT) immunization for pregnant women (1975/76), polio and typhoid vaccination (1980/81), BCG vaccination (1981/82), and measles vaccination (1985/86) had already been launched in Kerala. The expansion of immunization into the whole of Kerala in the 1980s must have played an important role in bringing down infant mortality.

Immunization can explain the decline in infant deaths caused by exogenous factors. The nearly one-third of infant deaths that were neonatal also declined substantially in Kerala during this period. Causes of death peculiar to infancy, such as malposition, birth injury, cord infection, and malnutrition, have obviously been controlled in Kerala. One factor accounting for this could have been the availability of medical attention during pregnancy and childbirth. Evidence to this effect is available, in terms of institutional deliveries and medical attention during childbirth. In Kerala in 1973, 26% of rural childbirths took place in a medical institution, rising to 47% by 1980 and over 80% by 1990. Thus, immunization and medical attention during pregnancy and childbirth largely explain the infant mortality reduction in Kerala beyond 1976.

Overall, Kerala's success in health outcomes is traced not so much to government expenditure on the health sector, nor to the geographical distribution of health-care facilities, but rather to better utilization of health-care facilities and strong emphasis on immunization programs. As better utilization emerges as the core explanation of Kerala's success, it is increasingly important not to ignore the role of the private health-care sector. Studies focus on programs spearheaded by government health departments and on attendance at government health facilities, but not on the use of health-care facilities overall. A hint of the existence of a large private health-care sector is evident in Krishnan (1975); Panikar (1985) elaborated it and Caldwell (1986) quoted it approvingly. The private health-care sector in Kerala has been expanding, and its utilization has been increasing. How large is the private sector, and what proportion of the population uses private health care?

KERALA'S HEALTH INFRASTRUCTURE IN THE MID-1990s

Over the past four decades, Kerala's health-care environment has become a vast and complex infrastructure, a mix of public and privately owned facilities, with the private growing rapidly in both urban and rural areas. The vast health infrastructure is also characterized by various systems. In this section we describe the health infrastructure in its complexity across the districts of the state as observed in the mid-1990s.

The health infrastructure under the state government includes over 6 000 medical institutions, including subcentres. A medical institution is defined as an establishment where patients are examined or diagnosed for diseases and where medical treatment is prescribed and provided. Places where only consultation facilities are available, such as consulting rooms and institutions engaged in selling medicines, are not treated as medical institutions.

At the apex of the system are the medical colleges, geographically dispersed over the length of the state. The 14 districts each have a general/district hospital and numerous subdistrict hospitals. The most numerous are the primary health centres (PHC) and the subcentres under them. There are also institutions for women and children, and others for infectious diseases, such as tuberculosis and leprosy. There are hospitals attached to most of these institutions, with beds totaling over 46 800 in 2002.

As mentioned, the medical institutions are distributed over the districts of the state. Over 90% of government medical institutions are located in the rural areas (Table 1), and about 40% of hospital beds are in the rural areas. Rural concentration is very high (>65%) in the districts of Idukki, Malappuram, and Wayanad, and very low (<30%) in Kannur, Kozhikode, and Thiruvananthapuram.

TABLE 1. DISTRIBUTION OF GOVERNMENT INSTITUTIONS AND BEDS (ALLOPATHY) BY DISTRICTS AND LOCATION IN KERALA, 1997

District	Medical institutions			Hospital beds		
	Rural	Urban	Total	Rural	Urban	Total
Alappuzha	81	9	90	1 706	2 300	4 006
Ernakulam	95	21	116	1 397	2 641	4 038
Idukki	62	2	64	566	274	840
Kannur	94	9	103	573	1 542	2 115
Kasargod	56	4	60	288	401	689
Kollam	83	5	88	1 151	919	2 070
Kottayam	77	7	84	1 228	2 126	3 354
Kozhikode	83	12	95	487	3 908	4 395
Malappuram	114	9	123	990	1 171	2 161
Palakkad	105	7	112	1 311	877	2 188
Pathanamthitta	59	4	63	467	474	941
Thiruvananthapuram	92	23	115	1 559	5 657	7 216
Thrissur	112	10	122	1 990	2 129	4 119
Wayanad	37	2	39	768	43	811
Kerala total	**1 150**	**124**	**1 274**	**14 481**	**24 462**	**38 943**

Source: Government of Kerala, Economic Review 1998.

The government has also supported the traditional systems of medicine—ayurveda and homeopathy—by establishing medical colleges and setting up dispensaries and hospitals. There are altogether 690 ayurvedic and 415 homeopathic institutions in the state. The total number of beds is less compared to the allopathic system, but they are fairly well distributed over the districts (Table 2).

TABLE 2. DISTRIBUTION OF GOVERNMENT INSTITUTIONS AND BEDS (AYURVEDA AND HOMEOPATHY) BY DISTRICTS IN KERALA, 1995

District	Medical institutions		Hospital beds	
	Ayurveda	Homeopathy	Ayurveda	Homeopathy
Alappuzha	52	33	180	75
Ernakulam	62	44	230	75
Idukki	30	28	110	50
Kannur	50	27	211	25
Kasargod	35	20	100	75
Kollam	47	30	170	75
Kottayam	41	34	150	175
Kozhikode	45	35	170	75
Malappuram	65	34	200	50
Palakkad	59	27	130	25
Pathanamthitta	37	20	80	25
Thiruvananthapuram	64	41	255	175
Thrissur	82	28	223	25
Wayanad	21	14	100	25
Kerala total	**690**	**415**	**2309**	**950**

Source: Government of Kerala, Economic Review 1996.

The private sector has grown phenomenally in Kerala, with facilities in all three systems of medicine. Of the 12 618 private medical institutions (in 1995, the most recent data available), 4 288 are allopathic, 4 922 ayurvedic, and 3 118 homeopathic (Table 3). Although the three systems are almost equal in number at the aggregate level, across the districts there is considerable variation in their relative positions. Whereas the districts south of Ernakulam have almost equal numbers of institutions among the three systems, the northern districts have relatively more ayurvedic and homeopathic facilities. In the south, Thiruvananthapuram is an exception, with a large number of ayurvedic and homeopathic institutions.

In contrast to the number of institutions, the number of hospital beds is largely confined to the allopathic hospitals (Table 3). Of the 70 924 hospital beds in the private sector, 67 517 are under the allopathic system. Nearly 50% of all private-sector hospital beds are located in the four districts of Ernakulam, Kollam, Kottayam, and Thrissur. Fewer than 25% of the total beds are located in the six northern districts.

TABLE 3. DISTRIBUTION OF PRIVATE MEDICAL INSTITUTIONS BY DISTRICT, KERALA, 1995

District	Medical institutions				Hospital beds			
	AL	AY	HO	Other	AL	AY	HO	Other
Alappuzha	367	346	328	9	3 633	168	22	24
Ernakulam	542	406	444	25	11 418	78	75	31
Idukki	239	180	123	13	3 944	54	6	0
Kannur	264	391	260	16	3 952	122	25	0
Kasargod	157	209	44	13	1 290	3	0	20
Kollam	369	397	230	11	7 194	231	74	20
Kottayam	474	501	440	17	7 642	206	0	40
Kozhikkode	372	549	366	42	3 714	246	36	57
Malappuram	237	554	165	23	3 313	561	41	33
Palakkad	180	452	105	23	2 105	111	15	0
Pathanamthitta	257	187	167	17	4 391	40	26	39
Thiruvananthapuram	431	232	221	46	4 807	302	31	85
Thrissur	288	455	171	30	8 345	436	43	69
Wayanad	111	63	54	5	1 769	37	0	0
Kerala total	**4 288**	**4 922**	**3 118**	**290**	**67 517**	**2 595**	**394**	**418**

Source: Government of Kerala. Report on the Survey of Private Medical Institutions in Kerala 1995.

Key: AL = allopathic, AY = ayurvedic, HO = homeopathic

Taking into account public and private facilities under all three systems of medicine both for Kerala as a whole and for the districts, there is one medical institution per 2 000 population and one hospital bed per 250 population (Tables 4 and 5). On average, a person could theoretically access a medical institution within a distance of one kilometre. However, variation in the density of medical institutions across the districts is considerable. The density of government medical institutions (per 100 000 population) is higher in Idukki, Kasargod, Pathanamthitta, and Wayanad, largely because population density is lower, as is evident from the area covered per government medical institution. The density of private medical institutions is lower than the state average in Malappuram, Palakkad, Thiruvananthapuram, Thrissurand, and Wayanad. It is significantly higher in Kozhikode and in the geographical belt from Pathanamthitta in the south to Ernakulam in the central region. The distribution of total (public and private) medical institutions across the districts shows that Kozhikode and the geographical belt from Pathanamthitta to Ernakulam have a density of over 58 institutions per 100 000 population. The districts of Thiruvananthapuram and the Malappuram, Palakkad, and Thrissur belt stand at the lower end, with around 40 institutions per 100 000 population. The other districts are close to the state average.

TABLE 4. GEOGRAPHICAL DENSITY OF HEALTH CARE FACILITIES (ALL SYSTEMS) IN KERALA, 1995

District	GMI	Area/GMI	PMI	Area/PMI	TMI	Area/TMI
Alappuzha	8	8.78	52	1.35	60	1.17
Ernakulam	8	10.89	50	1.70	58	1.47
Idukki	11	41.14	51	9.04	62	7.41
Kannur	8	16.66	41	3.19	49	2.64
Kasargod	11	17.32	39	4.71	50	3.70
Kollam	7	15.10	42	2.47	49	2.13
Kottayam	9	13.68	78	1.54	87	1.38
Kozhikode	7	13.47	51	1.76	58	1.56
Malappuram	7	15.99	32	3.63	39	2.96
Palakkad	8	22.74	32	5.89	40	4.68
Pathanamthitta	11	19.57	53	4.21	64	3.46
Thiruvananthapuram	7	9.92	32	2.36	39	1.90
Thrissur	9	13.01	34	3.21	43	2.58
Wayanad	11	28.80	35	9.15	46	6.94
Kerala total / average area distributions	**8**	**16.34**	**43**	**3.08**	**51**	**2.59**

Sources: *PMI*: Government of Kerala. Report on the Survey of Private Medical Institutions in Kerala 1995. *GMI, areas*: Government of Kerala, Economic Review 1996.

Key: GMI = government, PMI = public, TMI = total, medical institutions per 100 000.

Area in square kilometres.

TABLE 5. DENSITY OF BEDS (ALL SYSTEMS) PER 100 000 POPULATION IN KERALA, 1995

District	Government	Private	Total
Alappuzha	208	192	400
Ernakulam	150	412	562
Idukki	93	371	464
Kannur	104	182	286
Kasargod	79	122	201
Kollam	97	312	409
Kottayam	202	432	634
Kozhikode	177	155	132
Malappuram	77	128	205
Palakkad	94	94	188
Pathanamthitta	96	378	474
Thiruvananthapuram	250	177	427
Thrissur	159	325	484
Wayanad	139	269	408
Kerala total	**143**	**244**	**387**

Sources: *PMI*: Government of Kerala. Report on the Survey of Private Medical Institutions in Kerala 1995. *GMI, areas*: Government of Kerala, Economic Review 1996.

The distribution of hospital beds follows a pattern slightly different from that of medical institutions. The districts south of Thrissur report over 400 beds per 100 000 population while the northern districts report fewer than 300 beds per 100 000 population, with the exception of Wayanad, which reported 408 beds per 100 000 population. The inequality in the distribution of beds in government institutions across the districts would explain only part of the overall inequality in distribution. Generally, the southern districts have a higher density of institutions and beds than do the northern districts.

The geographical area to be covered per government institution in the southern districts is well below 15 km², with the exception of Idukki and Pathanamthitta. In the northern districts, only Kozhikode reports the area per government institution below 15 km². With regard to geographical area covered per private institution, the picture is similar. All districts south of Thrissur, except Idukki and Pathanamthitta, report a figure below 3.2 km². In the north, only Kozhikode has a lower figure. Putting the two together, it may be seen that in the south, five out of the eight districts have a medical institution at an average distance of less than 0.8 kilometres, whereas in the north, only Kozhikode falls into this category.

Overall, Kerala reports a fairly high density of medical institutions and hospital beds, together with considerable inter-district variation, with the southern districts reporting densities higher than in the northern districts. Whereas Alappuzha reports the best physical access both for government and private institutions, Kasaragod reports fairly poor access for both.

No doubt a long tradition of education (especially among females), female autonomy, and public-action driven political processes have facilitated higher utilization of health-care facilities in Kerala. However, this higher utilization has not been of services provided by the public sector, as since at least the mid-1960s people have been exiting from it and seeking services from the large and growing private sector. This exodus has reduced the role of the public sector in every aspect of health care, while the private sector has come to fill the increasing demand. For outpatient services, about one-third of people seeking treatment are seen in government facilities, and fewer than 10% receive free treatment. There is not much difference between the rural (29.8%) and urban (30.5%) areas in the proportion of population using public health-care services in Kerala. In the case of inpatient treatment, the percentages of hospitalized cases treated in government facilities were higher at 39.5% (rural) and 37.3% (urban) (NSSO 1998). Thus, over the years, the private health-care sector has emerged as the dominant care provider in Kerala.

PERCEIVED QUALITY OF HEALTH-CARE SERVICES

Why do people turn to the private health-care sector in Kerala? Physical access does not appear to be a major consideration. As noted in the previous section, except for a few locations, physical distance to the public service is not very great, and the state has fairly good roads and transportation networks. This leads us to question whether perceptions of quality could be a factor in the choice of care.

In this study, perception of quality was measured using a scale where respondents were asked to grade a specific aspect of quality from very good (5) to very unfavourable (1). Both the head of the household and the spouse were asked 20 questions, independently and separately. The questions have been organized into three groups for presentation in this section. The first five questions are on service delivery, the next six on the attitude and behaviour of health-care workers, and the remaining nine on health-care facilities.

The data on quality and cost of care (presented in the next section) are from two districts, Kasaragod and Alappuzha, where 555 and 569 households, respectively, were surveyed in 1999. The household questionnaire had four modules, of which Module 2, on perceived quality, was canvassed on 1 015 and 942 individuals, heads of household, and spouses in the two districts, respectively. In Kasaragod, two villages and a town were selected and, in Alappuzha, one village and one town. In Kerala, villages and towns have wards as administrative units, which were selected randomly for the survey, and households were selected from wards.

The first and foremost finding is that in none of the locations surveyed does the average score for quality surpass 3 for any of the three dimensions of public health care: quality of service delivery, health worker quality and health facility quality (Table 6). In rural Kasaragod, the upper range value just crosses 3 with regard to health worker quality and health facility quality. In Alappuzha, the aspect with regard to which the score exceeds 3 is health-care delivery, indicating that the respondents have faith in the diagnostic and treatment abilities of the physicians in the public facilities. However, their ratings of health worker quality and health facility quality are unfavourable. Thus, by and large, the quality of public health care services is rated between moderate and unfavourable with regard to all three dimensions of quality.

TABLE 6. PERCEPTION OF HEALTH CARE QUALITY IN KERALA, 1999

Quality aspect	Males		Females	
	Private	Public	Private	Public
	Kasaragod – urban			
HC delivery	3.45–3.72	2.60–2.95	3.18–3.67	1.87–2.19
HC worker	3.46–3.71	2.53	3.11–3.57	1.87–2.05
HC facility	3.17–3.63	2.42–2.44	2.82–3.36	2.07–2.19
	Kasaragod – rural			
HC delivery	3.71–4.40	2.35–2.86	3.04–3.70	1.89–2.47
HC worker	3.73–4.45	2.35–3.04	2.91–3.41	1.61–2.18
HC facility	3.11–3.73	2.34–3.29	2.69–3.24	2.03–2.38
	Alappuzha – urban			
HC delivery	4.00–4.34	2.86–3.48	3.95–4.31	2.81–3.41
HC worker	3.71–4.14	2.59–2.85	3.75–4.16	2.50–2.61
HC facility	3.39–3.49	2.91–3.05	3.33–3.43	2.89–2.95
	Alappuzha – rural			
HC delivery	3.67–3.82	3.53–3.56	3.61–3.82	3.50–3.52
HC worker	3.59–3.68	2.64–2.93	3.59–3.62	2.66–2.93
HC facility	3.19–3.27	2.81–2.96	3.23–3.25	2.81–2.97

Source: MAPHealth primary survey (1999).
Key: HC = health-care; private = private health-care facility; public = public hospital.

In striking contrast is the rating of private health-care facilities in both districts. The quality of private health-care service is rated above 3 with regard to all three aspects of quality in almost all locations. The only exceptions are averages in three locations in Kasaragod that are below 3, all by women and almost all having to do with the quality of the health-care facility. In some locations in Kasaragod, the average measure stood close to or above 4. Especially high is the rating of service delivery and health worker quality. In Alappuzha all the averages are above 3, and are either close to or above 4. Thus, while the quality of public health-care service is rated as moderate or unfavourable, that of private service is rated as good or very good.

Is there a difference in the perception of health-care quality between men and women? In Alappuzha, there is hardly any difference, except in two urban wards. In one of these, women rate health worker quality lower in the public hospital, and in the other, women rate all three aspects lower. In Kasaragod, women rate the quality of public services significantly lower than do men on all three aspects. Especially striking are the large differences with regard to health worker quality. For public hospitals in Kasaragod, the average rating for health worker quality by women is nearer to or lower than 2 in almost every ward selected. Such differences are almost non-existent for private facilities, with few exceptions.

Two findings stand out. First, the overall quality of public health-care service is rated moderate to unfavourable, whereas that of private service is rated good to very good. Second, the quality ratings of public service in Kasaragod by women are significantly worse than the ratings given by men, especially for health worker quality. It therefore seems likely that perceived poor quality is one of the major reasons for the low utilization of public health care.

THE BURDEN OF HEALTH-CARE COST

In previous sections, we have seen that utilization of private health-care facilities is high in Kerala, and that one of the reasons for this is the perceived poor quality of public health-care services. What are the cost implications of using private services?

When using private health-care services, in the absence of any form of health insurance, households will incur out-of-pocket expenditure. In both districts surveyed, the average health-care expenditure per household is significantly lower in rural than in urban areas—about 35% lower in Alappuzha and about 20% in Kasaragod (Tables 7 and 8). Health expenditures in Alappuzha are almost twice what they are in Kasaragod, a significant difference. Thus, health expenditure per household shows considerable variation between rural and urban areas and between districts.

TABLE 7. ANNUAL HEALTH EXPENDITURE BY HOUSEHOLDS IN ALAPPUZHA, 1999

Income class (Rupees)	Urban			Rural		
	Distribution (%) of households	Average health expenditure	Health expenditure (% income)	Distribution (%) of households	Average health expenditure	Health expenditure (% income)
<12 000	11.19	4 416	106.61	13.43	2 768	41.64
12k-15k	2.45	9 850	70.79	6.36	1 428	10.29
15k-20k	6.64	3 384	18.10	15.19	2 077	11.52
20k-30k	12.59	4 986	19.33	32.16	2 699	11.31
30k-40k	14.34	5 402	15.15	14.49	3 555	10.21
40k-50k	7.69	3 753	8.23	8.48	2 792	6.22
50k+	45.10	4 167	2.85	9.89	4 683	5.87
All	100 (286)	4 516	5.66	100 (283)	2 852	9.86

Source: MAPHealth primary survey (1999).

Note: Figures in brackets are the total number of households surveyed.

TABLE 8. ANNUAL HEALTH EXPENDITURE BY HOUSEHOLDS IN KASARAGOD, 1999

Income class (Rupees)	Urban			Rural		
	Distribution (%) of households	Average health expenditure	Health expenditure (% income)	Distribution (%) of households	Average health expenditure	Health expenditure (% income)
<12 000	3.48	1 067	16.55	10.70	840	8.85
12k-15k	2.33	1 550	11.19	2.35	790	5.59
15k-20k	5.81	1 120	6.11	5.48	1 130	6.17
20k-30k	11.63	1 430	5.55	23.24	1 144	4.60
30k-40k	15.12	2 200	6.21	16.71	3 016	8.55
40k-50k	6.40	1 236	2.70	11.49	1 250	2.71
50k+	55.23	2 094	1.66	30.03	1 386	1.30
All	100 (172)	1 867	2.26	100 (383)	1 478	2.88

Source: MAPHealth primary survey (1999).

Note: Figures in brackets are the total number of households surveyed.

The existence of significant variation in health expenditure between rural and urban areas does not imply any significant variation in expenditure across income classes. In both districts, health expenditure shows hardly any variation across income classes within rural and urban locations. In other words, health expenditure does not increase with household income; rich and poor spend almost equally on health. Consequently, although the overall share of health spending in annual income varies between 2% and 10% across locations and between districts, for certain income classes at the lower end, it represents 40% to 70% of their incomes. In the urban areas of Alappuzha, for the poorest income class, health expenditure is more than their annual income. Thus, the utilization of private health-care service and the associated out-of-pocket expenditure is a heavy burden on the poorer segments of population.

A comparison of the three regions in India taken for the MAPHealth study shows that the cost of health care per episode of illness and the health expenditure as a percentage of income is lowest in Kerala. However, the percentage of households spending over 20% of their annual income on health-care expenditure is close to 15% in Kerala, the highest among the three states studied (Narayana 2001). Especially high is the percentage of households in Kerala spending over 100% of their annual income on health care (>9%).

Annual household expenditure on health care is a product of the cost of consultation per episode of illness and the number of household members falling ill during the year. A regression of the cost per episode of illness showed that among the three variables considered (age of the household member falling ill, household income, and the use of private or public facilities), the use of private facilities is the only significant explanatory variable in Kerala. The use of private health-care facilities results in a higher cost of consultation, being higher by a fixed amount across the selected wards. Neither the age of the ill person nor household income is a significant explanatory variable. Especially striking is the lack of variation in cost of consultation across income classes.

The number of household members falling ill during a four-week reference period shows significant similarity among households within a randomly selected ward, whereas the between-ward variation in the number of persons falling ill is high. The variation in morbidity among households is explained by household size, number of members above 60 years of age, number of members below five years of age, quality of drinking water, and number of rooms in the house. The association of higher morbidity with the number of members above 60 years and below five years of age is well known. What is striking, however, is that as the number of rooms in the house increases, the number of members falling ill decreases, and also that income is not a statistically significant explanatory variable. Thus, the age composition of the household and the living environment are important explanatory variables of the incidence of illness in a household, but not the level of household income.

The use of private health-care facilities is an important factor explaining the cost of health care and is not influenced by age, sex, education, or work status of the member falling ill. Income of the household and distance to the facility also do not have an influence on the utilization of private facilities. The overall picture regarding utilization of public or private facilities may be summarized as follows:

> Some important differences could be observed in the utilization of PHC, private health care facilities, and public hospital in Kerala. Individual characteristics such as age, household income, sex and education do not seem to play a role in the utilization, except for the role of sex in the utilization of public hospital. The lower utilization of public facilities by women is a striking result with some serious implications. Perceived quality of care is a very important aspect in the decision to use a facility, but the specific aspect

of care influencing the decision is different across facilities. In the case of PHC, the health worker quality is an important explanatory factor; in the case of private facilities, the health facility quality and health delivery quality is important; and in the case of public hospital, the health facility quality is important (Narayana 2001, p. 80).

The perceived quality of care seems to play an important role in the choice of the provider, irrespective of household income. As the quality of public service is perceived to be poor, people increasingly seek private care. The cost implications of this are serious, with the poorer segments of the population devoting a sizable proportion of their income to health care.

CONCLUSION

Low mortality, high morbidity, and high utilization of private care summarize the story of health care in Kerala. The use of private care, with the associated out-of-pocket expenditure, is a heavy burden on the poorer segments of the population. As in the other states of India, only a small proportion of Kerala's population is gainfully employed in the organized sector with some financial protection against the cost of ill health. The large unorganized sector—farming, household manufacturing, and services—provides no financial protection against the cost of illness, leading to high levels of financial distress and dragging down productive investment and income generation. Furthermore, the lack of access to health care belies Kerala's image of providing good health at low cost.

The developments of the last 10 years in decentralized governance and the phenomenal growth of self-help groups (SHGs) in Kerala provide opportunities for evolving some mechanism of financial protection. SHGs have been the focal point of rural credit, self-employment programs, and poverty alleviation in India since 1995. In 1999, the Ministry of Rural Development restructured the numerous programs and introduced a new self-employment program called Swarnjayanti Gram Swarozgar Yojana (SGSY), implemented through SHGs. Usually, SHGs have between 10 and 20 members, and their basic functions are to mobilize savings that go into a common fund, obtain credit from banks, and extend loans to members. Over 80% of SHGs are made up of women and, interestingly, about two-thirds of SHGs are located in the southern region of the country. Since 2001, local governments in Kerala have actively promoted SHGs. Our impression is that about 20% of the borrowings from members' own savings go to pay for health-care expenses.

Thus far, there is little evidence of efforts on the part of policymakers, administrators, or social workers to exploit opportunities for developing effective financial protection mechanisms. With the aging population and the rising incidence of chronic diseases, the level of financial distress is bound to increase unless appropriate measures are implemented soon.

Note

1. Scheduled caste (SC) and scheduled tribe (ST) are population groups listed in the schedules of the Indian Constitution for special consideration owing to their social backwardness.

References

Berman, P.A. 1998. Rethinking health care systems: private health care provision in India. World Development, 26(8), 1463–1479.

Caldwell, J.C. 1986. Routes to low mortality in poor countries. Population and Development Review, 12(2), 171–220.

Dreze, J.; Sen, A. 1989. Hunger and Public Action. Clarendon Press, Oxford, UK. 373 pp.

_____ 1995. India: Economic Development and Social Opportunity. Oxford University Press, Delhi, India. 292 pp.

Government of Kerala. 1958. Second Five Year Plan: Kerala. Government Press, Trivandrum, Kerala, India.

_____ 1996. Report on the survey of private medical institutions in Kerala 1995. Department of Economics and Statistics, Thiruvananthapuram, Kerala, India.

_____ 1997. Economic Review 1996. State Planning Board, Thiruvananthapuram, Kerala, India.

_____ 1999. Economic Review 1998. State Planning Board, Thiruvananthapuram, Kerala, India.

_____ 2001. Economic Review 2000. State Planning Board, Thiruvananthapuram, Kerala, India.

Halstead, S.B.; Walsh, J.A.; Warren, K.S., ed. 1985. Good health at low cost. Proceedings of a conference held at the Bellagio Conference Center, Bellagio, Italy, April 29–May 3, 1985. Rockefeller Foundation, New York, NY, USA.

Jeffrey, R. 1992. Politics, women and well-being: how Kerala became 'a model'. The Macmillan Press, London, UK. 285 pp.

Krishnan, T.N. 1976. Demographic transition in Kerala: facts and factors. Economic and Political Weekly, 11(31–33), 1203–1224.

_____ 1985. Health statistics in Kerala State, India. In Halstead, S.B., et al., ed., Good health at low cost. Rockefeller Foundation, New York, NY, USA. pp. 39–46.

Nag, M. 1983. Impact of social and economic development on mortality: a comparative study of Kerala and West Bengal. Economic and Political Weekly, 18(19–21), 877–900.

_____ 1985. The impact of social and economic development on mortality: a comparative study of Kerala and West Bengal. In Halstead, S.B., et al., ed., Good health at low cost. Rockefeller Foundation, New York, NY, USA. pp. 57–77.

_____ 1989. Political awareness as a factor in accessibility of health services: a case study of rural Kerala and West Bengal. Economic and Political Weekly, 24(8), 417–426.

Narayana, D. 1999. Public expenditure reform without policy change: infrastructure investment and health care provision under fiscal squeeze in Kerala. In Mackintosh, M.; Roy, R., ed., Economic decentralization and public management reform. Edward Elgar, Cheltenham, UK. pp. 106–121.

Narayana, D.; Hari Kurup, K.K. 2001. Decentralisation of the health care sector in Kerala: some issues. Working paper no. 298. Centre for Development Studies, Trivandrum, Kerala, India.

National Sample Survey Organisation (NSSO). 1998. Morbidity and treatment of ailments. NSS fifty-second round, July 1995–June 1996, Report no. 441 (52/25.0/1). Government of India, New Delhi, India.

Panikar, P.G.K. 1985. Health care system in Kerala and its impact on infant mortality. In Halstead, S.B., et al., ed., Good health at low cost. Rockefeller Foundation, New York, NY, USA. pp. 47–55.

_____ 1979. Resources not the constraint on health improvement: a case study of Kerala. Economic and Political Weekly, 14, 1802–1809.

Panikar, P.G.K.; Soman, C.R. 1984. Health status of Kerala. Centre for Development Studies, Trivandrum, Kerala, India.

Sen, A. 1981. Public action and the quality of life in developing countries. Oxford Bulletin of Economics and Statistics, 43(4), 287–319.

_____ 1983. Development: which way now? Economic Journal 93, 745–762.

Sen, G. 1992. Social needs and public accountability: the case of Kerala. In Wuyts, M.; Mackintosh, M.; Hewitt, T., ed., Development policy and public action. Oxford University Press, Oxford, UK. pp. 253–278.

United Nations. 1975. Poverty, unemployment and development policy: a case study of selected issues with reference to Kerala. United Nations Department of Economic and Social Affairs, Document ST/ESA/29. New York, NY, USA. 235 pp.

World Bank. 2004. World development report 2004: making services work for poor people. World Bank and Oxford University Press, Washington, DC, USA, 288 pp.

CHAPTER 8

REFORM WITHOUT STRUCTURAL CHANGE: CONSERVING TRADITIONAL SOURCES OF POWER AND PRESTIGE IN MEXICO'S SEGMENTED HEALTH MARKET

Luis Durán, Sofía Arjonilla, Viviane Brachet-Márquez, Jeannie Haggerty

INTRODUCTION

Mexican health care is highly segmented in both delivery systems and quality of care. A variety of social insurance institutions, the major players in the health system, cover the majority (55%) of the population, followed by public services provided by the Secretary of Health (*Secretaría de Salud – SSA*) to the uninsured (45%), and finally, private services for those who can afford to pay (5–15%), some of whom are also covered by the other two sectors. Social insurance institutions provide health care and retirement benefits to their members in facilities jointly financed through government grants and employee–employer contributions. At the end of 1994 and throughout 1995, Mexico underwent a severe economic crisis during which the proportion of the population employed in the formal economy diminished, and the unemployed lost their health-care coverage.

In response to this crisis, health sector reforms between 1995 and 2000 reflected policy directions outlined in the seminal World Bank report, *Investing in Health*: providing a package of essential health services to the poor, opening up social insurance to a wider group, and integrating private delivery systems into the health system (World Bank 1993). Expanding services to the poor and decentralizing public health services to the state level were major directions of the 1995–2000 health policy cycle. Our study was carried out at the conclusion of that cycle to determine how the population and providers were experiencing these health reforms in the context of the economic crisis. This study used multiple methods to examine the following hypotheses:

i)   The economic crisis would cause a shift in patterns of health care use. Loss of employment, with concomitant loss of membership rights to social insurance services, was expected to increase the use of public (SSA) services.

ii) Health sector reform would improve access to health services for the poorest strata in society through targeted programs.

iii) The reform would not adequately redress existing inequities in the health system, such that there would continue to be marked differentials in scope and quality of care among public, social insurance, and private health-care systems.

OVERVIEW OF MEXICO

Politically, Mexico is a federation of 32 states with six-year national election cycles and state elections every four years. It has been classified as a middle-income country, with a gross national product (GNP) of 4 020 USD per capita in 1998 (World Bank 2004). Mexico's population of about 98 million is the second largest in Latin America, with three-quarters living in urban areas. Although its population is still growing, the rate of growth has slowed from over 3% in the 1970s to 1.53% between 1995 and 2000. Life expectancy at birth has been steadily increasing, reaching 74.03 years by 2000 (CONAPO 2000), such that the population over age 60 has gained in both size and policy relevance.

After six decades of one-party rule, Mexico's long democratic transition led to the victory of the opposition in both the 1997 parliamentary and 2000 presidential elections. This political transition coincided with the move from an import-substitution to a market-based economy, while the new government also had to contend with an increasing burden of poverty and inequality.

Health, in this regard, is one of the main arenas of social inequality. In 1995, 10 million Mexicans, principally in remote geographical areas, had no access to health services. Despite various health coverage schemes, most health care entails significant direct and indirect costs for the users. Mexico is also facing complex epidemiological challenges. Common infections have decreased but the frequency of chronic diseases and injuries is increasing, creating a double burden of morbidity from acute and chronic illnesses. The country is also confronted with emerging problems such as AIDS and the diverse health effects of environmental pollution, as well as re-emerging infections like dengue and cholera, all of which compete for the scarce resources of the national health system.

STUDY METHODS

The study in Mexico followed the general multiple methods design outlined in Chapter 3: a retrospective review of macroeconomic and health policies, evaluation of trends in resource allocation and in the amount and types of service provided at health facilities, and a major household survey. However, two additional substudies were added to provide in-depth understanding of the reform process and its impacts. The first was a policy analysis of reform processes at state and local levels, with special emphasis on political processes and the managerial capacity to decentralize the health sector (Brachet-Márquez 2002). In-depth interviews were carried out with 60 key informants including the respective state health secretaries, managers, and providers in the social insurance institutions, as well as private providers of both allopathic and alternative medicine. The second was a qualitative study of providers and users of health care in both rural and urban areas to gauge knowledge of the reforms and perceptions of changes in recent years. Semi-structured interviews were conducted with 137 public and private providers, principally phy-

FIGURE 1. MEXICAN STATES INCLUDED IN THE MAPHEALTH STUDY: GUANAJUATO, OAXACA, SONORA

sicians and nurses. The user perspective was obtained through focus groups of women: 12 urban—grouped into high, middle, low, and marginal socioeconomic levels—and 12 rural groups in 12 distinct localities.

The study was conducted in three states that represent distinct economic and cultural contexts: Sonora in the north, the richest and most developed zone of the country; Guanajuato in the centre, a region of medium development; and Oaxaca in the south, the poorest region in the country (Figure 1).

These regions also experienced varying degrees of implementation of health sector reform. Guanajuato and Sonora started decentralization in 1985, and Oaxaca, in 1994. Table 1 outlines some of the salient differences among the three states.

Due to budget limitations, the household survey and health facilities studies were conducted only in Sonora and Oaxaca. For the household survey, urban households were randomly selected from basic geostatistical areas that had been stratified by socioeconomic criteria, and rural households were randomly selected within municipalities of different population size. Data was col-

TABLE 1. KEY CHARACTERISTICS OF THE THREE MEXICAN STATES INCLUDED IN THE STUDY

	Guanajuato	Oaxaca	Sonora
Population (1995)	4 406 568	3 228 825	2 085 540
Population density	144/km²	34/km²	11/km²
Rural population	33%	56%	19%
Adult literacy rate	18%	75%	95%
Per capita income (USD, 1994)	$1 624	$1 092	$3 029
Percent employed in primary (1°), secondary (2°) and tertiary (3°) sectors	1°: 22% 2°: 33% 3°: 45%	1°: 51% 2°: 14% 3°: 34%	1°: 18% 2°: 28% 3°: 54%
Health coverage by social insurance	36%	27%	57%
Distinguishing policy features	Opposition governor from the PAN and 2000 presidential candidate. Health care extended to poor as showcase.	60% indigenous. Majority of local governance according to native traditions and customs. Formal political processes quite chaotic.	Shared border with United States, high levels of industrial investment under NAFTA. Transition to pluralistic but stable political environment.

Sources: INEGI: Banco de información económica, Sistema de cuentas nacional de México, 1995; Anuario estadístico del estado de Sonora, México, 1998; Anuario estadístico del estado de Guanajuato, México, 1999; Anuario estadístico del estado de Oaxaca, México, 1998.

NAFTA = North American Free Trade Agreement, effective as of 1994 between Mexico, the United States, and Canada. PAN = Partido Acción Nacional.

lected between June and September 1999 from 2 074 households in Oaxaca and 2 063 in Sonora, representing a total of 16 801 individuals (response rate 98%).

For the health facilities study, 45 primary care facilities were visited in both urban and rural areas. In these facilities, we applied the health facilities inventories and obtained administrative data on resource inputs and the amounts and types of services provided. We also conducted 222 surveys of providers and 319 user exit surveys.

MACROECONOMIC CONTEXT

From the early 1950s to the early 1970s, Mexico followed an economic model of imports substitution that developed the industrial sector through protectionist policies and transfer prices from the agricultural sector, where low prices maintained low wages, such that the agricultural sector essentially subsidized industrial growth. This period of the so-called "Mexican economic miracle" was characterized by low inflation, high growth rates, and stability in public finances and balance of payments. The average annual growth rate during this period was 6.5%, with inflation around 4%. In this protectionist scheme, current account imbalances were minimal, fluctuating between 1.05% and 3.55% of GNP. The public sector even registered a small budget surplus during the early part of the period, but after 1965 the deficit began to increase, reaching 3% of GNP in 1970 (Figure 2).

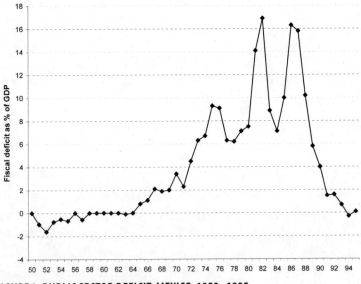

FIGURE 2. PUBLIC SECTOR DEFICIT, MEXICO, 1950–1995
Source: INEGI, National accounts (various years).

Following the worldwide oil crisis in 1973, high prices made Mexican oil exports the new fuel of the economy throughout the 1970s. During the oil boom, high GNP growth made it possible to leverage loans to finance the country's development. The state actively pursued economic growth through public investment (averaging 9% growth from 1970 to 1980, as against 5% for private investment) and created a whole new set of social policy instruments, particularly in health, to alleviate the burden of poverty. However, inflation was increasing, reaching 28% by 1980, and the excellent credit rating masked serious underlying economic problems. By 1982, the international price of oil plummeted, bringing this process of public sector growth and private investment to a halt.

As the price of oil went down, international interest rates shot up, and the country's external credit was severely reduced. Initial attempts at adjustment in 1982 were met with reactive policies that often contradicted the adjustment policies (Pánuco-Laguette and Székely 1996). In this atmosphere of uncertainty, capital flights increased, leading in the last trimester of the year to nationalization of the banks, establishment of exchange controls, and conversion of dollar accounts to pesos in Mexico (Gurría 1994). With external debt at 30% of GNP and a soaring fiscal deficit (Figure 2), the government declared a moratorium of 90 days on external debt payments.

In 1983, to deal with the lack of internal and external equilibrium and the financial volatility, the government undertook a radical adjustment, implementing drastic reductions in public spending and a more radical devaluation of the rate of exchange, together with a gradual deregulation and lowering of import tariffs. This reduction of the public deficit was accompanied by a strategy of privatization of state-owned organizations (Rogozinski 1993). A major anchor of the reforms was a pact, or broad social agreement, among the government, the private sector, and labour unions that controlled wages and prices and stabilized the exchange rate.

The market-oriented policy environment favoured international investment and controlled inflation. By 1988 investment confidence had recovered, and between 1988 and 1994 real growth averaged 2.7%. Fiscal balance was attained in 1992, inflation was 8%, and the reforms had cleared away the bureaucratic layers of protection and regulation. At the beginning of 1994, Mexico's economic outlook was very positive. Trade with the United States and Canada had increased substantially in anticipation of the North American Free Trade Agreement and was poised to increase further after NAFTA's inception in January 1994. International reserves increased early in the year, reaching 28 billion USD by the end of February 1994.

However, the economic recovery actually experienced by the population after 1988 was modest. Real wages had barely returned to their 1980 level by 1993, and the gap between rich and poor widened. Additionally, there was a significant imbalance in the current account because Mexico's inflation rate was consistently higher than the sum of US inflation and peso depreciation. Consequently, the prices of Mexican goods were increasing at a faster rate than those of US goods, encouraging imports and discouraging exports. The current account deficit went from 6 billion USD in 1989 to 15 billion in 1991, and 20 billion in 1993. The total balance of payments remained stable, however, because the current account deficit was offset by a rapid increase in capital investments during the same period. The peso was indexed to the US dollar, allowing for gradual depreciation, but in price-adjusted terms the value of the peso was increasing. These conditions meant the economic recovery was still superficial and fragile.

Over the year 1994, the dream of an economic boom evaporated as Mexico underwent a series of political shocks. At the beginning of the year, a guerrilla conflict in the southern state of Chiapas initially raised doubts about political stability. On March 23, the presidential candidate for the official party, the *Partido Revolucionario Institucional* (PRI), Luis Donaldo Colosio, was assassinated, heightening fears of political instability and setting off a brief financial panic. International reserves dropped sharply to 17 billion USD as the government intervened to maintain the value of the peso. The political climate seemed to stabilize and the presidential election continued relatively smoothly, with the investiture of Ernesto Zedillo from the PRI as president in August 1994. However, in late September the PRI's general secretary, Francisco Ruiz Massieu, was also assassinated, and in mid-November his brother, the Deputy Attorney General, claimed that high-level officials in the ruling party had ordered the assassination and were obstructing its investigation. This culmination of political shocks severely undermined confidence in the country's political and economic stability. There were enormous flights of capital over the next few weeks, such that international reserves dropped to 12.5 billion USD by the end of November and 6.1 billion USD by the end of December.

Because of the atmosphere of uncertainty, on 20 December 1994 the government devalued the peso by 15% to 3.5 pesos per dollar (USD). Within days, the value of the peso plummeted, going from 5 pesos per dollar on December 22 to 7.7 pesos per dollar by the end of the month. The drop in international reserves meant the government could not meet its short-term obligations, let alone intervene in the currency crisis. A 50 billion USD rescue package from diverse international sources was required to stall the economic free fall.

In the first months of 1995, interest rates soared, impelled by massive inflation that resulted from currency devaluation. The average Interbanking Interest Rate went from 28.02% in December 1994 to 109.72% in the third week of March 1995. This harmed internal debtors, whose interest and capital payment obligations grew considerably, and led to the financial instability of banking institutions. Meanwhile, foreign investment continued to leave the country—10 billion USD in 1995 alone—and international reserves were reduced to nearly 3 billion USD. The GNP went from positive growth (4.4%) in 1994 to negative (−6.2%) in 1995.

The 1995 economic crisis and measures implemented to contain it led to profound deterioration in socioeconomic conditions among the population of limited resources. Compared to the beginning of 1994, real minimum wage diminished by 15%, 13% and 23.4% in 1995, 1996, and 1997, respectively (CONASAMI 2004). Unemployment in the formal sector grew from 4% in 1994 to 6% in 1996 (INEGI 2004). By 1999, at the time our study was conducted, macroeconomic indicators showed that although the worst of the crisis was over, the population was still in the grip of a severe recession.

THE MEXICAN HEALTH-CARE SYSTEM

The segmented nature of health care in Mexico reflects the history of its institutions and the values underlying their development. During the colonial period, after independence and into the 1930s, health-care institutions were built either to cater to those who could pay, or in charitable response to the needs of the poor. Private medical care dominated, with care of the needy and destitute undertaken principally by Catholic charities.

In 1937, the federal government formally assumed responsibility for the care of the needy with the creation of the Secretary of Public Assistance. When the latter merged with the newly created Secretary of Health (SSA) in 1943, the scope of the mandate expanded to include provision of health services in rural areas, governance of national referral institutions (e.g. Children's Hospital and Cardiology Institute), public health, and epidemiological surveillance. Today's SSA is responsible for providing health services to those not covered by private means or social insurance. The SSA delivers mainly primary care services, although it has a network of 250 hospitals, most of them understaffed and undersupplied. The secondary and tertiary centres are concentrated in urban and semi-urban areas, posing a problem of geographical accessibility for those in rural areas. Even so, their capacity and level of use by the population are considerably lower than what would be expected given the proportion of uninsured. Only 29.4% of hospital birth deliveries are carried out by SSA facilities, which charge user fees, compared to 57.5% by the Mexican Institute of Social Security (SSA 1994).

The Mexican Institute of Social Security (*Instituto Mexicano del Seguro Social – IMSS*) was created in 1943 to provide health care and pension funds for salaried workers and their families in the growing industrial sector. Its financing base included a formula of contribution by both employee and employer as well as government subsidy. Affiliation was mandatory for salaried workers. The institution also managed pension funds, which enhanced its financial stability and allowed for capital investment in health infrastructure. Health care was provided in a network of primary and secondary care facilities by personnel belonging to the IMSS. In 1959, an equivalent social insurance institution was created for government workers, the Institute of Social Security and Services for Federal Employees (*Instituto de Seguridad y Servicios Sociales de los Trabajadores del Estado – ISSSTE*). Other well-endowed social insurance institutions were also created to provide health care for smaller but influential groups (e.g. oil workers and the military). The infrastructure and delivery of care under all these various institutions were concentrated in cities and oriented toward curative services.

IMSS is the major player among social insurance institutions, covering close to 50% of the general population and having almost 35% of all physicians on its payroll (SSA 1994). The population covered by IMSS is composed of two distinct groups: salaried workers (around 42 million people) and those enrolled in IMSS-Oportunidades, a program for the rural poor that covers approximately 8.2 million people (IMSS 2003). Approximately 10% of the population is covered by ISSSTE. Social insurance benefits include life, disability, retirement, and family health coverage for primary, secondary, and tertiary care.

Figure 3 shows the distribution of the population according to their coverage by different social insurance and health-care agencies in 2004. These percentages mask the fact that some people are covered by more than one agency (e.g. university professors who also hold government positions) and that a large proportion of users from all categories also use private providers.

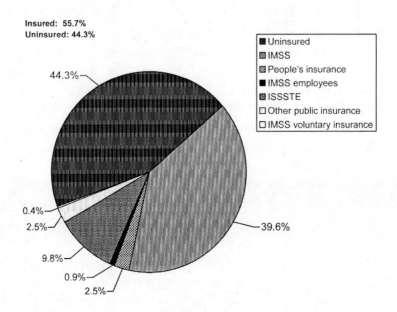

Total population: 104 213 503

FIGURE 3. DISTRIBUTION OF HEALTH-CARE COVERAGE, MEXICO, 2003

Sources:

Instituto Mexicano del Seguro Social. Informe ejecutivo federal al Congreso de la Unión. June 2004. www.imss.gob.mx.

Instituto Nacional de Salud Pública. Evaluación del Seguro Popular. January–August 2003. Mexico, 2003.

Banco Mundial (World Bank). La pobreza en México. July 2004. http://www.banco-mundial.org.mx/pdf/estudiosporsector/lapobrezaenmexico

The private sector is composed of a myriad of different types of health-care units. Its real capacity is unknown, and there are no good estimates of the population covered by it. However, in the National Health Survey of 1994, 23.1% of respondents enrolled in social insurance institutions reported a private provider as their usual source of care, as did 46.6% of the uninsured. Service payments are mainly out-of-pocket. Voluntary medical insurance is growing, but slowly (3.5% of the population in 1999), due to the relatively high fees. The potential for expansion of voluntary insurance is concentrated in the upper 10% of the national population. Although the private system is quite heterogeneous in the complexity and quality of care it offers, there are 72 private hospitals with a high level of complexity that the population generally regards as being the most prestigious. As is reflected in the National Health Survey, most Mexicans, regardless of their social status, would prefer to receive care in a private sector facility (especially in one with a high complexity) than in an SSA or social insurance institution facility.

Power and prestige in the health system of Mexico are related to: the level of complexity of health care provided at a facility; the amount of financial, material, and human resources available to the institution; and the socioeconomic strata of the system's main constituency (Durán 1996). By these criteria, SSA facilities rank lowest in prestige and power, followed by social insurance institutions, with private health-care facilities being accorded the highest value and trust by the population.

HEALTH POLICY ENVIRONMENT

Although Mexico has the second highest gross domestic product (GDP) in the Latin American region, the proportion allocated to health care is considerably lower than in other middle-income countries of the region. In 1990, total health expenditure—private and public—amounted to 5.4% of GDP in Mexico, compared to Barbados (6.4%), Chile (8.0%), Costa Rica (8.6%), Jamaica (5.0%), Panama (9.2%), and Uruguay (10.0%), all of which also had lower infant mortality rates than Mexico at that time (FUNSALUD 1994; OPS/OMS 1998).

Public expenditure in health in Mexico was negatively affected by adjustment policies designed to counter the economic crisis between 1982 and 1988. Public expenditure in health, for social insurance agencies and services for the uninsured, declined by 3% annually in real terms after 1982 and reached its lowest level in 1987, equivalent to 2.7% of GDP. In subsequent years, the expenditure level slowly recovered, reaching 4% of GDP—albeit a decreasing GDP—in 1995 (Frenk 1997).

Starting in 1980, efforts to expand coverage to the uninsured, especially to peasants in rural areas, were intensified through a special program administered by IMSS that created over 3 000 primary health-care centres and dozens of rural hospitals throughout the country. In return for financial credits and continued management autonomy, the IMSS administered this special initiative of building and staffing these rural health units. The initiative was named IMSS-Coplamar; it was renamed IMSS-Solidaridad in 1988 and IMSS-Oportunidades in 2000. Although some of these centres were incorporated into the Secretary of Health system in 1984 in the wake of the decentralization of health services, most remained under IMSS administration and carried out their own decentralization thereafter.

One of the main goals of the 1982–1987 policy cycle was to create a National Health System to address perennial problems in the health sector, among them the disorderly expansion of medical care in both the public and the private sectors, inequitable segmentation, and inter-institutional rivalries. A national body was entrusted with coordinating and integrating the different health-care delivery systems to ensure reasonable quality and national health coverage. Although the Secretary of Health was formally confirmed as head and major health policy decider for the whole sector, it had no real means of ensuring that social insurance institutions would follow through on its directives (Brachet-Márquez 2001, 2005). In 1984, the General Health Law enshrined the protection of health as a constitutional right and defined the private health-care system as part of the National Health System, an innovation that brought it under the jurisdiction of the Secretary of Health and prepared the ground for the private sector's subsequent participation in public health institutions. It also mandated the devolution of IMSS-Coplamar clinics to the jurisdiction of the Secretary of Health, but only about a third of the clinics in that system followed that route, due to resistance to this policy by IMSS and IMSS-Coplamar users, who stood to lose benefits such as free medicine.

During the 1988–1994 policy cycle, the decentralization policies were put on hold because of their unpopularity with many states and the IMSS. Instead, the Salinas government concentrated on targeted poverty alleviation programs that encouraged grassroots participation in improving basic community services in health, education, nutrition, housing, and employment. The National Solidarity Program (*Programa Nacional de Solidaridad – Pronasol*), into which former IMSS-Coplamar health centres were incorporated, was a multidimensional program providing matching federal grants and raw materials to local Pronasol committees in poor communities that submitted proposals (mainly for infrastructure), obtained funds, and carried out the projects. Policy analysts charged that the program was a means of enhancing political loyalty in grassroots organizations while allowing the formal services of the public health-care sector to deteriorate because of reduced federal financing and continuing problems of excessive centralization and bureaucratic rigidity.

HEALTH SECTOR REFORM, 1995–2000

The presidential term of 1994–2000 saw the completion of the move to decentralization and the implementation of poverty alleviation programs targeted to the extremely poor, under the name of Progresa (*Programa de educación, salud y alimentación*). An attempt was also undertaken to streamline health services for the uninsured.

The health sector reform presented in the 1995–2000 National Development Plan was aimed at improving the quality and efficiency of health services and extending health-care coverage, especially among the uninsured (SSA 1996). Its orientations and strategies follow closely those recommended for developing countries by the World Bank in 1993 (Cassels 1995). The Plan recommended that the role of the state be limited to financing access to primary health care by delivering a free package of essential health services (*Paquete Básico – PAB*), whereas secondary and tertiary level services should be financed through prepayment mechanisms. The report also calls for more public–private partnerships under the assumption that private delivery systems are more efficient than state-run services.

The PAB was to be managed by the now decentralized state secretaries of health responsible for its delivery to their respective health clinics and to the new areas reached by mobile units. Operating resources were allocated to the state level according to a formula based on mortality and poverty indicators as well as on historical funding that diminished the difference in resources between poorer and wealthier states. Even so, poorer states were unable to carry out their new responsibilities, such that in 1991, a 250 million USD international loan was used to distribute funds through the Program of Support to Health Services for the Uninsured Population (*Programa de Apoyo a los Servicios de Salud a Población Abierta – PASSPA*) in Chiapas, Guerrero, Hidalgo, Oaxaca, and the Federal District, for services to the poor. The IMSS and ISSSTE systems also decentralized their administration to the states within their respective jurisdictions.

The provision of essential services was focused exclusively on the primary care level, as can be seen from the 13 essential health services of the PAB listed in Table 2, many of which are educational and promotional rather than curative. The PAB was delivered in heretofore unserviced rural areas via mobile units traveling to villages once or twice monthly. Additionally, the Progresa poverty alleviation program was selectively directed to the extreme poor, with the health component being delivered at SSA facilities.

Another strategy for extending health care was to expand social insurance coverage by opening up affiliation to non-salaried workers, whose families could be affiliated to health-care services for an annual fee of three months' minimum wages payable in one lump sum, or about 430 USD in 2004—something beyond the reach of most non-salaried workers. This provision was part of a sweeping reform of the IMSS law carried out in 1996, of which the most radical components were lengthening

TABLE 2. ESSENTIAL HEALTH SERVICES PACKAGE (PAC) DELIVERED BY THE SECRETARY OF HEALTH TO THE UNINSURED POOR IN MEXICO

Interventions

1. Family hygiene and waste disposal
2. Family planning
3. Prenatal care and birth delivery
4. Nutritional and growth surveillance of children
5. Immunizations
6. Home management of diarrhea
7. Anti-parasitic treatment for family unit
8. Acute respiratory disease management
9. Prevention and control of pulmonary tuberculosis
10. Prevention and control of diabetes mellitus and high blood pressure
11. Prevention of accidents and early management of injuries
12. Community participation for self health care
13. Prevention and control of cervical cancer

Source: SSA (1996).

the requirement of active contribution to the pension fund from 10 to 20 years, creating individual pension deposit accounts, and allowing private agencies (*Afores*) to manage them (Brachet-Márquez 2001).

In an attempt to stimulate the creation of employment, the 1996 reform also reduced employers' contributions while increasing that of the government. Increases in employment and affiliation were expected to compensate for the reduced revenue from employers. The modification also contemplated fee reversals for firms opting to take care of their workers' health-care needs through medical facilities other than the IMSS. This last element was blocked in Congress, however, as it actively encouraged movement toward private care while potentially eroding the financing base of social insurance institutions. There was a 1997 proposal to introduce user fees for all public health services, but these were never implemented in social insurance institutions. However, user fees continued to be charged for health services provided by the state SSAs.

STUDY RESULTS

Implementation of reforms

The Secretary of Health stepped back partially from being a service provider by decentralizing the delivery of public services to the state level. However, this decentralization was incomplete because financial and allocative powers were not completely transferred to the state level. The federal government decentralized operating resources and management while retaining control over capital expenditures and the creation of new human resource positions. Consequently, the states' margin for manoeuvre was severely limited, giving them only the capacity to implement policy directions dictated by the central level and to use other state funds to finance local initiatives. States varied considerably in their capacity and political will to manage public health services, and political factors were a predominant consideration in their management. In Guanajuato, the presence of an opposition governor (who became president of Mexico in 2000) provided strong policy direction that maximized the margin for manoeuvre and ensured better implementation of expanded services for the poor (Brachet-Márquez 2002).

At the operational level, providers in both social insurance and SSA facilities tended to be unaware of the content of health reforms and the new policy directions, except when these had a direct impact on their work by requiring them to provide free preventive care and disease monitoring services to the poor. They also noted that although availability of supplies had improved over the previous year, they were not sufficient to meet increased demand for services.

Shifts in utilization of health care

In the household survey, 850 people (5%) indicated they had had a health problem in the past month, a lower prevalence than expected, in view of the 2000 National Health Survey's finding that 14.6% of respondents had experienced a health problem in the past two weeks (SSA-INSP 2003). The difference in prevalence rates might reflect the facts that our survey was conducted in the low-morbidity summer season and that the National Health Survey specifically included accidents and violence, whereas our study asked about health problems generally, so accidents and violence may have been overlooked by the population as a health problem. The prevalence of recent health problems was higher in Oaxaca, where sanitation conditions were considerably poorer, and where 57% of households had bad quality water supply. Recent health problems were more prevalent among women, the elderly, and the less educated. Overall, 60% of those with a health problem had sought medical assistance, with no significant differences between Oaxaca and Sonora.

In our household study, we found that among those who had consulted a physician for a health problem in the past month, 63.8% in the rich state of Sonora reported that it was in a social insurance institution facility, followed by 18.8% who reported using private services and 17.4%, SSA facilities. In the poor state of Oaxaca, use of the three institutions was more evenly distributed, with 38.8% reporting the use of SSA facilities, followed by private services (32.5%) and social insurance institutions (28.6%). The qualitative study indicates there had been a major shift in utilization patterns in Sonora among the middle class and the near-poor, who are not usually targeted by SSA programs. The shift to using SSA facilities was related to loss of employment and inability to pay for private care, whereas among the middle class the economic crisis led to reduced use of the private sector and preferential use of services offered by social insurance institutions to which they were affiliated.

The shift in utilization patterns is easy to understand in light of the differential cost of services. For example, in our survey (1999), the average cost for a prenatal care visit, including consultation, laboratory exams, and medications, was 507 pesos (53 USD) in private care, free of charge in social insurance, and 189 pesos (20 USD) in SSA facilities. For their most recent pregnancy, the 22% of women who used the private system cited trust in the provider as the principal reason for their choice, the 40% who used social insurance cited affiliation as the main reason, and the 16% who used the SSA facility cited its availability. Of the 23% of women who had not received prenatal care for their pregnancy, one-third cited lack of money as the main reason and another 11% cited unavailability of a health professional. For the more expensive service of delivery of the baby, utilization shifted toward public facilities: 51% used social insurance institutions; 22%, SSA; 19%, private services; and 7%, non-medical personnel.

The qualitative study revealed that when the decision is made to seek medical care, the principal considerations in choosing the type of facility were availability of facilities and ability to pay. Recourse to the formal medical system was reserved for conditions perceived to be serious (diabetes, injury, cancer) or that did not resolve with home management. Self-treatment with traditional and over-the-counter medicines was the first line of management for all illnesses, regardless of socioeconomic strata. This was often followed by resorting to the social network or to traditional healers and then to the formal health-care system as a last resort.

Access to health services for the poor

In rural areas, the new programs designed to reach the extreme poor have resulted in access to the PAC (*Programa de Amplicación de Cobertura*) for people who previously had nothing. This was particularly clear in Oaxaca. In the health facilities study, users were asked to rate their perceptions of quality in various dimensions of care (infrastructure, accessibility, technical and interpersonal quality), contrasting their current perceptions with their recalled perceptions of care in the previous year. Users in Oaxaca noted improvement in all dimensions of care, whereas in Sonora no improvement was noted in the conditions of the buildings or the availability of medicines and vaccines. This finding seems consistent with the effort conducted from 1997 to 1999 to improve the structure of health-care services in public institutions and to provide more resources to states with the worst conditions, based on the federal government's funding formula. One should keep in mind, however, that owing to the extreme geographical dispersion of the habitat in Oaxaca, most of its 9 000 localities still lack health facilities. Thus, although accessibility improved in available facilities, we cannot conclude that it did so for the whole population.

Although access to primary care has improved for the rural population through targeted programs, the qualitative study reveals great frustration among both users and providers regarding the limited capacity to resolve health problems at the primary level and the poor access to secondary care services. The initial primary care consultation became more accessible, but patients were often referred to an urban or private facility for follow-up tests, and the additional indirect and direct costs caused some patients to forgo continuing care. Access to medical care for the rural population and the poor therefore remains clearly inadequate.

The household survey showed that a higher proportion (49%) of users of health care in the poorer state of Oaxaca paid for physician consultations than in the rich state of Sonora (28%), where social insurance institutions covered a higher percentage of the population. The absolute average consultation cost was lower in Oaxaca than in Sonora, but was higher relative to household revenue. In addition, 43% of users in Oaxaca purchased medication following consultation, compared to 27% in Sonora, with no difference in average medication cost between the states. Essential medications are covered by the social insurance institutions packages but often are not available. So, despite the expansion programs, ability to pay remains a determining factor in accessing medical care in poor regions.

Persistent differentials in quality of care

The population consistently identifies private care as best quality, followed by social insurance institutions, with SSA services being perceived as the most limited in scope and quality. In the private system, there is enormous variation in quality and type of care, but the institutions at the pinnacle of the system have the reputation of providing the best quality and most technologically advanced care in the health-care system. The segmentation of the market emerges particularly in urban areas, with different levels of access to technology and health-care services and clear differentials in quality.

Many providers work in both the public and private systems, a situation that aggravates the limited availability of services in the two public systems. Many of the SSA and social insurance institutions have short office hours so that providers can carry out their private practice in the late afternoons and evenings. They claim their public salaries are inadequate, requiring them to resort to private practice to maintain their desired standard of living. Users perceive public system office hours to be inconvenient for working people, obliging them to choose between losing one day of work to obtain care at a public facility or paying to get care at a more convenient time. Qualitative interviews with the users indicate that providers sometimes offer different or faster possibilities for care in their private practice than they can offer in the public services, thereby actively creating a competition and using the public forum to generate private clients.

Providers were also asked to contrast quality of care between the previous (i.e., pre-reform) and current situations. They perceived that availability of medicines and vaccines had improved but not the physical plants, nor the technical quality of care. In the qualitative study, providers expressed frustration at the poor maintenance of diagnostic and therapeutic equipment as well as at the lack of some supplies.

The household survey showed the perceived quality of amenities and of the technical and interpersonal aspects of care to be higher in Sonora than in Oaxaca. Overall, mean quality scores were not significantly different for SSA and social insurance facilities, but scores for private facilities were substantially higher. When asked to compare current quality to that of the previous year, improvement was noted in all facilities, but improvement in the private sector was perceived to be significantly greater. The difference was particularly noted in the quality of buildings and in the technical quality of both preventive and curative services.

Providers at social insurance and SSA facilities identified their work environment as negatively affecting the quality of care, and of interpersonal care in particular. They felt their salary levels were too low, with particular resentment being expressed by SSA providers who perceived their salaries to be lower than those of their social insurance counterparts. However, dissatisfaction was more consistently expressed with the organizational environment that did not offer a clear career path or a transparent system of rewards and incentives.

Users also sensed providers' dissatisfaction, perceived as lack of respect toward patients, which in turn generated a lack of trust in the providers. The lack of trust in public resources extended in some users even to a perception that the medicines offered in public facilities were less efficacious than those purchased at the pharmacy. The association between interpersonal quality of care and other dimensions of quality was very strong, underlining the importance attributed to interpersonal quality. Trust in the provider was the most important reason for preferring to use private services.

The qualitative study, which purposely targeted health care users from low, middle, and upper-middle socioeconomic strata, further suggests that even within the same social insurance institution, perceptions of quality differ markedly across groups. Several participants in the upper stratum made allusions to having had their care facilitated by social connections to physicians in the institution. Participants from all strata referred to the scarcity of resources but agreed that those from the upper-middle class enjoyed more rapid access to a larger scope of services compared to the poorest, who were treated with less respect and even denied services.

CONCLUSION

In this study, we found evidence of major shifts in utilization due to economic pressures. Indeed, use of public services increased, but the major increase was in use of social insurance services by members who, in better economic circumstances, would have preferred to use private services. Access to targeted primary care services improved for the poor, especially those in rural areas and poor states; however, secondary care remained largely inaccessible. Both providers and users indicated that the public, social insurance, and private health-care subsystems remained segmented in terms of availability of resources and quality of care. The private sector continued to provide the most comprehensive care to the wealthiest, followed by the social insurance institutions with their network of clinics and hospitals providing primary through tertiary care, and lastly, services offered by the SSA subsystem, which remained largely limited to primary and preventive care in community clinics, with limited access to tertiary care in poorly equipped hospitals located in urban areas. Overall, the reforms expanded the reach of the formal health-care system but did not significantly reduce existing inequities in access to quality care.

Up to the year 2000, it would be fair to say that little had changed in the value system underlying the organization of the health-care sector, despite the reforms. The public health-care functions of the system became more decentralized and basic access improved, but not to the degree desired by proponents of the reform. The Secretary of Health had decentralized operation of health services to the state secretaries of health, but as of 2000 it still maintained the same profile and influence that it had in 1995. At the same time, social insurance institutions continued to function in a centralized way. While the private sector has come increasingly under the regulatory influence of the Secretary of Health, concrete actions have been focused on integrating care in the prestigious hospitals and their affiliated institutions through managed care.

The policy of maintaining, and in some cases extending, the network of primary health care to the uninsured based on the PAC may have contributed to improving overall health status and confronting major health problems (e.g. diabetes, cardiovascular diseases, tuberculosis, child mortality) in the uninsured population. However, for some of these problems, medication is unavailable in most cases, and special diets are not practical in the environment of the rural poor, as indicated by results obtained from the qualitative part of the study. Yet given the short time frame since implementation, concrete impacts cannot yet be corroborated by this research study. It is a concern of policy analysts and of this team of researchers, however, that many of the interventions in these programs stop at education and early detection, without ensuring ongoing care for conditions such as diabetes and cardiovascular disease that require lifelong medical treatment. The reform has not led to a more comprehensive set of primary care services or specialized care, resulting in high levels of frustration in users and providers alike. Despite the PAC's emphasis on preventive measures, the capacity for resolving health problems at the primary level remains limited, hence the population's general lack of confidence in public providers.

Social insurance services were the big losers in the economic crisis and the health reforms. Their financing base weakened, while demand for their services increased. Because of the economic crisis, the middle class—who clearly prefer to use private services when they can afford to—shifted toward use of social insurance services, placing enormous pressure on resources that were insufficient to cope with the increased demand. The freezing of social insurance budgets for infrastructure improvements and medical equipment exacerbated the problem.

The health reform did not include any mechanism to level the playing field in terms of quality of care among the private, social insurance, and SSA systems. The lack of active policy on this front, accompanied by incomplete decentralization of public resources and erosion of the financial base of social insurance institutions, actually increased pre-existing differences in quality and scope of care. After two cycles of health policy reform since 1988, the system continues to reflect and reinforce the established segmentation of power and prestige. Social protection of the poor through preventive care has increased, but the complexity and quality of curative care continues to be a function of the patient's ability to pay.

One final note is in order. Since the study data was collected, at least two important changes in the health-care sector have taken place. First, a new prepaid health insurance for the poor (*Seguro Popular*) was introduced in 2004, co-financed by users, the federal government, and the states, which participate on a voluntary basis. The service scope of this new program is much broader than the PAC, a welcome improvement. It is hoped that this initiative will improve the infrastructure and funding of SSA health services. Second, IMSS has embarked on a major modernization effort in equipment and essential inputs, as well as organizational changes aimed at strengthening managerial capabilities in the system. However, the impact of this reform remains to be seen, since IMSS's annual report for 2003 describes the institution to be in dire financial straits (IMSS 2004). Even if both changes may contribute to improve overall quality, the first threatens to create new categories of users and quality within the Secretary of Health system, separating states that have entered the *Seguro Popular* program from those that have not and, within enrolled states, prepaying from non-prepaying patients.

In sum, the reforms undertaken in the 1990s, although often sweeping, have remained within the framework of the pre-existing health system, leaving untouched the inequities inherent in an institutionally fragmented structure of unequal benefits. It should be made clear, however, that reformers made no attempt to create a unified health system through these reforms, and if they had tried, they would probably have failed. Each step of the reform process was met with opposition and staunch resistance from the more privileged groups, terrified at the prospect of being lowered to the level of those receiving fewer benefits. Also, existing, better-endowed programs lacked the fiscal capacity to incorporate the less privileged.

Faced with this institutional and financial impasse, reformers have had to make changes within existing compartments, based on the tacit assumption that something had to be done to fill existing lacunae, even if only piecemeal and insufficient. Through these efforts, minimal PAC coverage has been extended over the whole territory, social insurance has averted financial breakdown, and the health needs of the extremely poor have been incorporated into a very considerable effort to diminish poverty. Nevertheless, the PAC is grossly insufficient to guarantee treatment of a very large number of common conditions, the majority of the population is still without secondary and tertiary health coverage, service delivery in the public sector remains of low quality, and a high proportion of the next generation of social insurance affiliates may end up without retirement benefits owing to the near impossibility of complying with even minimal stipulations in the new law. As long as Mexico's economy remains incapable of growing substantially and creating some wealth at the bottom (as opposed to exclusively at the top, as presently), these problems will likely be subject to more piecemeal, and mostly unsatisfactory, but nevertheless useful reforms. The *Seguro Popular* currently being launched is one such partial reform that will both raise expectations on the user side and create pressures for further changes in existing practices on the delivery side, hopefully for the better.

What have we learned? First, that multiple methods and approaches are necessary to understand fully both the complexity of processes underlying health reform and the joint impacts of reform and macroeconomic adjustments on the health system. The policy analysis approach, in particular, is key to interpreting findings obtained from different survey methods.

Second, the democratic process presently underway in Mexico and other countries is a major determinant of both the shape and the pace of health reform. In the future, both the study and the design of health-care reform must avoid being imposed from above and must enter the fray of democratic debate, competition, and negotiation peculiar to Mexico's endogenously developed democracy, with the principles and values defining citizens' entitlements in this context (Brachet-Márquez 2001).

Finally, the study cautions against the application of master recipes for policy around the world. Attempts to homogenize the health systems of different countries should be recognized as increasingly inappropriate. Historical, cultural, and political differences cannot be ignored, at least not to the extent implied in model policies offered by experts from international organizations. For example, in the political analysis we found evidence that democratization had become an obstacle to reform—at least, to reform imposed technocratically from above, as happened in the past. Greater political freedom, in turn, creates variations in the direction of reforms in each context, marking the limits of single approaches. In brief, it challenges the one-size-fits-all homogeneity sought in the reforms of the 1990s around the world, calling for new ways of contextualizing this process.

References

Brachet-Márquez, V. 2001. La reforma de los sistemas de salud y previsión social en México, 1982–1999. Socialis. Reflexiones sobre Política Social, 5(Nov),103–130.

_____ 2002. Elementos para investigar la capacidad estatal político-administrativa en materia de salud pública. Los casos de Guanajuato, Oaxaca y Sonora. Research note. Estudios Sociológicos, XX(58), 239–252.

_____ 2007. Mexico's welfare state: birth, growth and retrenchment (1822–2002). *In* Riesco, M., ed., Social policy in a development context. Latin America: a new developmental welfare state model in the making? Palgrave, Houndsmill, UK. pp. 117-147.

Cassels, A. 1995. Health sector reform: key issues in less developed countries. Journal of International Development, 7(3), 329–347.

CONASAMI (Comisión Nacional de los Salarios Mínimos). 2004. Salario mínimo general promedio de los Estados Unidos Mexicanos: 1964–2004. Government of Mexico, México, DF, Mexico, http://www.conasami.gob.mx/estadisticas/docs/Salminprom_64_04.pdf, cited July 2004.

CONAPO (Consejo Nacional de Población). 2000. La situación demográfica de México, 2000. Consejo Nacional de Población, Government of Mexico, México, DF, Mexico, http://www.conapo.gob.mx/publicaciones/2000/pdf/1Preliminares.pdf, cited July 2004, 10 pp.

Durán, L. 1996. Determinants of professional status of physicians in urban areas of Mexico. University of Michigan, Ann Arbor, MI, USA. PhD dissertation, 215 pp.

FUNSALUD (Fundación Mexicana para la Salud / Mexican Foundation for Health). 1994. Economía y salud: propuestas para el avance del sistema de salud en México. FUNSALUD, México, DF, Mexico. 401 pp.

Frenk, J., ed. 1997. Observatorio de la salud, necesidades, servicios, políticas. FUNSALUD, México, DF, Mexico. 122 pp.

Gurría, J.A. 1994. La política de la deuda externa. (Policy on external debt). Serie: Una visión de la modernización de México. Fondo de Cultura Económica, México, DF, Mexico. 304 pp.

IMSS (Instituto Mexicano del Seguro Social). 2004. Informe al Ejecutivo Federal y al Congreso de la Unión sobre la situación financiera y los riesgos del Instituto Mexicano del Seguro Social. IMSS, México, DF, México. 104 pp.

INEGI (Instituto Nacional de Estadística, Geográfica e Informática). 2004. Banco de información económica. Encuesta nacional de empleo urbano. México, DF, Mexico, www.inegi.gob.mx/est/default.asp?c=1801, cited July 2004.

_____ 1995. Banco de información económica, Sistema de cuentas nacional de México, México, DF, Mexico.

_____ 1988. Anuario estadístico del estado de Oaxaca, México, DF, Mexico.

_____ 1998. Anuario estadístico del estado de Sonora, México, DF, Mexico.

_____ 1999. Anuario estadístico del estado de Guanajuato, México, DF, Mexico.

OPS/OMS (Organización Panamericana de la Salud / Organización Mundial de la Salud). 1998. La salud en las Américas. Vol. 1, Publicación Científica No. 569, OPS/OMS, Washington, DC, USA. 334 pp.

Pánuco-Laguette, H.; Székely, M. 1996. Income distribution and poverty in Mexico. *In* Bulmer-Thomas, V., ed., The new economic model in Latin America and its impact on income distribution and poverty. University of London Institute of Latin American Studies and St. Martin's Press, New York, NY, USA. pp. 185–222.

Rogozinski, J. 1993. La privatización de empresas paraestatales. Serie: Una visión de la modernización de México. Fondo de Cultura Económica, México, DF, Mexico, 208 pp.

SSA (Secretaría de Salud). 1994. Boletín de información estadística. Vol.1, no. 13. Secretaría de Salud, México, DF, Mexico. 91 pp.

_____ 1994. Encuesta nacional de salud II. México, Secretaría de Salud, México, DF, Mexico. 65 pp.

_____ 1995. Programa de reforma del sector salud 1995–2000. Secretaría de Salud, México. DF, Mexico, 14 pp.

_____ 1996. Plan nacional de reforma del sector salud. Secretaría de Salud, México, DF, Mexico.

SSA; INSP (Secretaria de Salud; Instituto Nacional de Salud Pública). 2003. Encuesta nacional de salud 2000. Tomo 1. INSP, México, DF, Mexico. pp. 80–86.

World Bank. 1993. World development report: investing in health. Report no. 12183. Washington, DC, USA. 344 pp.

_____ 2000. World development report 2000/2001: attacking poverty. Oxford University Press, New York, NY, USA. 352 pp.

_____ 2004. World development indicators data base, http://www. worldbank.org/data, cited February 2006.

CHAPTER 9

THE EVOLUTION OF THAILAND'S HEALTH SYSTEM AFTER THREE CRISES, THREE ADJUSTMENTS, AND THREE DECADES OF GROWTH

Sanguan Nittayaramphong, Yaowarat Porapakkham, Supattra Srivanichakorn, Sunee Wongkongkathep, Enis Barış

COUNTRY BACKGROUND

Over the past 30 years, Thailand has achieved remarkable and consistent economic growth, transforming itself from an inward-looking agrarian economy into an export-oriented industrialized economy. This transformation has had considerable impact on the society overall, and more specifically on how the State and the people have responded to rapidly changing needs and expectations, both in terms of political rights and obligations and of health and health care.

Thailand is divided into four geographical regions: (i) the North, mostly mountainous; (ii) the Central Plain, a fertile valley called the Rice Bowl of Asia, which includes Bangkok; (iii) the Northeast, or the Korat Plateau, mostly arid with harsher climate; and (iv) the South, including the Southern Peninsula, mostly tropical.

The population of Thailand, about 62 million in 2002 (or 121 persons/km^2), is a mosaic of most of the ethnic groups of the Mekong Basin. Buddhism is the national religion, professed by 95% of the population. Islam, Christianity, and Hinduism are also practiced freely. The official language is Thai, a tonal and monosyllabic language; Chinese and Malay are also spoken.

Thailand has had a checkered political history since the end, in 1932, of 700 years of absolute monarchy in favour of a constitutional monarchy. Though the monarchy plays an undeniably important and stabilizing role in Thai society and in the governance structure, the country has, over the past 60 years, been ruled by a series of military governments and a civilian bureaucracy. As a result of several constitutional changes, most recently in 1997, and subsequent political reforms, citizens now enjoy greater freedom, enhanced transparency and accountability, more pluralistic and participatory democracy in governance, and all the essential political, civil, and human rights. At the national level, legislative power is vested in an elected House of Representatives and an appointed Senate.

The country is divided into 76 provinces, each administered by an appointed governor, and further subdivided into 156 municipalities, 774 districts, and 6 500 tambons, or subdistricts. Although there are four levels of subnational governments, the power is firmly vested in the central government, which controls most sources of revenue and has the authority to allocate resources. Several reform initiatives are underway that would devolve some authority to subnational levels for raising revenues and allocating resources. Administrative authority has been the first function devolved to Tambon Administrative Organizations, which now have more control over the resources allocated to them from the central government.

Thailand is a middle-income country with a gross national product of 1 980 USD (Atlas method in current USD, or PPP 6 680 USD), a literacy rate of about 95%, and a life expectancy of about 70 years. Access to an improved water source is 84% and to sanitation, 96%. While still highly rural, more so than many countries at the same level of socioeconomic development, Thailand is becoming increasingly urban. The country has undergone profound transformation, having made significant progress in terms of both economic and human development.

Even if Thailand's economic growth over the past three decades has been remarkable, averaging 8% annually up to the 1997 crisis, its policies and interventions to improve the status of the poor have been uneven. Indeed, a distinguishing feature of this rapid transformation has been the evolution of inequalities across various segments of the population and the evolution of poverty in particular. The fight against poverty has been a focus since the late 1950s, when the country adopted the policy of having quinquennial national development plans. Nonetheless, and despite many pro-poor policies adopted since then, the Gini index in 2001 was 42.4%. As a corollary, the increase in the national share of the highest income quintile—from 49.8% in 1962 to 59% in 1992—has been more prominent than the reduction in poverty, albeit without any further increase, but rather a slight decrease to 57.6% in 2001. As for the lowest quintile, their share decreased from 7.9% in 1962 to 3.9% in 2001 (NESDB 2002).

In addition to the rising inequalities, rapid industrialization also brought with it social strains resulting from rural to urban migration, greater drug use and abuse, violence, and sexual promiscuity. For instance, although prostitution is officially illegal, laws are not enforced because commercial sex has become an integral part of the country's tourist industry. Consequences of this rapid transformation include the HIV/AIDS epidemic, although curtailed to a large extent thanks to a successful national program; widespread child labour, despite a recent law establishing 15 as the minimum legal working age; and immigration of an estimated two million labourers from Myanmar, Laos and Cambodia.

MACROECONOMIC CONTEXT AND PERFORMANCE

In Thailand, the macroeconomic crises and ensuing reforms in recent history are closely linked with global events beyond its control, namely the first (1973–1975) and second (1979–1985) oil crises, the economic boom (1990–1995) resulting from the structural transformation of the economy in response to regional economic developments, and the subsequent currency crisis (1997–1999).

A sudden increase of 284% in the price of oil between 1973 and 1974 affected the Thai economy—heavily dependent on the petroleum import—considerably. Real economic growth slowed from 9.9% to 4.3% between 1973 and 1974, due to a trade balance reversal and the related increase in the current account deficit (4% of the GNP), as well as an increase in inflation to 24.4% in 1974. Fortunately, the inflation rate was back to normal in 1975 at 5.2%, but this period marked, for the first time, an increase in foreign indebtedness to finance the deficit (although small by today's standards), amounting to 8% of the GNP.

The second oil crisis in Thailand, when oil prices rose by 131% in 1979 to 29.92 USD per barrel, lasted longer and created more macroeconomic instability. The GDP growth rate was slowed, and implementation of the social agenda foreseen in the fourth National Economic and Social Development (NESD) Plan (1977–1981) was postponed to the next (1982–1986).

Between 1979 and 1987, real economic growth remained around 5% (Figure 1); although inflation peaked at 19.7% in 1980, it decreased to one-digit rates soon thereafter. Importation of expensive oil resulted in a current account deficit and higher costs of production of good and services. Fearful of extensive debt financing fueling the inflation, the Bank of Thailand raised the nominal interest rate from 13% in 1979 to 16.3% in 1980, then to 17.3% in 1981. Even if the increase in 1980 was able to contain credit growth at first, a loss of public confidence rendered subsequent increases ineffective in stopping recourse to further financing and subsequently to a higher debt/GDP ratio. Also during this period, Thailand received two structural adjustment loans from the World Bank totaling 325 million USD.

Following the oil crises, Thailand enjoyed a decade of sustained economic growth, mostly in the manufacturing sector, recording an average annual growth rate of 12.4%. This was mainly

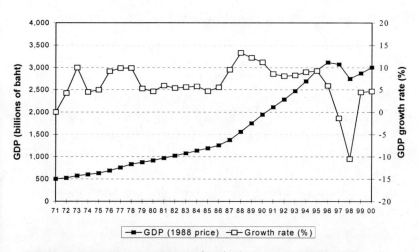

FIGURE 1. GROSS DOMESTIC PRODUCT (GDP) AND ANNUAL GROWTH RATE, THAILAND,1971–2000 (1988 PRICES)

Source: National and Economic Social Development Board, Thailand (2002).

due to appreciation of the Japanese currency and the subsequent increase in offshore Japanese investment destined toward Thailand, because of the success of the Board of Investment (BOI) in attracting foreign direct investment of about two billion USD per year. This led to gross capital formation, especially in the areas of telecommunications and electric power. It also further opened the Thai economy to foreign trade and speculative investment in real estate, used as collateral for borrowing money from foreign banks. The proportion of short-term foreign debt rose from less than 40% in 1993 to over 45% in 1995, and between 1989 and 1996, borrowing from overseas commercial banks rose more than 16-fold, leading to Thailand's third economic crisis.

This crisis, a consequence of heavy borrowing and speculative investing in non-productive sectors, was actually, macroeconomically speaking, self-inflicted—a result both of the liberalization of capital markets following the establishment of the Bangkok International Banking Facility (BIBF) with a mandate to allow and regulate foreign financial institutions operating in the country, and of the abandonment of foreign exchange control.

Lower interest rates charged by foreign institutions encouraged borrowing under a fixed currency exchange regime, such that the flow of foreign capital into Thailand increased substantially in 1995. However, foreign currency speculators seized the opportunity to speculate on the devaluation of the Thai currency. The Bank of Thailand at first countered attacks on the baht (THB), which began in November 1996, by dipping into its foreign reserves to defend the value of the currency, but on 2 July 1997, as its foreign reserves dwindled, it had to let the baht float.[1] The currency depreciated rapidly and considerably—up to 100%—although not for long.

The main features of the crisis were severe economic contraction, from almost 5.5% GDP growth in 1996 to –5.5% in 1998, and increased unemployment, going from 1.5% of the total labour force in 1997 to 4.4% in 1998. A survey in May 1999 estimated the unemployment rate at about 5.7% of the active labour force, or 1.87 million people.

Government policy responses to crises were as different as the reasons that brought them about. The government reacted to the first oil crisis by increasing its budget by 23% in 1974, and by another 29% in 1975, nominally to counter the slowdown of the economy. In real terms, these increases corresponded to 7% and 11%, respectively, with the additional funding mainly directed to economic sectors, at the expense of social sectors such as education and health, to stimulate the economy. This led to increased public spending, reduced taxation, and consequently larger budget deficits. Although there was an attempt to cut expenditure and raise the prices of public utilities, the budget remained in deficit until after 1987 when the trend was reversed, registering continual surpluses, with a record high in 1995, until the 1997 currency crisis (Figure 2).

The government's first response to the currency crisis was a tight fiscal policy focused on containing public expenditures to stabilize the economy. However, after being criticized for following the IMF program, which was deemed inappropriate for

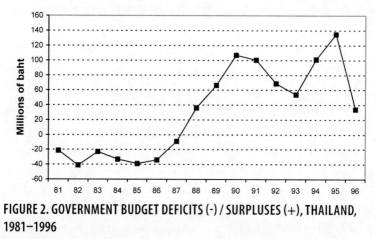

FIGURE 2. GOVERNMENT BUDGET DEFICITS (-) / SURPLUSES (+), THAILAND, 1981–1996

Source: Government of Thailand, Bureau of the Budget.

the Thai situation, the government reversed its macroeconomic policy. Once the exchange rate was stabilized and the capital flight was over, it relaxed the fiscal discipline it had imposed, to stimulate aggregate demand and economic activity. Again, it turned to international finance institutions (IFIs) for financial and economic adjustment loans of 1 350 million USD, from the World Bank alone. Then it launched a new economic stimulation package intended to bring the economy out of recession and resume economic growth.

DEMOGRAPHICS AND TRANSITION IN HEALTH

Thailand has been quite successful in managing its demographic and health transitions with good policy choices and effective interventions. There has been a considerable increase in life expectancy at birth, from around 40 years for both sexes in 1937, to 70 years for males and 75 years for women in 1996. After the adoption of the national population policy in 1970, the annual population growth rate declined substantially. Four demographic surveys carried out during this period showed reduction in the crude birth rate from about 40 per 1 000 population in the early 1960s to about 16.2 in 1995. During the same period, the crude death rate fell to the lowest level ever recorded, approximately 5.5 per 1 000 population.

Most of the gain in life expectancy is attributable to a remarkable reduction in infant mortality, from 141 per 1 000 live births in 1960 to 24 in 1996. In addition, the maternal mortality ratio also registered a significant decrease, from 200 per 100 000 live births in the late 1980s to 45 in the late 1990s.

Although overall socioeconomic development should account for most improvements in health status, Thailand appears to be one of the few examples of middle-income countries where health gains have been more prominent due to significant government investment in the health sector and various pro-poor health financing and insurance schemes, such as the Fee Exemption Scheme and the Low Income Card Scheme introduced since the early 1970s. These schemes, both part of the special budget allocation by the Ministry of Public Health (MOPH), provided the poor with access to care and pharmaceuticals, either totally free of charge or at highly subsidized prices. The benefit package was quite comprehensive, including almost all essential care services and pharmaceuticals. Over time, what had begun as rather simple schemes based on eligibility at the discretion of medical staff evolved into large-scale programs with explicit eligibility criteria, guaranteed packages of services, restrictions in the first point of contact and referrals, and issuance of low-income cards.

HEALTH-CARE SYSTEM IN TRANSITION AND HEALTH SECTOR REFORM

The development of the health-care system in Thailand is marked by three major reform cycles, often referred to as the first health sector reform (HSR) (1975–1980), the second HSR (1990–1995) and the third, or present, HSR (1996–present).

The first HSR was characterized by a radical restructuring of the MOPH in 1974 to integrate all health activities under a single administration, as well as by the adoption of the community-based primary health care (PHC) model, in line with the

Alma Ata Declaration adopted by all member states of the World Health Organization (WHO) in 1978.

The second HSR, which occurred during the economic boom of the early 1990s, was characterized by a high level of investment in health care and increased financial protection for the poor under the Medical Welfare Scheme, often at the expense of the MOPH's own operational budget, representing therefore a proportionally higher share of total public health outlays, reaching 19% in 2000. Some achievements of this period were the creation of an extensive network of public facilities reaching each subdistrict and increases of 50% in total beds and of 75% in the number of physicians between 1985 and 1995.

The 1997 economic crisis brought about large-scale reform initiatives in many sectors, including health, with a view to increasing efficiency and sheltering the poor from negative effects of the crisis. These initiatives included autonomous management of public hospitals, reform of the Civil Servant Medical Benefits Scheme (CSMBS) and introduction of the Universal Coverage Scheme, or the so-called 30 Baht Scheme, replacing all previous pro-poor financing schemes (Table 1). The latter, implemented nationwide in April 2002 after one year piloting in six provinces, covers all who are not covered by the Social Security Scheme (SSS) or the CSMBS—some 45 million Thais. It offers a very comprehensive package at par with the other two schemes. The scheme is financed by the MOPH, except for a 30 baht co-payment (about 75 cents US). Those who are eligible receive a gold card that entitles them to care, although only in public facilities. Providers are paid on the basis of capitation for ambulatory care and of DRGs for inpatient care.

MACROECONOMIC POLICIES AND HEALTH SECTOR REFORM—EXPLORING THE LINKAGES

This section focuses mainly on linkages between health-care outcomes and the macroeconomic environment under which health sector reform initiatives have been carried out. As

TABLE 1. HEALTH REFORM INITIATIVES IN THAILAND

Changes	First reform 1975–1980	Second reform 1990–1995	Third reform 1996–present
Structural changes	Restructuring of MOPH	Restructuring of MOPH	Autonomy (self-management) of hospitals
Policy changes	Primary Health Care policy Redefinition of role of hospitals National EPI program	Expansion of health welfare Public–private health care mix National HIV/AIDS program Private sector involvement	De-concentration of budget management to provincial level Civil society involvement Civil Servant Medical Benefits Scheme reform
Resource changes	Training of community-based health personnel Increased coverage of health facilities Free care scheme for the poor	Increased production and recruitment of high-level health professionals Changes in healthcare financing	Cut in public health budget, changes in allocation of resources between categories Reform of payment of free care scheme for the poor Introduction on a pilot basis of Universal Health Coverage

Source: MAPHealth study (2001).

explained in Chapter 3, both primary and secondary qualitative and quantitative data were collected and triangulated to explore potential linkages between macroeconomic policies and health care. Primary data collection in Thailand involved two field surveys: a health facility survey covering 6 urban, 60 rural, and 24 peri-urban health centres; 14 district and 8 provincial public hospitals; and 35 private clinics and 6 private hospitals; and a multistage stratified cluster survey covering 7 800 individuals in 1 950 households. A community survey was also conducted, including key informants, to collect ecological data on community characteristics and perceptions about health and health care. Most of the economic data is compiled from government documents and reports, mainly those regularly published by the National Economic and Social Development Board, the National

Statistics Office, the Bank of Thailand, the MOPH, and IFIs such as the World Bank and the Asian Development Bank.

Austerity measures and macroeconomic policies adopted in times of crisis are often criticized as having deleterious effects on the health sector in general, and on people's access to and use of services in particular, but the evidence from Thailand does not support any such broad-brush conclusion. Rather, it provides useful insight into how good policies, even if adopted in difficult times, can lead to improved access and expanded coverage. In this section, we examine linkages between macroeconomic policies and changes in health financing, health-care coverage, resource allocation, and increasing pluralism in the sector.

Sustained increase in health-care financing and coverage for the poor

Since 1986, all governments of Thailand, irrespective of their ideology, have increased, or at least maintained, the amount of financing for the Low Income Card Scheme.

These increases not only provided adequate financial coverage for the poor, but also expanded it to vulnerable populations such as the elderly, the disabled, and children below five years of age, as well as to the 4.4 million workers under the SSS, run by the Social Security Organization for those formally employed in the private sector and financed through a 1% payroll tax from both employee and employer. Indeed, in the 1990s, there was a considerable increase in health-care coverage, from 32.9% of the population in 1991 to 80.3% in 1998, including the expanded implementation of a national program aimed at increasing access to health-care services, the Voluntary Health Card Scheme, which added another 14 million people (Table 2).

Management of resource allocation

As in many low- and middle-income countries, personnel expenditures account for about half of total public health-care expenditures, followed by operating costs and capital investment. In relative terms, the latter declined during and after the oil crises

TABLE 2. EVOLUTION OF HEALTHCARE COVERAGE (%) IN THAILAND IN THE 1990S

Scheme	1991	1992	1995	1997	1998
Health welfare for general population	**16.6**	**35.9**	**43.9**	**44.7**	**45.1**
Low income	16.3	20.7	15.5	13.4	13.5
Elderly	-	6.2	4.6	4.9	5.5
Children <5 yrs	-	-	7.1	7.3	7.3
Primary and secondary school	-	9.0	8.9	11.1	11.1
Veterans	0.3	-	0.4	0.3	0.3
Community leaders, health volunteers	-	-	5.0	5.4	5.4
Handicapped	-	-	1.8	1.8	1.5
Religious	-	-	0.6	0.5	0.5
Civil servants	**10.2**	**11.3**	**11.0**	**10.8**	**10.8**
Civil Servants Medical Benefits Scheme	8.7	9.9	9.6	9.4	9.4
Public enterprise	1.5	1.4	1.4	1.4	1.4
Compulsory health insurance	**3.2**	**7.6**	**7.3**	**7.6**	**8.5**
Social security	-	4.4	7.3	7.6	8.5
Workmen's compensation	3.2	3.2	-	-	-
Voluntary health insurance	**2.9**	**3.9**	**9.8**	**15.3**	**15.9**
Health card project	1.7	2.3	7.8	13.3	13.9
Private insurance	1.2	1.6	2.0	2.0	2.0
Covered	**32.9**	**58.7**	**72.0**	**78.4**	**80.3**
Uncovered	**67.1**	**41.3**	**28.0**	**21.6**	**19.7**

Source: Bureau of Policy and Strategy, MOPH, Thailand (2002).

and bounced back significantly during the boom period, reaching 40% of total expenditures in 1996. Figure 3 shows how, in times of crisis in Thailand, the MOPH has been able to absorb fiscal constraints by cutting down on new investment.

Increased pluralism in service provision

With the advent of the PHC movement in the late 1970s, and as a result of the MOPH's policy to provide grants to community groups and non-government organizations (NGOs), there has been a steady increase in the number of projects and budget requests, mostly for health services aimed at the poor. In 1996, 150 NGOs made funding requests for 491 projects, amounting to some 193 million THB, and received 49.2 million THB (approximately 1.9 million USD) (Medical Registration Division 1997).

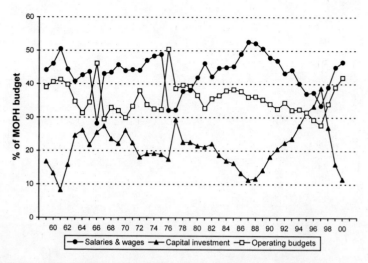

FIGURE 3. MOPH BUDGET PATTERN, THAILAND: PERSONNEL, OPERATING, AND CAPITAL BUDGETS, 1959–2000
Source: Bureau of Policy and Strategy, MOPH, Thailand (2002).

After the second health reform and the establishment of the Social Security Scheme, the involvement of private service providers increased considerably, leading to various public–private mixes in service delivery, albeit mostly confined to the greater-Bangkok metropolitan region. Between 1991 and 1996, the number of contractual arrangements for purchasing health-care services from private providers grew from 18 to 68, resulting in an even larger increase in the number of sub-contractors, from 69 to 1609, during the same period, a large majority involving the MOPH itself. In 1996, the number of contracted hospital networks reached 151, with an ever-increasing public–private network of providers, accounting for 15% of the total and mostly confined to Bangkok, its vicinity, and the central region (Nittayaramphong and Pannarunothai 1988).

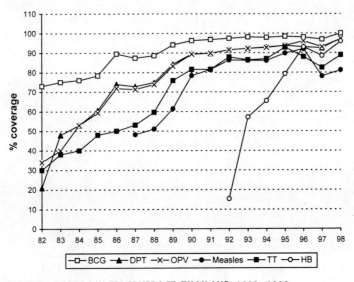

FIGURE 4. TRENDS IN EPI COVERAGE, THAILAND, 1982–1998
Source: Bureau of Policy and Strategy, MOPH, Thailand (2002).

HEALTH SECTOR REFORM AND ACCESS TO, USE, AND QUALITY OF HEALTH-CARE SERVICES

What impacts have these reforms and changes had on the supply, demand, use, and quality of health-care services? As a result of the first health sector reform and increased public participation, there has been a steady improvement in the provision and coverage of preventive and primary health-care services; food hygiene and nutrition; maternal and child health; family planning; immunization; safe water supply; and sanitation. Figure 4 shows the positive trends in immunization coverage for children and pregnant women.

Similarly, Thailand launched a successful national HIV/AIDS program with an ambitious goal of 100% condom use among commercial sex workers. The results were impressive—an increase from 25% condom use in June 1989 to 92% in December 1994. This increase proved to be sustainable; the very high proportion of condom use remains stable, as evidenced by the steady decrease in the prevalence of sexually transmitted diseases over the same period, from about 6 per 1 000 in 1989 to 0.49 in 1996.

Expanded health-care coverage has resulted in an increase in the use of both outpatient and inpatient services by the poor and disenfranchised (Table 3). This was accompanied by gradual changes in patterns of use, with an increase in the demand and use of services at subdistrict health centres and district-level hospitals, at the expense of outpatient clinics in provincial hospitals. This shift was a result of the MOPH's policy of expanding the network of health facilities to subdistrict level and increasing the availability of health personnel, mainly physicians, at the subdistrict and district levels to strengthen the system hierarchy (Figure 5).

TABLE 3. TRENDS IN SERVICE USE UNDER VARIOUS INSURANCE SCHEMES, THAILAND, 1988–1997

Scheme	1988	1991	1992	1992	1993	1994	1995	1996	1997
Health card									
OP/person/year	1.07[a]	0.88[b]	0.93[b]	2.11[c]		1.99[c]	1.25[c]	2.15[c]	2.67[c]
IP/person/year	0.05[a]	0.88[b]	0.93[b]	0.07[c]		0.09[c]	0.05[c]	0.09[c]	0.11[c]
IP/day/admission		3.48[b]				4.4[c]	4.53[c]	4.33[c]	4.34[c]
Social Security Scheme									
OP/person/year		0.32[b]	0.78[b]		0.87[d]	1.08[d]	1.22[d]	1.34[d]	1.52[d]
IP/person/year		0.02[b]	0.04[b]		0.04[d]	0.04[d]	0.03[d]	0.03[d]	0.03[d]
IP/day/admission		4.23[b]	3.74[b]			4.32[d]	4.59[d]	5.6[f] public 4.0[f] private	
Low Income Card[g]									
OP/person/year					1.182[h]	1.607[h]		1.91[h]	
IP/person/year								0.03[f]	
IP/day/admission								5.1[f] private	

Sources:

a: Kiranandana, T. et al. (1990).

b: Singkaew, S. (1992).

c: Supachutikul, A. et al. (1993).

d: Social Security Office, Ministry of Labour and Social Welfare.

e: Insurance Health Office, MOPH.

f: Supachutikul, A.,Tanscharoensathien, V. (no date) and Supachutikul, A. (1996).

g: Sonkhla, M.N. et al. (1997).

h: Low Income Card (LIC) data from annual reports 1993 and 1994 of the PHC office, MOPH.

Note: OP: outpatient visits; IP: inpatient visits.

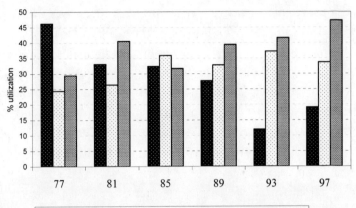

FIGURE 5. PATTERNS AND TRENDS IN SERVICE UTILIZATION BY TYPE OF HEALTH FACILITY, THAILAND, 1977–1997

Source: MOPH, 1998

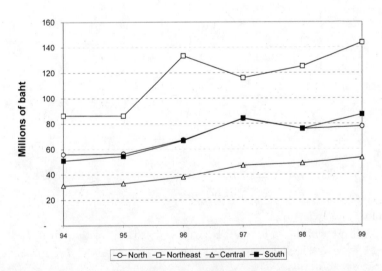

FIGURE 6. EVOLUTION OF HEALTH-CARE BUDGET ALLOCATED FOR LOW INCOME POPULATION IN FOUR REGIONS, THAILAND, 1994–1999

Note: Based on data from eight provinces.

Source: Health Facility Survey, MAPHealth study (1998).

Access to services is primarily determined by the availability of resources, their geographical accessibility and the affordability of services. Geographical access in Thailand has improved considerably over the past 20 years; most health centres and hospitals are easily accessible in terms of both distance and time (Table 4).

TABLE 4. GEOGRAPHICAL ACCESSIBILITY MEASURED IN DISTANCE AND TRAVEL TIME TO SERVICE POINT BY TYPE OF FACILITY AND TO THE CLOSEST HOSPITAL, THAILAND, 1998

	Service area		To the closest hospital	
	Distance (km.) min. – max.	Travel time (minutes) min. – max.	Distance (km)	Travel time (minutes)
Health facility				
Public health centre				
Rural	0.4 – 7.4	5.3 – 24.5	12.4	28.9
Peri-urban	0.3 – 10.2	6.8 – 33.9	10.7	26.9
Urban (municipal)	0.4 – 5.7	6.7 – 28.7	2.2	10.0
Public hospital				
Rural (community)	0.4 – 24.1	6.5 – 55.0	39.6	41.3
Urban (general)	0.4 – 22.5	6.0 – 96.0		
Private clinic				
Rural	0.04 – 38.0	2.5 – 12.0	6.4	7.7
Peri-urban	0.4 – 23.6	4.8 – 52.0	8.9	20.6
Urban	0.6 – 92.0	6.5 – 121.3	4.6	15.2
Private hospital	0.75 – 72.5	4.5 – 197.0	14.2	2.8

Source: MAPHealth study, health facility survey (1998).

As explained earlier, the 1997 economic crisis was weathered by shifting funds from the investment budget line to operations and by safeguarding the budget allocated to provide services to the poor, including those living in peri-urban slums (Figure 6).

There has been no discernable negative impact on the utilization of preventive or curative health-care services. Indeed, the volumes of outpatient and inpatient services at district hospitals and provincial hospitals have gradually increased, subject to regional variations (Figure 7).

Table 5 shows that in 1998, in the midst of the economic crisis, there was no shortage of either essential or non-essential drugs in public or private health facilities. Meanwhile, the quality

FIGURE 7. EVOLUTION OF SERVICE USE BY TYPE OF SERVICE AND FACILITY, THAILAND, 1988–1998

Source: MAPHealth study (2001).

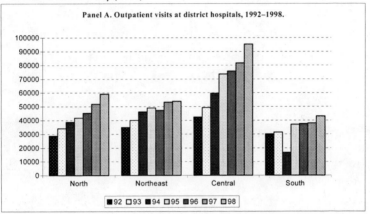

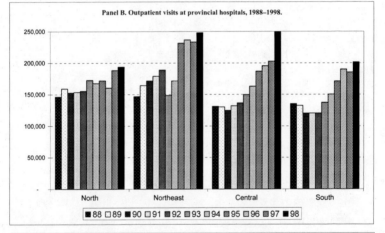

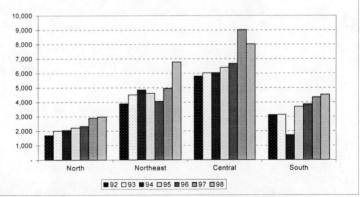

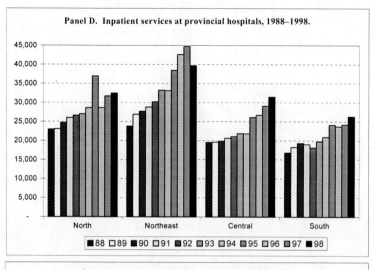

Panel D. Inpatient services at provincial hospitals, 1988–1998.

Legend: ■ 88 □ 89 ■ 90 ■ 91 ■ 92 ▨ 93 ▨ 94 ▨ 95 ■ 96 ▨ 97 ■ 98

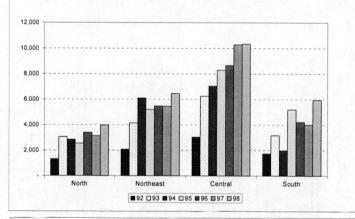

Panel E. EPI services at district hospitals, 1992-1998 .

Legend: ■ 92 □ 93 ■ 94 □ 95 ■ 96 ▨ 97 □ 98

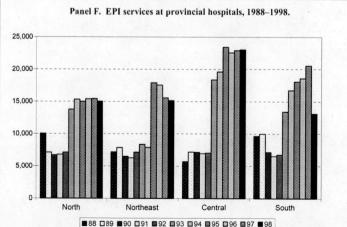

Panel F. EPI services at provincial hospitals, 1988–1998.

Legend: ■ 88 □ 89 ■ 90 □ 91 ■ 92 ▨ 93 ▨ 94 ▨ 95 ■ 96 ▨ 97 ■ 98

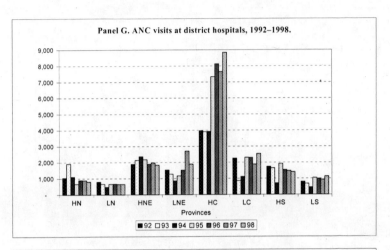

Panel G. ANC visits at district hospitals, 1992–1998.

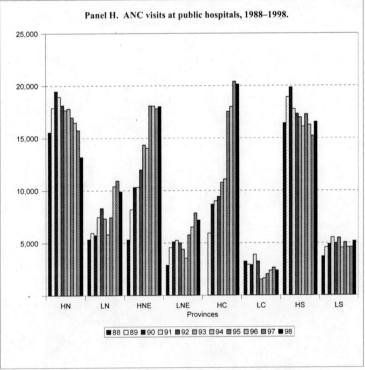

Panel H. ANC visits at public hospitals, 1988–1998.

TABLE 5. AVAILABILITY OF DRUGS, THAILAND, 1998

Health facility	Total drug items	Essential list	Non-essential list
Health centre			
Urban	64.6	53.5	-
Peri-urban	65.8	51.4	1.0
Rural	70.3 (p>.05)	67.0 (p>.05)	9.4 (p>.05)
Public hospital			
Community	151.5	138.4	15.3
General	65.8 (p>.05)	288.3 (p>.05)	58.3 (p>.05)
Private clinic			
Urban	107.4	36.0	24.2
Peri-urban	8.8	51.6	19.5
Rural	20 (p>.57)	6.7	0
Private hospital	752	N/A	N/A

Source: MAPHealth study, health facility survey (1998).

TABLE 6. PERCEIVED QUALITY OF HEALTH SERVICE EXPRESSED AS AVERAGE SCORES ON QUALITY OF HEALTH CARE DELIVERY, HEALTH WORKERS, AND HEALTH CARE FACILITIES, THAILAND, 1998

		Mean scores			
Type of facility	N	Health care delivery	Health workers	Health care facilities	Total score
Health centre	736	90.87	82.85	93.79	89.18
Private clinic	728	92.98	91.17	87.79	90.68
Religious health service	14	81.54	72.73	82.77	79.64
Traditional service	59	83.05	78.95	83.94	82.18
Pharmacy	422	86.92	82.40	88.11	85.87
General Stores	221	82.51	76.07	87.55	82.28
Government hospital	986	90.87	90.77	87.93	89.85
Midwife / traditional birth attendant	13	84.62	75.38	86.81	82.27

Source: MAPHealth study, household survey (1998).

Note: Quality score ranges from 0 to 100; average = mean of unweighted sum.

of services as perceived by the users remained high, irrespective of the type and nature of the facility, although scores were higher in rich provinces (Table 6).

IMPACT ON THE HOUSEHOLD: COPING AND HEALTH EXPENDITURES

While the accessibility and affordability of public health services were safeguarded, the economic crises and ensuing austerity programs did have an effect on household welfare and coping strategies. This was observed particularly in households that were larger,

TABLE 7. COPING STRATEGIES OF HOUSEHOLDS WITH FINANCIAL PROBLEMS DURING THE PAST FIVE YEARS, THAILAND, 1998

Groups		Heled score (p-value)	Asset score (p-value)	New loan % (p-value)
Gender, head of	M	.178 (.000)	.594 (.09)	19.3 (.99)
household	F	.456	.469	19.3
Household size	≤4	.201 (.004)	.56 (.95)	17.8 (.02)
	4+	.416	.56	23.3
Household income	Q1	.369 (.027)	.553 (.114)	16.8 (.10)
	Q2	.189	.483	21.8
	Q3	.427	.705	23.9
	Q4	.226	.678	19.6
	Q5	.108	.454	15.2
Education, head of	None	.459 (.006)	.281 (.028)	13.3 (.059)
household	Primary	.302	.61	21.1
	Secondary+	.000	.500	16.3
Location	Rural	.169 (.000)	.737 (.000)	23.5 (.001)
	Urban	.143	.433	14.3
	Slum	.764	.439	21.3
Province	Poor	.170 (.002)	.671 (.05)	19.9 (.57)
	Rich	.381	.478	18.6
Region	Central	.442 (.002)	.655 (.32)	22.7 (.05)
	North	.172	.47	16.6
	Northeast	.336	.565	22.3
	South	.108	.54	16
	Mean (SE)	.266 (1.216)	.572 (1.245)	19.3%

Source: MAPHealth study, household survey (1998).

Note: Heled score measures lack of access to health or education by any member of household (range 1, 10). Asset score measures disposal of any asset during past 5 years (range 1, 10). New loan is the percentage of households having received a new loan in the past 5 years.

headed by women, poorer, less educated, and living in slum areas and the northeastern region, with regard to access to health and education (measured by the Heled Score), disposal of assets (measured by the Asset Score), and recourse to a new loan (Table 7). Overall, access to health care and education and disposal of assets remained low at 2.66% and 5.72%, respectively, and there was a significant 19.3% increase in the number of households obtaining new loans.

TABLE 8. ANNUAL HOUSEHOLD HEALTH EXPENDITURES, THAILAND, 1998

Groups		N = 1951 Interviewees with health expenses (%)	N = 1159 Health expenses (in baht) for those who paid for care		N = 1123 Health / total expenses (%)
			Mean	SE	
Gender, head	Male	60.5	7 772.99	914.93	5.41
of household	Female	64.3	7 177.46	1 204.63	6.15
Household	Q1	61.2	5 788.27	*1 476.52	5.93
income	Q2	63.1	5 731.67	*1 449.58	5.43
	Q3	67.3	6 990.93	1 372.02	5.51
	Q4	65.1	9 441.68	1 383.76	6.48
	Q5	70.0	9 423.56	1 375.66	5.54
Education, head	None	74.8	7 548.28	1 871.63	6.45
of household	Primary	64.0	7 402.53	830.2	6.06
	Secondary +	65.8	7 603.36	1 358.62	4.82
Occupation,	None	68.8	7 548.28	1 321.36	*7.14
head of	Professional	62.4	6 867.44	1 851.68	4.65
household	Trader	70.9	12 016.13	*1 453.54	*6.66
	Farmer	61.5	5 873.45	1 423.26	5.9
	Laborer	63.8	5 070.82	1 372.97	4.54
Location	Rural	62.9	6 772.66	1 219.4	5.59
	Urban	67.5	8 469.06	1 057.7	5.96
	Slum	65.6	7 183.95	1 412.4	5.78
Province	Poor	62.0	6 491.80	*1 031.30	*5.26
	Rich	68.4	8 458.65	987.72	*6.30
Region	Central	73.5	8 264.67	1 222.7	6.03
	North	73.1	8 529.97	1 244.2	5.28
	Northeast	51.7	6 871.80	1 434.6	5.21
	South	63.7	6 234.46	1 256.3	6.59
Total		65.3	7 249.90	2 641.3	5.09

Source: MAPHealth study, household survey (1998)

* Significant at p< 0.05

Note: I USD = 40 baht

Table 8 shows the financial burden on households of out-of-pocket health expenditures. On average, 65% of all households had incurred health expenditures during the past year, averaging 7 249 THB per household (180 USD in 1998), or 5.1% of all household expenditures. Interestingly, there were no discernable differences by any of the household attributes.

Although not presented here, according to the household survey, the ratios of health expenditures to food and education expenditures were 0.343 and 3.784, respectively, with no significant difference by income quintiles or any of the other attributes. This is not surprising, given the fact that almost all preventive services and close to 80% of curative services provided in health centres were free of charge (Table 9).

TABLE 9. PROPORTION OF SERVICES PROVIDED FREE OF CHARGE ACCORDING TO TYPE OF FACILITY AND NATURE OF CONSULTATION, THAILAND, 1998

Type of facility	Moderate illness	Severe illness	Antenatal care	Delivery	Vaccination
Health centre					
Rural	71.8	73.2	90.3	90.0	97.5
Urban	61.7	72.5	87.9	82.4	94.8
Slum	76.4	80.6	97.0	83.3	97.0
Public hospital					
Rural	63.4	61.3	61.5	47.3	92.9
Urban	52.1	54.5	64.5	48.2	87.4
Slum	60.8	63.7	61.7	50.8	89.1
N	1 621	1 489	710	710	1 175

Source: MAPHealth study, health facility survey (1998).

However, there were significant differences in willingness to pay depending upon the respondent's gender and education, the wealth of the household, and the types of services. More specifically, women were willing to pay more for delivery than men; those in the poorest quintile were less willing to pay for antenatal care; the higher-educated were less willing to pay for all services, except for delivery; and the rich were willing to pay more for all except for delivery. It should be noted that the service fees were set in accordance with the perceived purchasing power in the provinces or regions (Table 10).

TABLE 10. WILLINGNESS TO PAY AT HEALTH CENTRE (AMOUNT PAID IN BAHT), THAILAND, 1998

Groups	Adult illness Moderate N = 450	Severe N = 73	Child illness Severe N = 53	Antenatal care N = 48	Vaccination N = 30	Delivery N = 22
Gender, head of household						
M	104.08	201.19	222.22	113.50	88.57	*208.33
F	98.30	250.27	247.06	186.45	126.83	448.13
Household income						
Q1	92.45	306.54	327.74	*68.44	40.00	295.71
Q2	79.80	175.26	210.00	169.00	128.00	418.75
Q3	125.96	277.50	200.00	66.25	112.86	440.00
Q4	92.72	120.63	108.00	560.00	168.36	400.00
Q5	120.47	216.67	256.00	200.00	65.00	400.00
Education, head of household						
None	56.97	150.00	246.67	173.75	126.28	566.67
Primary	105.51	255.83	248.45	180.88	76.00	326.25
Secondary+	94.58	169.00	74.67	72.50	117.90	500.00
Location						
Rural	101.50	264.89	253.66	110.61	159.69	361.33
Urban	100.40	190.45	211.25	319.29	60.83	416.67
Slum	91.10	221.43	230.00	100.00	150.00	500.00
Province						
Poor	*73.06	*95.24	195.38	172.29	*64.38	470.00
Rich	127.92	296.06	252.68	170.21	179.07	350.00
Region						
Central	102.50	67.50	145.83	137.50	*152.50	380.00
North	99.16	280.00	238.26	155.00	212.83	415.00
Northeast	105.33	282.69	293.16	198.95	33.57	283.33
South	84.38	199.29	266.67	180.83	196.67	500.00
Mean	100.25	238.29	238.62	171.25	117.90	382.73
SD	151.34	388.97	216.44	373.25	165.35	238.53
Min	5.00	10.00	20.00	5.00	10.00	50.00
Max	2 000.00	3 000.00	1 000.00	2 400.00	777.00	1 000.00

Source: MAPHealth study, household survey (1998)

* Significant at p < .05

Note: 1 USD = 40 baht.

In general, users were willing to pay higher fees in private clinics regardless of the type of services. Predictably, there was a significant association between the amount of the fee and household income, education, and area of residence. Fees in private facilities, though higher in general, are often close to those in public facilities (Table 11).

TABLE 11. WILLINGNESS TO PAY AT PRIVATE CLINIC (AMOUNT PAID IN BAHT), THAILAND, 1998

Groups	Adult illness Moderate N = 1235	Severe N = 310	Child illness Severe N = 241	Antenatal care N = 207	Vaccination N = 142	Delivery N = 31
Gender, head of household						
M	420.97	*1 243.33	1 255.56	845.80	359.38	5 666.67
F	379.30	873.85	988.46	676.99	337.29	3 517.14
Household income						
Q1	*296.57	*717.41	*526.49	846.87	*400.00	1 300.00
Q2	395.78	924.10	776.43	527.39	631.67	5 000.00
Q3	344.69	728.63	1 242.64	850.34	232.27	3 768.75
Q4	435.96	847.31	366.57	876.13	465.62	4 725.00
Q5	439.10	1 588.55	1 808.64	638.28	296.76	4 022.22
Education, head of household						
None	*278.12	*488.40	*833.33	605.00	300.00	*2 150.00
Primary	380.66	921.05	902.78	751.95	309.80	2 923.53
Secondary+	457.41	1 545.71	1 518.09	703.16	366.14	5 100.00
Location						
Rural	*302.13	990.68	*663.50	846.97	375.56	1 550.00
Urban	431.54	1 107.17	1 417.63	685.82	344.44	3 938.64
Slum	474.45	612.50	566.00	754.64	326.88	4 470.00
Province						
Poor	408.19	81.65	1 014.60	717.76	333.54	*1 900.00
Rich	375.95	1 080.53	1 106.65	724.73	358.10	4 152.00
Region						
Central	*358.56	*968.21	*744.71	603.59	378.48	3 500.00
North	403.10	1 521.55	1 679.86	683.38	369.82	5 166.67
Northeast	477.36	662.54	774.61	884.00	379.09	1 925.00
South	349.15	1 147.02	1 123.63	869.23	258.33	3 250.00
Mean	394.38	999.00	1 073.80	720.82	3 716.13	344.44
SD	575.25	1 497.39	1 697.01	931.95	2 538.94	348.38
Min	10.00	20.00	40.00	80.00	200.00	50.00
Max	8 000.00	9 600.00	9 000.00	5 000.00	8 000.00	2 000.00

Source: MAPHealth study, household survey (1998)

* Significant at p < .05

Note: 1 USD = 40 baht.

The willingness to pay for hospital-based services was, as expected, more than that for services provided in public health centres, but not so different for services provided in private clinics

(Table 12). Once again, level of education, income, and area of residence were significantly associated with the amount one would be willing to pay for either preventive or curative services.

TABLE 12. WILLINGNESS TO PAY AT PUBLIC HOSPITAL (AMOUNT PAID IN BAHT), THAILAND, 1998

Groups	Adult illness Moderate N = 1235	Severe N = 310	Child illness Severe N = 241	Antenatal care N = 207	Vaccination N = 142	Delivery N = 31
Gender, Head of Household						
M	*625.55	155.59	1403.37	505.60	310.71	1 830.20
F	451.66	1 358.86	1109.73	375.10	277.06	1 647.36
Household income						
Q1	504.17	*1 293.36	1 191.43	371.11	340.00	*1 490.11
Q2	545.58	1 052.55	1 120.77	256.96	252.22	1 391.31
Q3	428.68	1 288.37	1 042.01	346.00	253.00	1 587.01
Q4	529.01	1 542.68	951.44	473.14	220.00	1 644.04
Q5	499.53	1 810.76	1 456.44	396.73	321.13	2 185.00
Education, Head of Household						
None	402.13	1 387.5	1 138.46	348.67	203.33	*1 190.63
Primary	521.03	1 424.78	1 124.69	411.73	229.23	1 576.51
Secondary+	538.64	1 485.44	1 535.59	384.53	451.88	2 149.54
Location						
Rural	501.92	*1 322.77	*1 178.90	*516.29	348.00	*1 432.99
Urban	570.79	1 611.28	1 400.71	372.12	388.27	1 949.42
Slum	389.70	1 286.61	724.88	276.61	120.62	1 695.57
Province						
Poor	*447.33	1 440.37	*1 438.35	357.15	328.37	1 732.94
Rich	582.47	1 429.53	1 054.14	440.90	251.67	1 649.19
Region						
Central	*477.28	1 477.32	1 209.90	*497.28	*182.22	*1 874.82
North	436.78	1 415.79	1 107.97	348.68	407.92	1 902.87
Northeast	580.00	1 505.05	1 222.24	287.58	365.11	1 345.53
South	652.59	1 153.13	1 398.28	433.72	130.83	1 658.64
Mean	514.90	1 434.86	1 208.62	402.33	284.54	1 689.09
SD	654.57	1 419.04	1 300.99	460.29	345.99	1 529.25
Min	10.00	50.00	50.00	15.00	10.00	50.00
Max	8 000.00	8 000.00	7 000.00	3 000.00	2 000.00	8 000.00

Source: MAPHealth study, household survey (1998)

* Significant at $p < .05$

Note: 1USD = 40 baht.

CONCLUSION

Thailand's sustained economic growth has raised the socioeconomic level of its entire population without significantly increasing inequalities. Indeed, between 1990 and 2001, the Gini index remained steady at around 42.4, as did the share of the highest income quintile in national income, at about 58%. The proportion of the poor dropped from 32.6% in 1988 to 14.2% in 2000, and that of the near poor (i.e., with income 100–120% of the poverty line) went from 9.1% to 6.5% during the same period.

The health sector was a beneficiary of this economic growth, receiving its fair share and more, as the growth rate of health expenditures has consistently outpaced GDP growth rate since the 1970s. Consequently, the relative share of health expenditures in the GDP has increased, reaching close to 4% in 2000. Moreover, the ratio of public to private expenditures has also increased over time, and in 2000, close to 60% of health expenditures were public. Finally, since the inception of national economic development plans in early 1970s, health insurance coverage has always been aimed at the poor, culminating in universal insurance as of 1 April 2002, in the 30 Baht Scheme.

Not surprisingly, health indicators have improved dramatically. Indeed, with lower infant, under-five and maternal mortality rates, Thailand compares favourably with other middle-income countries.

It might be contended that the three economic crises described here caused considerable macroeconomic and social setbacks and undoubtedly eliminated some gains in standard of living for the whole population, and disproportionately so for the poor and the rural. Nevertheless, they were also instrumental in triggering radical reforms in the health sector. In times of crisis, and subsequently, the health sector has had to adjust to the reduced growth of sectoral investments by greater efficiency in the use of resources, or by reallocating them from investment to recurrent budget in a such a way as to mitigate the effects of funding shortages. Meanwhile, population health-care coverage continued to increase, privileging coverage of the poor. As the economy moved from crisis to economic boom, the amount of investment in the health sector also increased, more often at a higher rate than in other sectors.

Other favourable effects were the adoption of policies leading to greater community and civil society participation in system development and health services management, as well as increased involvement of private providers, even as financing has increasingly become public.

Accordingly, it would be fair to say that macroeconomic adjustment polices and austerity measures adopted as a result of economic crises did not result in reduced access and utilization, a finding equally applicable to all segments of the society regardless of income, education, area of residence, or type of services demanded.

One could argue that maintaining the same volume and intensity of services may have brought about a reduction in quality, but our findings do not corroborate this conjecture. Measured in terms of the availability of essential and non-essential drugs and of patients' perceptions, the quality of health care had not changed, as the system was able to adjust itself by adopting measures to increase productivity and efficiency, such as autonomy and accreditation of hospitals.

At the household level, however, we observed a number of effects, particularly in those headed by women, larger in size, and located in slums and poorer areas. There is evidence from the household survey that economic crises increased health needs and resulted in delays in seeking health care especially by the poor, women, and the uneducated.

In summary, macroeconomic changes do have an effect on the health-care system as well as on the community and on household welfare. The effects vary much less on the supply or system side, barring small variations across regions in terms of financing, but are more discernible on the demand side, with poorer households being less able to cope with the financial consequences of illness.

RECOMMENDATIONS

A number of recommendations follow from our findings and observations:

— Economic crises can present opportunities for health sector reform that in times of economic expansion may not be popular or even considered. The increased emphasis on primary care, and particularly on a system hierarchy with health centres and district hospitals as the first points of service, might not have happened to the same extent if there had not been budgetary pressures for increased efficiency and a preoccupation with safeguarding accessibility during economic crises.

— Economic crises also sensitize policymakers to be aware of and to seize opportunities in better times to increase investment in the sector, as Thailand aptly did in late 1980s and most of the 1990s.

— Ultimately, reforming the health sector becomes a continuous process, with different leverages exerted at different times according to the macroeconomic situation, focusing on intersectoral efficiency in times of contraction and constantly increasing the coverage and reach of services (gradual incrementalism) in times of expansion. Similarly, the nature of policy responses also changes, with rapid shifts in budgetary allocations to safeguard the availability of drugs and the workforce in times of contraction, as well as longer-term outlooks to increase coverage and improve health-care system performance.

— There is a limit to how much sectoral measures can mitigate the untoward effects of economic crises on demand for, access to, and use of services, in a system where there is no universal coverage and where outlays for health care are still primarily out-of-pocket. This is all the more an issue for the poor and for vulnerable groups such as women and children. That is why pro-poor financing policies are needed not only in times of crisis, but also on a more permanent basis, to ensure access to most essential services. This requires both an institutional capacity with an effective intelligence base for collecting data and information on poverty and health status, and effective leverages to ensure the unperturbed flow of funds to facilities that predominantly serve the poor.

Ideally, pro-poor policies should go beyond the health-care sector to encompass other services such as nutrition, safe water supply, and sanitation, but these are often neglected in times of crises. Because investing in health alone will not be sufficient, it is all the more essential to safeguard investments in education and social protection that have been painstakingly achieved in better times.

Note

1. In November 1996, 1 USD equaled 25.46 THB, and in January 1997, 53 THB.

References

Bureau of Health Policy and Planning. 1998. Annual report 1997–1998. Ministry of Public Health, Nonthaburi, Thailand.

Bureau of Health Policy and Planning. 1999. Report of Health Resources. Ministry of Public Health, Bangkok, Thailand: Express Transportation Authority Press.

Bureau of Policy and Strategy. 2002. Thailand Health Profile 1999–2000. Ministry of Public Health, Bangkok, Thailand: Express Transportation Authority Press.

Bureau of the Budget. 1997. Government Financial Statistics. Office of the Prime Minister, Bangkok, Thailand.

Medical Registration Division. 1997. Annual report 1996–1997. Ministry of Public Health, Nonthaburi, Thailand.

NESDB (National Economic and Social Development Board). 2000. Press release, June 17, 2000. National Economic and Social Development Board, Bangkok, Thailand, 8 pp. www.boi.go.th/english/download/business_analysis/15/nesdb_pr_1quart2002.pdf

Nittayaramphong, S.; Pannarunothai, S. 1998. Achieving universal coverage of health care through health insurance: the Thai situation. *In* Nittayaramphong, S.; Mills, A., ed., Achieving universal coverage of health care: experiences from middle and upper income countries. Office of Health Care Reform, Ministry of Public Health, Nonthaburi, Thailand. pp.257–280.

Primary Health Care Office. 1994. Annual report 1993–1994. Ministry of Public Health, Nonthaburi, Thailand.

CHAPTER 10

STRIVING TO SAFEGUARD A HEALTH SYSTEM UNDERMINED BY ADJUSTMENT: POLICY LESSONS FROM ZIMBABWE

Stephen K. Chandiwana, Tapiwa Jhamba, Charles Mutasa, Brian Chandiwana, Boy Sebit, Henry Chikowa, Paulinus L.N. Sikosana, Levon Arevshatian

DESCRIPTION OF THE COUNTRY

Zimbabwe, a landlocked country in southern Africa bordered by Zambia, Mozambique, the Republic of South Africa, and Botswana, occupies an area of 390 756 km². Its population in 1992 was 10.4 million, reaching 12.3 million in 1997. Despite growing urbanization, about 70.4% of the population live in rural areas (UNDP 2000). The population is youthful, with a dependency ratio of 94.4% in 1992 made up of 45% below 15 years and 3% over 65 years. Almost the entire population (98.8%) is of African origin, with MaShona and Matabele ethnic groups predominating.

In 1890, the MaShona and Matabele territories, which comprised what we now know as Zimbabwe, fell under the influence of the British empire, and the country was renamed Southern Rhodesia after Cecil Rhodes, a prominent colonialist leader. After suppressing widespread uprisings in the early 1890s, the settlers went on to establish a network of rail and road communications on the fertile highveld, forcibly displacing the African population to make room for commercial agriculture and mining. In 1923, the British government granted the small population of Europeans self-governing status that excluded the

African majority. Then, in 1931, the colonial regime passed the Land Apportionment Act reserving half of the arable land area to the white population, who numbered less than 1% of the total population. This land imbalance laid the foundation for future discord among the first independent government of Zimbabwe, the British government, and white commercial farmers.

Militant nationalistic parties emerged in the 1960s clamouring for restoration of land rights and independence. To pre-empt the granting of majority rule, the white settlers rebelled against the British government, and in 1965, Ian Smith, the Prime Minister, issued a Unilateral Declaration of Independence. Nationalist parties were banned and went underground, forming guerilla armies that made incursions into the country from bases in neighbouring Mozambique and Zambia. After nearly a decade of armed struggle, the Smith regime capitulated in 1979. A year later, the British government conducted a plebiscite that brought Robert Mugabe's Zimbabwe African National Union Patriotic Front (Zanu(PF)) into power on 18 April 1980.

Zimbabwe remained a multi-party democracy, but the Zanu(PF) party dominated political life throughout the 1990s, despite the presence of about a dozen opposition parties. However, in February 2000, the Movement for Democratic Change (MDC), a broad-based party led by Morgan Tsvangirayi, a former leader of the Zimbabwe Congress of Trade Unions, campaigned successfully against a referendum supported by government to introduce a new Constitution. It won 57 parliamentary seats in the general elections of June 2000, against 62 won by Zanu(PF). Although the MDC lost the hotly contested 2002 presidential election to Mugabe, it won important urban councils, including the mayorship of Harare, the capital city. The two main pillars of MDC support are urban workers, who have borne the brunt of deteriorating economic conditions since the 1990s, and white commercial farmers, whose farms were expropriated by government for fast-track land resettlement of peasant and black farmers. The MDC, the British government, and its allies are strongly opposed to the government fast-track land reform program, arguing that land reforms were disorderly and done for political opportunism, without regard for agricultural productivity and human rights. Government has retorted that land reforms were necessary to alleviate land hunger and poverty among peasants and to deracialize commercial agriculture.

DEVELOPMENT AND HEALTH INDICATORS

At independence in 1980, Zimbabwe inherited a socioeconomic structure with gross inequalities in health status between whites and blacks, and between rural and urban residents. Social and geographical inequalities were indicative of a colonial health system designed to provide health care to the minority settler population. There were marked income disparities between whites and blacks in formal employment and peasant farmers. This system ignored major health problems of the 70% majority black population living in rural areas, where health services were inadequate and where nutritional deficiencies and communicable diseases were rife. About a third of rural children were malnourished and only a quarter were immunized. The incidence of preventable conditions was much lower among the white population.

Access to education and jobs followed the same trend, with better educational facilities and opportunities available to whites, followed by urban blacks, whereas rural blacks had little or no access. Almost all urban residents had access to potable water and sanitation facilities, as opposed to 10% among the rural population. Distribution of arable land was even more skewed, with about 4 500 white farmers owning 75% of the land, while five million peasants lived in overcrowded and low-rainfall areas with poor soils. Overcrowding in communal lands led to environmental degradation due to inappropriate or intensive use of generally marginal land.

The new government adopted a policy of "Equity in Health," using the primary health-care (PHC) strategy to redress inequities between rich and poor, black and white, and urban and rural communities. Public health expenditures were increased, shifted toward rural areas, and focused on primary and preventive services, nutrition, and family planning. Basic health indicators such as nutrition, contraceptive use, life expectancy, and infant mortality showed dramatic improvements from 1980 to 1990 (Sanders and Davies 1988). Previously deprived rural and urban populations saw their life expectancy increase from 56 years in 1980 to 61 in 1990, and 85% had access to a health facility within eight kilometres. Immunization rates for children rose from 25% in 1980 to 77.9% in 1991, while the weight-for-age indicator for malnutrition in children fell from 22% to 16%. There was a dramatic reduction in the infant mortality rate from 80 (1978) to about 55 (1994) deaths per 1 000 live births.

Public sector investments in PHC, family planning, female education, and improved access to safe water and sanitation were important tools in promoting equity in health among the rural poor. Women and children benefited most, and universal access to primary education further strengthened the program. Literacy rates increased. It was estimated from the 1992 census that over 80% of the population were literate (86% among males and 75% among females). Female education is a key proxy for household socioeconomic status, bringing better understanding of health issues, particularly of disease and its prevention. The combined effects of increased family planning services, high literacy, and education also brought about a significant decline in total fertility rate from 7 in 1969 to 4.3 in 1994. Maternal health services were among the key areas developed in the 1980s.

However, Zimbabwe's second decade of independence (1990–2000) saw an increase in child and adult mortality while maternal and child health indicators stagnated. Some analysts claim this deterioration was a result of the introduction of structural adjustment programs (SAPs), which dramatically curtailed resources to the social sector. Others point to poor governance and the failure to respond effectively to the AIDS epidemic. In

1997, it was estimated that 20% of the adult population (about 1.4 million people) were HIV-infected (NACP 1998). The national crude death rate, which had dropped from 10.8 in 1982 to 6.1 in 1987, rose to 9.5 in 1992 and 12.2 in 1997. Some projections even suggested that life expectancy would fall below 40 years in the absence of effective behaviour change (Gregson et al. 1996, 1998; Gregson et al. 1997). AIDS is now the primary cause of adult and child mortality, which led the government to introduce an AIDS Fund in 1999 through a statutory 3% levy on taxable income. It is estimated that about 15 million USD has been raised each year.

ADJUSTMENT POLICIES

In 1980, the government adopted a policy of "Growth with Equity" and at the same time promoted national reconciliation with the white minority population. The international community responded favourably and pledged about one billion USD to support the 1981 Zimbabwe Conference on Reconstruction and Development (ZIMCORD). In the first two years of independence, gross domestic product (GDP) grew in real terms, at 11% in 1980 and 13% in 1981, most likely in response to pledges made at ZIMCORD. The "Growth with Equity" policy was intended to reduce deep inequities in wealth distribution inherited from the colonial government. Foreign direct investments available to the private sector were limited. The policy was successful in promoting social equity in national development, but proponents of market forces felt it crowded out the private sector, limiting economic growth. The consequent mismatch between expenditure and revenue precipitated budget deficits of up to 10% of GDP. Other consequences included balance of payments problems, rising unemployment, inflation, and low levels of investment.

To secure balance of payments support, government was forced to undertake SAPs with the assistance of the International Monetary Fund (IMF) and the World Bank. The first of these, known locally as an Economic Structural Adjustment Programme (ESAP), was launched in 1991. Its main objective was to redress imbalances in the economy and promote growth through fundamental reforms of the economy to make it market-based. Measures were put in place to move from an inward-looking, protectionist, and state-controlled economy to one that was outward-looking and competitive, based on market forces, that would accelerate growth and lead to higher employment and improved standards of living. Poor people were cushioned from negative effects of ESAP through a Social Development Fund to assist with social services like health and education and to provide funds for income generation activities. Poor people also needed government support in dealing with the devastating droughts of 1991–92 and the growing problem of HIV/AIDS. Recent studies suggest a direct link between the deteriorating economic situation and increased disease in the population (Woelk and Chikuse 2001).

To stimulate broad-based macroeconomic stability, accelerate poverty reduction, and alleviate hardships arising from ESAP, in 1995 the government formulated a second phase of reforms embodied in the Zimbabwe Programme for Economic and Social Transformation (ZIMPREST), the focus of which was to alleviate poverty directly through land reform, indigenization, fostering small-scale enterprises, and an effective national HIV prevention strategy. However, weak implementation, droughts, HIV/AIDS, and policy differences with the international community militated against the success of the reform, such that confidence in the economy remained low. This was compounded by a slowdown in the global economy that saw a sharp decline in commodity prices, especially that of tobacco, responsible for about 30% of foreign currency earnings. Manufacturing and tourism declined by 7.5% and 3.5%, respectively.

The net effect of the reforms was to liberalize the economy, especially the financial services sector, but there was no increase in foreign direct investment, nor did unemployment or poverty decrease. Even more disturbing, the reforms ultimately led to decontrol of prices, removal of subsidies, poor supply response, high budget deficits, depreciating exchange rate, and high levels of inflation. Inflation rates had been erratic, going from 15.5% in 1990 to a peak of 42.1% in 1992, then down to 18.8% by 1997 and up again to 50% by 1999. The economy grew by less than 2% between 1991 and 1995 while inflation soared (ZIMCODD 2001). Population growth during the same period averaged 3.1%, explaining to a large extent the decline in GDP and in per capita GNP, from over 750 USD at the beginning of the 1980s to 500 USD in 1994. Earnings per employee declined 3% annually between 1980 and 1991, and unemployment went from 11% to 22% between 1982 and 1992, reflecting a significant deterioration in the standard of living. The situation was worsened in 1997 by huge, unbudgeted financial gratuities given to 50 000 veterans of the war of national liberation.

Even though the SAPs were considered by policy analysts to be good, implementation was poor and targets were often missed. This was due largely to differences between those in government who favoured the social welfare policies adopted at independence and those who had wholeheartedly accepted SAPs. The IMF, World Bank, and bilateral donors refused to bail out the government from its economic problems, because of reservations about its economic and land acquisition policies and its military commitments in the Democratic Republic of the Congo. This resulted in the steady decline of already low investments and erratic loan disbursements and precipitated the 2000 economic downturn (UNDP 2000).

Importantly, SAP policy issues were shrouded in secrecy. There was little public support for SAPs due to the lack of transparency, accountability, and public participation in their design and implementation. Indeed, after 10 years of SAP implementation (1990–2000), there was intense debate and criticism that the country's economy had been sluggish at best and otherwise contracting at an alarming rate. By the end of 2000, there were no signs of economic recovery, but rather mounting poverty and unemployment, compounded by a young population structure, the HIV/AIDS burden, rising foreign debts, and inflation. This continual deterioration forced government to adopt the Millennium Economic Recovery Programme, in a firefighting attempt to mobilize all economic stakeholders, public sector departments, business, labour, and civil society, to implement a package of synchronized macroeconomic stabilization measures that would be anticyclical and anti-inflationary.

STUDY DESIGN AND METHODOLOGY

Anecdotal evidence suggests that the health sector in Zimbabwe was seriously undermined by the SAPs, as described in the preceding paragraphs. Our aim was therefore to study the role of SAPs in health sector reform and their influence on access, utilization, and quality of health-care services. We also wished to assess the extent to which structural changes within the health-care system have arisen from socioeconomic pressures of adjustment policies, including any prejudice to the health sector under liberalization—as, for example, in the fact that its main input costs require foreign currency (e.g. drugs and equipment), while it produces for and is paid in the domestic market. The sector also lost highly skilled and experienced professionals (doctors, nurses, others) whose incomes became uncompetitive due to the rising cost of living during structural adjustment.

The existence of two distinct periods in the country's recent history facilitated the testing of the research hypothesis and related questions. First, in the decade of independence from 1980 to 1990, the country had a functioning and effective health delivery system that led to marked improvements in a number of health indicators. Then, in the decade from 1990 to 2000, when structural adjustment and health sector reform policies were introduced, there were marked declines in important health indicators.

Several methods were used to generate information, such as retrospective analysis of macroeconomic and health sector data to describe patterns and examine economic trends, social organization, and inventory of health facilities. We also reviewed the literature and analyzed reports and documents from government departments, academic and research institutions, non-governmental organizations, United Nations agencies, and related organizations. Interviews were conducted with key informants in economic and social sectors. Focus group discussions were conducted with representatives of rural and urban communities for cross-sectional understanding of the financing, delivery, and quality of health services at the local level. A household survey was carried out using a questionnaire administered to 2 000 respondents randomly selected throughout the country, with a non-response rate of 0.4%. The sampling frame for the household survey came from the 1992 Zimbabwe sample (ZMS92) developed by the Central Statistical Office (CSO) following the 1992 population census for use in demographic and socioeconomic surveys. The rural stratum consisted of communal land, large-scale farming, and small-scale farming and resettlement areas, and the urban stratum corresponded to the urban and semi-urban strata of the ZMS92.

The analytic challenge was to demonstrate linkages between SAPs and health sector reforms and to identify impacts on various aspects of access, utilization, and quality of care according to administrative and geographical location and socioeconomic status of the population. Such analyses provided insights into household economic indicators, ability to pay for health care, utilization of health services, perceptions, and health needs of different population groups. Interim findings and reports were prepared and discussed extensively at national meetings and workshops with key stakeholders (policymakers and planners, researchers, and public health experts) to get feedback and to attempt to reach consensus on the interpretations and conclusions.

FINDINGS AND DISCUSSION

The health system

As stated earlier, health policies, legislation, and regulations introduced after independence supported goals of equity and therefore promoted free health care to those who could not afford to pay. The key policy document, *Planning for Equity in Health*, and subsequent health-for-all action plans were based on PHC and thus included health as part of the development process. However, it remains difficult to assess the impact of traditional non-health inputs on health development and performance. Government demonstrated its commitment to PHC, keeping health expenditures as a percentage of GDP stable at 2–3% between 1980/81 and 1995/96, with 1990/91 being an exceptionally good year (Figure 1). During the period 1981–1994, the proportion of health expenditure as a percentage of total government expenditure was maintained at over 5%, except during the drought years of 1983–1985, when it dropped below this level. Between 1979 and 1987, public health expenditure grew by 94% in real terms and 48% in real capital terms. By the end of the

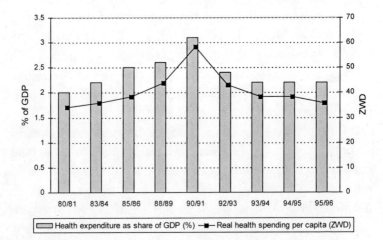

FIGURE 1. PATTERNS OF GOVERNMENT HEALTH EXPENDITURE, ZIMBABWE, 1980/81–1995/96
Source: MAPHealth study (2001).

1980s, the public health sector had undergone unprecedented expansion, such that recurrent annual levels of government financial allocations were inadequate to maintain existing services.

The Ministry of Health is the largest single provider of health care and preventive health services. It is directly responsible for 301 rural health centres (RHCs) and 55 rural hospitals, 50 district and general hospitals, 8 provincial hospitals, and 5 central hospitals.[1] It also provides subsidies to 600 health facilities of municipalities, missions, and rural district councils (RDCs) that adhere to government programs and health policies such as exempting the poor and indigent from fees for health care. Within this context, in 1980, government eliminated health services fees for those earning less than 150 ZWD (at that time, 100 USD) per month, effectively exempting 70% of the population and leading to a substantial increase in utilization of health services.

Introduction of reforms

Government initially insisted on its redistributive socialist model, but after severe foreign currency shortages in the late 1980s, it finally succumbed to the Bretton Woods institutions and introduced ESAP in 1991. Even though there is no clear documentation linking the introduction of health sector reforms to SAPs, local observers believe that once government accepted internationally-driven IMF and World Bank economic structural adjustment strategies, the link with health reforms became inevitable.

The corporate model and the management approach to health reforms were initiated internationally and introduced in Zimbabwe in the late 1980s as a package of externally funded workshops and technical assistance. The main reform objective was to decentralize power and decision-making in health services to the operational level. Under pressure from the World Bank, IMF, and bilateral agencies, cost-recovery and value-for-money policies were imposed on the public health system, with little internal consultation and debate to reach consensus. There was international pressure to increase access to health care and to improve quality by reforming and commercializing some services. This trend led to an increase in the health-care market of the private and non-governmental sectors.

There was no clear collaboration on the reforms between the Ministries of Health and of Finance, leading to dissonance between a strong political commitment to expand access to health services and a shift of national resources in favour of the private sector. Government's financial allocations to the public health sector in real terms were fairly consistent before and after the introduction of economic reforms. For example, in 1990/91, at the beginning of ESAP, public expenditure on health was 3.4% of GDP and 22 USD per capita, or 6.2% of total expenditure—one of the highest levels in sub-Saharan Africa. Indeed, allocations to the Ministry of Health increased from 6.1% of the total budget in 1990/91 to 10.4% in 1995/96. More recently, the share of expenditure on health as a proportion of public expenditure increased markedly, from 4.3% in 1996, to 10% in 2000 and 11.5% in 2001.

On the other hand, economic reforms were aimed at balancing the widening budget deficit partly caused by spiraling costs of public expenditures, including health care. With economic liberalization, the middle class, mostly urban, clamored for improvements in the quality of health care and for more responsiveness to consumer needs and preferences. Within the context of a disastrous economic situation and excessive inflation, the ensuing contradictory and confusing health policies gave the impression of a collapsed public health system. The decline was aggravated not only by unmanageable growth of the public health sector, but also by droughts, poverty, the HIV epidemic, and the decline in prices of export commodities. To complicate the picture, value-for-money and cost-recovery policies, which created barriers in access to public health services, were introduced without adequate examination of their impact on equity and on sustainability of the publicly funded health system (Hongoro and Chandiwana 1995).

Reform process

Content

Conventional wisdom suggests that health reforms were inevitable following the introduction of SAPs in the 1990s. However, we found no explicit government document or statement on the Ministry of Health's rationale for embarking on health sector reforms. Internal Ministry documents indicate that health sector reforms were being introduced in line with international trends to decentralize decision-making to the level of health service delivery. It is against this background that health sector reforms were introduced in Zimbabwe with the following objectives (Sikosana 2000):

— increase the effectiveness and quality of services, to achieve consumer satisfaction and ultimately improve health status;
— improve access to quality care for disadvantaged groups and ensure greater equity; and
— obtain greater value for money (cost-effectiveness) from health spending through targeting resources at priority activities, with better management and use of resources.

The Ministry of Health identified the following areas for reform: decentralization, health financing, regulation of the private medical sector, strengthening management, and contracting out of some services. Decentralization was aimed at providing flexible and adaptable management practices, inter-sectoral coordination, and community participation. From the perspective of central government, decentralization had political, administrative, and economic objectives. To support the reform process, the Ministry embarked on a project in 1990 aimed at developing management competency at district, provincial, and central levels.

The most important legislative changes associated with the reforms were under the Medical Services Act enacted in 1999, which provided the framework for the establishment and operation of private health providers and medical insurance schemes. The key elements of this act are:

— regulation of the establishment of private hospitals and of access to private and public hospitals;
— regulation of medical aid societies (private health insurance schemes);
— monitoring of the quality of care in private and public institutions; and
— establishment of hospital management boards (HMBs).

Hospital facilities were to be run by HMBs with strong representation from the community, and RDCs would be responsible for health delivery services in their respective districts. Initially, the HMBs or local authorities would receive grants from the central government awarded on an agreed formula for specified numbers and types of beneficiaries. In addition, the Health Services Fund (HSF) was established in 1996, allowing government institutions to operate bank accounts into which revenues from cost recovery and donor funds were deposited. This additional source of financing was characterized by flexibility and availability for addressing local priorities and needs. Up to then, all hospital fees had been remitted to Treasury's consolidated revenue fund, reducing the incentive for institutions to collect user fees. Another important aspect of reforms was the contracting out of non-core activities such as security, cleaning, and catering services.

Capital expenditure

Annual capital spending figures are difficult to compare because of high population growth and inflationary trends that eroded the value of the local currency. Thus, real per capita expenditure declined even as capital expenditure continued to grow. Large construction programs, such as the building of more than 90 new hospitals and clinics in 1992/93, placed a strain on current funding of staff, stock, and operating costs of the new facilities. Expansion of health services in the 1980s did not match the resources available—a major challenge compounded by the emergence of the HIV epidemic and periodic droughts. Signs of this gap between demand and resources included drug shortages, poor maintenance of infrastructure and equipment, understaffing, and real decline in salaries.

During the economic reforms, the share of donor agency contributions to health expenditures remained stable at 25% of Ministry expenditure over three fiscal years (1994/95–1996/97), then registered a slight increase to 27% in 1997/98. Despite government's commitment to primary health care, a disproportionate amount of spending is on higher-level facilities, accentuating the inequitable distribution of resources in favour of urban areas, where most tertiary institutions are located.

Stakeholders

The Ministry of Health adopted an incremental, rather than radical, approach to health sector reforms. Consultations on decentralization began in 1994 involving Ministry representatives from district, provincial, and central levels, culminating in a national workshop of stakeholders in 1996. Reforms were to proceed in stages to allow staff to gain experience and to create an enabling environment for implementation. However, recent interviews indicate that health workers at the periphery believe the consultation process was inadequate and that community groups felt they were not adequately apprised of the content and implications of the decentralization (Sikosana 2000).

Consultations with RDCs emphasized the need to build on existing structures and strengthen financial and information systems. Donors such as DANIDA (Danish International Development Agency) were actively enthusiastic about decentralization, with a view to reducing the influence of centrally-based structures. Health professionals and the public were concerned about how the reforms would affect the public health sector's ability to address identified health needs. The Ministry of Finance was more interested in how the economic reforms would reduce the widening budget deficit, partly caused by spiraling costs of public health care.

Implementation status

By 2000, key aspects of the reforms had been accomplished and included:

— establishment of a Health Services Fund;
— development of a resource allocation formula;
— enactment of legal statutes to strengthen the Ministry of Health's regulatory role;
— approval of a new organizational structure for the Ministry; and
— approval for the establishment of Hospital Management Boards (HMBs).

However, by the end of 2000, health personnel at the district level had still not been transferred to the RDCs and no new HMB was in place. Even though financing proposals for a social health insurance were complete, implementation was dependent on an enabling economic and social environment.

Mechanisms and implementation arrangements

The Ministry of Health established a Strategic Development Unit to coordinate health sector reforms within a hierarchy of institutions set up to manage the process. However, a major difficulty in achieving effective decentralization is that government ministries are sectoral in nature, whereas developing linkages between capacity-building and decentralization demands an intersectoral approach. Currently, RDCs do not have the capacity to administer a comprehensive decentralized system that involves taking over some of the functions of the Ministry of Health at a local level. For decentralization to be successful, the capacity of RDCs to manage projects, float tenders, contract out services, and manage personnel and finance must be built up.

Consequences of health reforms

Broader effects

The political commitment to the health sector was not significantly reduced, yet resources available declined in real terms due to high inflation. Thus, as had happened in economic reform, health reform was undermining the functioning of the health system. Nevertheless, health reforms did improve the efficiency and effectiveness of the annual planning process for health services. This planning was strengthened substantively through a bottom-up approach involving broad consultation at district level with key stakeholders, through which inputs from all 58 districts are consolidated into a national action plan before submission to the Ministry of Finance.

To ensure uniformity, a 10-year National Health Strategy (1997–2007) has been developed, with implementation based on three-year rolling plans resourced annually. However, the planning process has been negatively affected by economic reforms that reduced civil service posts, mainly clerical and maintenance, compromising efficiency and effectiveness as health professionals were burdened with additional responsibilities. Also, skilled administrators left the public health sector to join the private sector—an internal brain drain that increased markedly in the 1990s and affected the viability of the public sector.

It is clear that the long-term sustainability of the public health system requires a new value system and greater capacity to monitor and evaluate the delivery of health care. To accomplish this, the traditional supervision by monitoring must be replaced by a process of amicable dialogue among members of a health team around mutually agreed goals. Changes in management culture should entail on-the-job training, sharing of technical and managerial information with staff, and creating conditions for obtaining feedback from subordinates and the public. Staff morale would also benefit from regular performance appraisals with appropriate bonuses and incentives.

Impact on health-care functions

The Medical Services Bill of 1999 provided appropriate conditions for regulating health providers and institutions in the private and not-for-profit sectors. These encourage an optimal mix of private and public provision of health care aimed at effective use of scarce resources. The challenge is to implement agreed-upon financing and professional standards to protect members of the public from unscrupulous health providers. It is clear that a key role of the Ministry of Health is to administer a regulatory framework that facilitates an orderly and increased participation of the private sector in provision of health care. An optimal public–private sector mix increases the range of options available to patients, reduces pressure on government health services, and minimizes cost escalation to make health care affordable.

Since the early 1990s, the Zimbabwe health system has seen rapid and massive private sector expansion that includes private-for-profit, private-not-for-profit NGOs, mission hospitals, and health insurance schemes (Figure 2). Particularly, urban areas have seen steady growth in private-for-profit health-care facilities ranging from small consulting rooms and nursing homes to tertiary hospitals. This growth has spurred the exodus of experienced medical personnel into the private market at a time when the public health system is experiencing difficulties with morale due to low wages and poor conditions of service. The migration toward the private sector has been supported by economic policies encouraging investment and entrepreneurship through deregulation of the health sector. In 1996, the National Medical Aid Society (NAMAS) estimated there was demand for an additional 1 000 private beds at a 75% utilization rate (MOH 1996–1998).

In recent years, there has been growing cooperation between the public and private sectors, particularly those in the mines and in large-scale agricultural sectors, in management of human resources or in the sharing of physical infrastructure and equipment. HIV/AIDS has increased the number of patients such

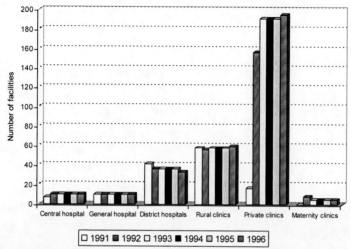

FIGURE 2. PATTERNS OF GROWTH OF PUBLIC AND PRIVATE HEALTH FACILITIES, ZIMBABWE, 1991–96

Source: MAPHealth study (2001).

that the public sector cannot cope. Those in the middle class on medical aid schemes find that private health providers are more convenient and that there is less waiting time before treatment.

Supply-side effects

Sharing the cost for utilizing services

The failure of economic reforms led to an increase in unemployment and in the level of poverty. In 1995, individuals contributed about 30% of health-care costs, approximately the same amount contributed by government. Employer-based benefits and private insurance schemes accounted for about 11.8% of expenditure, but this generally benefited those in urban areas. Government contribution was entirely devoted to public health facilities that benefited 80% of the population. Most beneficiaries live in rural areas and pay nominal consultation fees or are exempt from payments if they meet the criteria set by government for receiving free medical care: earning less than 400 ZWD per month (about 30 USD in 1997) and having a letter of recommendation from the Department of Social Welfare that they are eligible to have fees paid through the Social Development Fund (SDF).

Changes in provider payment mechanisms

With the introduction of user fees, individuals were expected to pay for health care at public institutions unless they met the above criteria for free services. In the health facilities survey, the majority of public health facilities in rural and urban areas reported having one or more mechanisms to provide free health services to those who were eligible. In urban areas, all surveyed facilities reported having mechanisms for patients to make direct cash payment for health services, whereas in rural areas, only half reported that patients could make direct cash payment.

Before economic reforms, most private health providers accepted payment through a health insurance scheme, but with the increasing difficulties insurance organizations have had since the reforms, many providers demand cash up front before service. Eighty percent of urban facilities had mechanisms to process payments made through medical insurance and the SDF, whereas only a third of the rural facilities could process payments through medical insurance and 16.7% through the SDF. The SDF was a form of safety net introduced to cushion the vulnerable population from the negative effects of the reforms. Access to a social welfare officer is better in urban areas, which explains why most rural people have limited access to the SDF.

Given the socioeconomic conditions in Zimbabwe, the proportion of patients who qualify for assistance through the SDF is high and has increased beyond the fund's capacity. There is a need to explore the potential for use of prepayment in rural areas where peasant families usually obtain funds seasonally from selling their agricultural produce. In the health facilities survey, only one rural facility had prepayment as a method of paying for health services.

Changes in system hierarchy

With health reforms, the central Ministry's responsibilities have been redefined as:

— health policy formulation;
— mobilization and allocation of resources, and budget analysis and formulation;
— human resources planning, development, and regulation;
— providing a regulatory framework for the operation of the private sector and other health providers;
— epidemiological surveillance, monitoring, and evaluation of the health status of the population; and
— liaison with international health organizations and aid agencies.

This has required streamlining the central structures of the Ministry of Health. With the devolution of authority, HMBs and provincial health administrations have more autonomy in revenue collection and administration of human and other resources. Donors have supported these reforms, particularly in providing resources to strengthen accounting procedures and developing strategies to enhance private–public sector collaboration in the delivery of health care. Since the establishment of the HSF in 1996, records indicate that fees retained at the institutional level have increased significantly. The funds have been used mainly to augment drug supplies from the government medical stores, contributing significantly to overall drug availability at the institutional level.

Changes in mechanisms for quality control and quality assurance

The health facilities survey examined a number of indicators used in quality control and quality assurance of health-care services at clinics in rural and urban areas. Health care was available at most facilities throughout the week. The majority (82%) of health facilities opened seven days a week, while 8% opened for six days and 10% opened for five days. In addition, about half (56%) of the facilities had an on-call system to attend to emergencies.

In the health facilities survey, staff members were asked about the existence of a therapeutic guide, whether in the form of a decisional tree or a medical practice guide. Staff at 83% of the facilities reported having a therapeutic guide. Of those facilities with a guide, 88% of the personnel were trained in its use and reported that it was used regularly. Most of these facilities (94%) had updated the guide, 42% within the last five years; about 40% could not give the updating date.

Regarding clients' average waiting time, health-care personnel interviewed were somewhat overly positive; only 7.5% estimated a waiting time of more than 30 minutes. This finding contradicts the view of a substantial proportion of respondents (26%) in the household survey, who indicated they had waited for more than 30 minutes before being served.

Public health interventions such as vaccinations are also indicators of the quality of the health delivery system. Gratifyingly, nearly 95% of 41 health centres surveyed provided daily vaccination services. About 66% of the facilities had a system to follow vaccinated children using follow-up cards, vaccination schedules, home visits, etc. The most common follow-up system was that of home visits by village community workers, who checked on children's vaccination cards and referred those unvaccinated to the health centre. This system was used by half of the facilities that reported a follow-up system.

Changes in cross-cutting issues

When ESAP was launched in 1991, the country had already made significant investments in human resources. There was steady growth in the number of health professionals registered with the Health Professions Council (HPC) from 1985 to 1997 (Table 1). Since the late 1990s, quality of care has been compromised through the large numbers of health professionals leaving the public health sector for the private sector or emigrating in search of better job opportunities, and the situation continues to deteriorate. The number of nurses per capita, for example, fell by 17% between 1988 and 1993. Shortages of drugs, consumables, and basic equipment continue to affect morale that is already low due to poor working conditions and low salaries. This led to stay-aways (not coming to work, but without a formal strike) and other job action, including a crippling strike by nurses and junior doctors in 1997 that negatively affected health delivery services.

TABLE 1. NUMBER OF HEALTH PROFESSIONALS REGISTERED BY CATEGORY, ZIMBABWE, 1985-1997

Category	1985	1990	1995	1997
Medical doctors	1 058	1 320	1 630	1 634
Dentists	94	131	152	148
Pharmacists	285	347	499	524
Psychologists	30	46	85	87
Radiographers	98	166	204	197
Medical scientists	7	11	30	-
Nurses (all grades)	9 533	12 518	14 108	16 407
Midwives	3 039	2 651	3 241	3 340
Laboratory technicians	-	-	225	259
Environmental health technicians	360	796	878	856
Dental technicians	14	22	33	36
Medical laboratory technologists	150	168	318	344
Environmental health officers	77	145	185	198
Pharmaceutical technicians	91	159	204	232

Source: Ministry of Health, Zimbabwe (1998).

Unfortunately, human resources development has been focused on doctors and nurses involved in medical care at the expense of environmental and other public health workers whose inputs have broader public health impact. This led to a stagnation, beginning in 1990, in development of the grade of environmental health staff, such that the role of this important cadre involved in preventive health services has fallen to the periphery. Since 1990, health services have been oriented more to curative than to preventive services.

The majority (85%) of health facilities reported that they had an updated essential drugs list and 94% of those with the list reported that it was available in the consultation room. On quality control, 24% of the health facilities estimated that quality of care was high, mainly due to good training and the use of therapeutic guides. On the other hand, 10% of the facilities complained that quality of care was low, mainly because some supervisory activities were not being done, due to staff short-ages. About two-thirds of the health facilities had a pharmacy where patients could procure prescribed drugs, suggesting that health centre based pharmacies are the most common source of prescribed drugs for patients.

Demand-side effects

Geographical accessibility

The results of the survey suggest that the government's policy of making health facilities available within eight kilometres of residence is working. The most common mode of transport to the nearest public health centre was by foot, followed by the use of vehicles. About 86% of urban respondents walked to the nearest public health facility, as did 72.5% of those in rural areas. A quarter of rural and about 12% of urban respondents used vehicles to get to the nearest health facility.

The proportion of respondents that had ever used a public health facility was high in both rural and urban areas, 87.9% and 82.2%, respectively. Similar utilization rates were recorded for public hospitals in rural (69.7%) and urban (73.7%) areas. On the other hand, urban respondents (67.1%) who used the nearest private health facility exceeded those in rural areas (43.9%). More rural respondents (44%) than urban (37.7%) used tradi-tional and religious facilities.

Surprisingly, in terms of time taken to access antenatal care, providers in rural areas were more accessible than those in urban areas: 61.1% of rural women had access to an antenatal care pro-vider within 30 minutes, compared to 54.2% of urban women. The explanation may be that these rural women live close to a health facility or a traditional birth attendant.

Financial accessibility

The household survey indicated that only a third of the study population were in formal employment. Data were analyzed by sector of employment and by gender to obtain an indication of an individual's economic status and likely ability to pay for health services. A higher proportion of rural respondents worked in the agricultural sector (86.1%), whereas urban residents worked in commercial, industrial, and service sectors. Women were predominantly employed in agricultural and domestic sectors and earned low wages hardly above poverty levels. Men dominated in commercial, public administration, and service industries, where wages were higher.

Interestingly, a high proportion of respondents (40–60%) spent considerable amounts of household income consulting doctors in the private sector or traditional healers. It is clear that many urban and rural households have the ability to pay for health services, an observation that supports the policy of user fees at government health facilities, as long as special arrangements are in place to ensure the poor have access to health care. Although government has stopped charging for primary care, clinics often lack basics such as drugs, trained personnel, and resources for physical maintenance. Some rural communities have started organizing themselves to generate funds for burial societies and even for upkeep of local clinics.[2] In spite of this effort, rural people have difficulty accessing modern health care and invariably are forced to rely on traditional healers, whereas urban people have some choice in the type of treatment.

Most of those who incurred traveling costs paid less than 50 ZWD (4 USD) per visit. For the majority of women in both rural (63%) and urban (50.4%) areas, no travel costs were incurred during antenatal visits, as the major mode of transport was by foot. Antenatal care (ANC), a key cornerstone of primary health care, has benefited from government policy on free medical care. For most rural women, ANC services were free, as their incomes were below the fee exemption threshold, which is generally not the case with urban residents. The proportion with free ANC was higher in rural areas (59.7%) than in urban areas (16.6%), while about a third of women in rural and urban areas paid less than 100 ZWD (7.5 USD). Nearly half of urban women paid more for ANC than rural women.

A majority of rural women (50.8%) thought prenatal care was inexpensive or very inexpensive, compared to 14.3% of the urban women. This is not surprising, given that the majority of women who received free treatment are from rural households. On the other hand, a significant proportion of women in urban areas (38.9%) thought prenatal care was expensive or very expensive, compared to only 18.7% in rural areas. Nevertheless, the majority from both areas indicated they were able to pay the cost of ANC.

Sociocultural accessibility

Local beliefs and customs influence access and utilization of health services. About 15% of health facilities personnel thought cultural beliefs had a negative impact on access to health services, and 9.8% noted a positive impact. For child vaccination, prenatal consultation, family planning, and nutritional follow-up of children, more than 70% of personnel reported a positive influence of local beliefs and customs. For prevention of HIV and sexually transmitted infections, 61% felt that local beliefs and customs played a positive role, and 14.6% observed a negative perception inhibiting the use of condoms in HIV prevention, as this was associated with increased prostitution in response to economic hardships.

Perceived service quality

Respondents of the household survey were asked to give their perceptions of different aspects of the quality of health care offered by providers closest to their homes, using a ranking scale from very good to very unfavourable. For the various aspects, a higher proportion of rural respondents than urban counterparts rated the public health centre and public hospital closest to their home as good or very good. Similarly higher proportions of rural respondents rated the quality of religious facilities as consistently good or very good for all aspects of quality examined. Traditional practitioners are also regarded more highly in rural areas.

Comparing private clinics with public health centres in urban areas, a higher proportion of respondents consistently rated private clinics as good or very good in most aspects of quality, except cleanliness and hygiene, for which only 55% rated the closest private clinic as good or very good compared to 69% of respondents using public health centres.

Among those who had had a health problem in the past four weeks and consulted a health facility, the majority were served within 15 minutes of waiting in both rural (42.6%) and urban areas (42.9%). The proportions of those waiting more than an hour were also similar, 12.8% in rural areas and 10.7% in urban areas. Generally, waiting time in all categories was similar in both areas. Waiting periods of more than 30 minutes were more common in public health facilities (30%) than in private facilities (18.2%) (Figure 3).

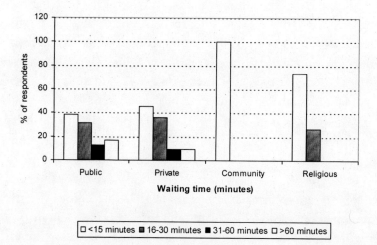

FIGURE 3. WAITING TIME BY OWNERSHIP OF HEALTH ESTABLISHMENT, ZIMBABWE
Source: MAPHealth study (2001).

More patients were not satisfied with the result of their visit in urban (21.1%) than rural areas (13.5%). At first glance, this suggests health facilities in rural areas offer better quality service than those in urban areas. A more plausible perspective, however, is that urban clientele are more sophisticated and have higher expectations than their rural counterparts, especially because they generally must pay a consultation fee, which is not the case at rural facilities.

Utilization of health services

Despite having limited resources and the least-trained health workers, the PHC level (rural hospitals, clinics, and health centres) handled an overwhelming proportion of new cases. Most were apparently minor ailments, as only a few were referred to the district level. Preventive health services constitute about a third of all health care, yet received only about 10% of public health resources. Over 50% of public resources continue to be expended at provincial and central hospitals in spite of clear evidence showing the benefits of investing in preventive care.

Temporal patterns in utilization of public health services show heavy workloads throughout the 1990s for new diseases or health conditions. Also, the number of inpatient deaths has been increasing, stretching hospital facilities, such as mortuaries, that do not have adequate capacity. This situation requires further strengthening of preventive and promotive health activities, especially against HIV and other preventable diseases like polio and measles, as well as of family planning and maternal health services.

Trends in the numbers of patients visiting health facilities for different consultations are shown in Figure 4. Vaccinations peaked in the late 1980s, then decreased steadily. Each type of consultation shows a different pattern that may be influenced by one or more factors. For example, health facilities use the "supermarket approach" for immunizations, using each visit by mother and child to vaccinate babies, thereby increasing immunization coverage. This includes curative or postnatal care, as well as growth monitoring visits.

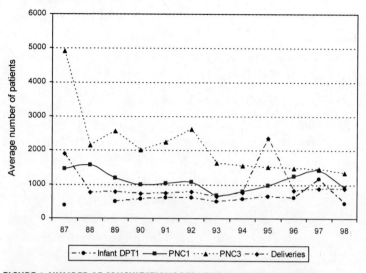

FIGURE 4. NUMBER OF CONSULTATIONS PER YEAR, BY TYPE OF SERVICE, ZIMBABWE, 1987–98
Source: MAPHealth study (2001).

Utilization of modern and traditional health services

The household survey showed that 77% of household members with a health problem had used some modern medicine since the onset of the illness; 76% had used modern medicines in the past four weeks, whereas the corresponding figures for traditional remedies were only 6% and 13%, respectively. The proportions of those using modern medicines or traditional remedies for self-treatment since the onset of illness were about the same in rural and urban areas. The proportion using traditional remedies in the past four weeks was substantially higher in rural (14.6%) than in urban (7.1%) areas.

Nearly a quarter of those who had been ill in the past four weeks used modern medicines without consulting a health professional. The use of stored modern medicines was more prevalent in urban (18%) than rural areas (11%). In urban areas, the majority of those who were ill in the past four weeks had purchased medicines from a pharmacy since the onset of the illness as well as in the past four weeks, 54.1% and 55.3%, respectively. In rural areas, however, only 12.2% of those ill in the past four weeks had bought medicines from a pharmacy, either since the onset of the illness or in the past four weeks. The purchase of traditional remedies was generally very low in both areas.

Reasons for not consulting a doctor or nurse

Respondents who were ill in the past four weeks but did not consult a health professional in modern health facilities were asked to give up to three reasons for their decision. For our analysis, we focused on respondents who did not consult a doctor or nurse in a public health centre, because these offer free services for PHC and are also readily accessible. The main reason given was that the respondents (27.7% in rural areas, 38.5% urban) did not think it was necessary, which may mean they did not think the illness was serious enough. The second most common reason (21.7% rural, 23.1% urban) was that it was either too expensive or they did not have enough resources. The cost element is an interesting paradox; as services are supposed to be free at public health facilities, this response may reflect a shortage of drugs at these facilities, requiring patients to travel elsewhere to purchase them.

Utilization of institutional health facilities

The proportion of people attended by a medical doctor was higher in urban (33.3%) than rural (14.9%) areas. In the majority of public, community, and religious health facilities consulted by those who had been ill in the past four weeks, care was provided by nurses, whereas in private health facilities care was mainly provided by doctors. The proportion of rural residents consulting a health facility for the first time exceeded that of urban residents, but the differences were reversed for second, third, and fourth visits. For example, 28.5% of urban residents had consulted a health facility for a fourth time compared with only 17.1% in rural areas. The difference indicates that urban residents are more apt to complete their treatment at modern health facilities and go for check-ups. This may be explained by the greater proximity of urban health facilities, the affordability of services (i.e., urban people being in a better economic position), and the higher level of literacy in urban areas.

Utilization of ANC and birth delivery services

Mothers who had prenatal care during their last pregnancy were asked to give reasons for choosing a particular ANC provider. In both rural and urban areas, the most common reasons for choosing an ANC provider were not linked to cost. The three most common reasons were proximity of the provider to home, availability of the necessary supplies and medicines, and competency of the care provider. The majority of women who had ANC for their last pregnancy were very satisfied with the care received, the proportion being slightly higher in rural (94.7%) than in urban (88.2%) areas. None of the women in either area reported they were unsatisfied.

The majority of birth deliveries reported by women in the sample (excluding miscarriages and abortions) occurred at public health facilities. However, more than 25% of births to rural women occurred at home, compared to only 5% among urban women. Home births were more common in rural areas, which may be an indicator of geographical differences in women's access to suitable health facilities with trained personnel. Urban women have more access to health education through radio and television and are aware of the potential hazards of home delivery. In fact, one of the reasons for providing free maternity services was the observation of very high numbers of home deliveries, reportedly up to 60% in some localities.

Private health facilities were used more by urban (10.5%) than rural (1.5%) women, likely because of differences in access, as well as differences in ability to pay. A significant proportion (11.5%) of births to rural women occurred in a religious health facility, compared to 3.1% among urban women, probably because most religious facilities are based in rural areas.

Utilization of health services for child immunization

The survey data revealed that 96.8% of children under 15 years old had been vaccinated at birth against major childhood immunizable diseases, suggesting continual high coverage since the launch of the Zimbabwe Expanded Programme of Immunization (ZEPI) in 1980. The overall difference in the proportions of vaccinated children in rural and urban areas was small, 96.4% and 98.7%, respectively.

The majority of children had been vaccinated at birth, except for hepatitis B, which was introduced into the national vaccination program later (1996–1998) than other antigens that had been part of the expanded program of immunization since independence. Also, due to the comparatively high cost of the hepatitis B vaccine, its supply has not been regular.

Contraception

The proportion of women who reported using contraception was high in both rural (56.5%) and urban (56.3%) areas. These usage rates are substantially higher than those reported in the 1988 (32%) and 1994 (35%) Zimbabwe Demographic and Health Surveys. The most common method in both areas was oral contraceptives, used by about 80% of urban and 77% of rural women. Injectables were the second most popular, used by 25% of urban and 17.2% of rural women.

Overall, oral contraceptives, injectables, condoms, and female sterilization were more popular in urban than rural areas; the "other modern methods," which include vaginal methods and implants, were also more popular in urban areas. More rural women used the IUD. Traditional methods were least popular, being used by fewer than 1% of rural women and none of the urban women surveyed. None of the respondents used male sterilization. About 45% of all women using contraception thought it was more difficult for women than for men to buy or use contraceptive methods without the permission of their parents or partner.

Women not using contraception were asked to give up to three reasons for not doing so. In both rural and urban areas, the most common response was that women did not need to use any contraception, or they cited a lack of knowledge of contraceptive methods; expense and lack of funds were the least common reasons given. The results show that economic changes have not had a major impact on the decision to use contraception.

Utilization of screening services for breast and cervical cancer

Overall, fewer than 7% of rural women had undergone a mammogram or a PAP test. Comparative proportions for urban women were slightly higher (mammogram, 8.5%; PAP test, 15.8%). This may indicate differences in knowledge about the need for such tests, or in ability to pay, or in the availability of services.

CONCLUSIONS

The impacts of macroeconomic and health sector reforms on access, quality, and utilization of health services were analyzed in the context of two main periods of Zimbabwe's recent history: the first decade of independence (1980–1990), with its expansionist social programs, and the second decade (1990–2000), when macroeconomic and health sector reforms were introduced. In the first period, the country had an effective health delivery system due to heavy investments in health and other social sectors, resulting in marked improvements in health indicators such as life expectancy, nutritional status, and infant and maternal mortality rates. The macroeconomic policies guiding government during the first decade were "Growth with Equity" and "Equity in Health". In the second period, structural adjustment and health sector reform had negative effects on the health system. Foreign currency and devaluation of the local currency affected supplies of drugs and related consumables. This demoralized health personnel at a time when conditions of service and remuneration were declining, precipitating the resignations of highly experienced personnel, strikes, and stay-aways by doctors and nurses. It is against this background that there were marked deteriorations in life expectancy and in infant and maternal mortality rates.

Thus, a key conclusion from this study is that the health sector in Zimbabwe has been seriously undermined by the effects of MAPs introduced with the aim of boosting economic growth through trade liberalization and institutional reforms. Since independence, the evolution of the health system has been part of the national development process, although inevitable links with economic structural adjustments were not acknowledged. The clearest correlation between MAPs and health sector reforms was seen in the deterioration of health systems at a time of worsening macroeconomic indicators. Health sector reforms based on decentralization involving cost-recovery and value-for-money policies were implemented without assessing the ability of communities or households to pay for services. Introduction of user fees in the 1990s, a key aspect of health sector reforms, led to marked reduction in utilization of health services (Hongoro and Chandiwana 1995). Analysis of data collected before and after the introduction of MAPs indicated increases in geographical and social inequities in delivery of health care and in population health status (Chandiwana et al. 1997).

Interestingly, the study revealed contradictions between the government's objectives of economic liberalization under SAPs and its strong political commitment to expand the public health sector and improve access to health care. Macro-level data suggest that MAPs and health reforms may have had profound effects on access and quality, and thus on utilization of health-care services. This situation has been aggravated by the pervasiveness of AIDS and poverty in Zimbabwean society since the 1990s. Even without economic reforms, the AIDS epidemic was bound to increase significantly the resources needed to meet the national health workload. There were also exogenous factors such as droughts and marked declines in world prices of primary commodities, particularly tobacco and gold, as well as policy disagreements with the IMF, the World Bank, and bilateral agencies that led to the withdrawal of balance of payments support. The combined effects of these factors precipitated the current economic downturn.

It is clear that SAPs had a negative impact on social equity in national development, as seen in the economic decline through devaluation and inflation, which eroded savings and spending power, including on health services. Under these circumstances, it can be argued that Zimbabwe has averted the total disintegration of its health services through the government's internal policy of maintaining high expenditures on health care, thus cushioning the poor from the negative effects of SAPs. Even in the midst of economic crisis, internal policies have thereby preserved some of the positive elements of the hitherto successful health system.

Paradoxically, the household surveys showed continued high utilization rates and general satisfaction with the health delivery system, particularly in rural areas. The better perception of public health services by rural people was likely reinforced by the government's fee exemption policy. However, this positive view may simply reflect a time lag between the adoption of MAPs and their eventual effects. Urban households felt the early direct effects of economic reforms as local authorities began to charge for most health-care services. Those who paid for health care expected a high standard of service and value for money spent. Nevertheless, urban residents preferred the private sector because of perceived higher quality and shorter waiting periods.

Utilization of findings

Initial and interim drafts of this report were discussed at the national level and widely disseminated to as many stakeholders as possible, particularly policymakers, researchers, and program planners. Key findings were also presented at seminars and public health meetings. The aim was to make policymakers and other stakeholders conscious of links between MAPs and health sector reform policies, on the one hand, and access, quality, and utilization of health care, on the other. From the ensuing debate and discussions, stakeholders at different levels have been able to extract lessons and information upon which to base changes in policies and programs to improve the health-care system. In this context, the MAPHealth research should be an integral element of strategic planning within the Ministries of Economic Planning and of Health, to ensure such research is linked with policy and action.

Future perspectives

Future directions of the MAPHealth study should build on the research databases developed over several years by a consortium of local institutions and a multidisciplinary study team. Country-specific expertise has been developed on MAPs, health sector reforms, and their impact on access, quality, and utilization of health care. Of significance are the large amounts of retrospective macro-level data on MAPs and health sector reforms collected mostly from fugitive sources that should form essential reference material for future studies. The nationwide health facility and household surveys provide hitherto unexplored insights into the local economy, social organization, inventory of health facilities, financing, delivery, and quality of health services. Valuable data was collected on household economic indicators, individuals' ability to pay, health services utilization, health perceptions, and health needs. This database offers vital baseline information to compare with subsequent surveys to assess the performance and effectiveness of national health systems. Such evaluation should promote transparency and accountability in planning and implementing sustainable health delivery systems under varying MAP regimes.

An agenda for future research could have as a starting point further analysis of the existing database to assess the impact of changes in health care brought about by MAPs and health sector reforms. Particularly pertinent is how current information can be used in shaping appropriate policies and best practices in different regions of the country and in different socioeconomic and sociocultural contexts. A number of key questions would set the framework for the agenda for future research:

— What have we learned about the links between structural adjustment, health sector reform, access, and utilization of services? How can we analyze the database to obtain additional information?

— Using available data, can policymakers and implementers find better options to put in place appropriate MAPs that enhance equity and improve health status?

— Where are the information and knowledge gaps? In particular, there is a need to explore roles for politicians and parliamentarians, researchers, health planners and program managers, civil society groups, and NGOs in relation to:

  • research to gather information, knowledge, and understanding;

  • policy to translate research into action; and

  • action to translate policy into programs (e.g. lobbying, advocacy, networking).

Notes

1. The country is divided into administrative subdivisions—eight rural and two urban provinces (six or seven districts comprise a province). A provincial administrator coordinates activities in a province, while a civil servant with the title of district administrator heads each district.

2. Edwin Zishiri, Ministry of Health, Provincial Medical Director, Midlands Province, Zimbabwe, personal communication, 2001.

References

Chandiwana, S.K.; Woelk, G.; Hongoro, C.; Sikosana, P.L.N.; Moyo, I.; Braverman P. 1997. The essential step: an interim assessment of equity in health in Zimbabwe. Mimeographed report, Blair Research Institute, Harare, Zimbabwe, 84 pp.

CSO (Central Statistical Office). 1994. Census 1992: Zimbabwe national report. Central Statistical Office, Harare, Zimbabwe. 226 pp.

CSO; IRD (Institute for Resource Development). 1989. Zimbabwe demographic and health survey 1988. Central Statistical Office, Harare, Zimbabwe, and IRD/Macro International, Columbia, MD, USA.

GOZ (Government of Zimbabwe), Ministry of Finance and Economic Development. 1981. Growth with equity: an economic policy statement. Government Printers, Harare, Zimbabwe.

Gregson, S.; Anderson, R.M.; Ndhlovu, J.; Zhuwau, T.; Chandiwana, S.K. 1997. Recent upturn in mortality in rural Zimbabwe: evidence for an early demographic impact of HIV-1 infection? AIDS, 11, 1269–1280.

Gregson, S.; Zhuwau, T.; Anderson, R.M; Chandiwana, S.K. 1996. The early socio-demographic impact of the HIV-1 epidemic in rural Zimbabwe: summary report of findings from the Manicaland Study of HIV-1 and fertility. Blair Research Institute, Harare, Zimbabwe, and Oxford University, Oxford, UK.

_____ 1998. Is there evidence for behaviour change in response to AIDS in rural Zimbabwe? Social Science and Medicine, 46(3), 320–330.

Hongoro, C.; Chandiwana, S.K. 1995. Study on the effects and impact of hospital user charges on health care delivery in Zimbabwe. Mimeographed report. Blair Research Institute, Harare, Zimbabwe.

Ministry of Finance and Economic Development. 1991, 1994, 1995, 2000, 2001. Estimates of expenditure. Harare, Zimbabwe.

_____ 1998. Zimbabwe programme for economic and social transformation 1996–2000. Government Printers, Harare, Zimbabwe.

MOH (Ministry of Health), 1982–2000: Epidemiology and Disease Control / Health Annual Statistics / PHC Review 1984, 1988, Government Printers, Harare, Zimbabwe.

_____ 1984: Planning for equity in health: a sectoral review and policy statement. Government Printers, Harare, Zimbabwe.

_____ 1995: Zimbabwe demographic and health survey 1994. Central Statistical Office, Harare, Zimbabwe, and Macro International, Calverton, MD, USA.

_____ 1995: Health sector reform in Zimbabwe: concept paper on decentralisation. Government Printers, Harare, Zimbabwe.

_____ 1996–1998. National annual health profiles. Government printers, Harare, Zimbabwe.

_____ 1997. National accounts, 1996–1997. Central Statistical Office, Harare, Zimbabwe.

_____ Nutritional surveys 1982–84, 1985, MCH/EPI Surveys 1991–1998. Government Printers, Harare, Zimbabwe.

Ministry of Health and Child Welfare. 1999. National health strategy for Zimbabwe, 1997–2007: working for quality and equity in health. Government Printers, Harare, Zimbabwe.

MPSLSW (Ministry of Public Service, Labour and Social Welfare). 1995. Report of the Poverty Assessment Study Survey (PASS). Social Dimension Fund, Government of Zimbabwe, Harare, Zimbabwe.

NACP (National AIDS Coordination Programme). 1998. HIV/AIDS in Zimbabwe: background, projections, impact and interventions. Mimeographed report. National AIDS Coordination Programme, Ministry of Health and Child Welfare, Harare, Zimbabwe. 75 pp.

Sanders, D.; Davies, R. 1988. The economy, the health sector and child health in Zimbabwe since independence. Social Science and Medicine, 27(7), 723–731.

Sikosana, P.L.N. 2000. Decentralisation of the health delivery system in Zimbabwe. MBA thesis submitted to Keele University, Keele, UK.

UNDP (United Nations Development Programme). 1980. Zimbabwe: towards a new order: an economic and social survey, working papers. Volumes 1 & 2. Programme Publications, Harare, Zimbabwe.

_____ 2000. Zimbabwe human development report. United Nations Development Programme Publications, Harare, Zimbabwe. 54 pp.

Woelk, G.; Chikuse, P. 2001. Using demographic and health survey data to describe intra-country inequities in health status: Zimbabwe. TARSC/EQUINET Monograph Series no. 8. Harare, Zimbabwe.

ZIMCODD (Zimbabwe Coalition on Debt and Development). 2001. The social effects and politics of public debt in Zimbabwe: impact of public debt management on development. Government Printers, Harare, Zimbabwe, 56 pp.

CHAPTER 11

POLITICAL WILL AND ADAPTIVE STRATEGIES: KEYS TO SAFEGUARDING THE HEALTH SECTOR IN TIMES OF MACROECONOMIC INSTABILITY

Slim Haddad, Delampady Narayana, Enis Barış

DIVERSE CASES OF MACROECONOMIC ADJUSTMENT

Between 1980 and 1999, the six MAPHealth countries received from the Bretton Woods institutions either structural or sectoral adjustment lending amounting to 36 operations and $13.1 billion USD. The Latin American countries, Mexico and Colombia, have been implementing adjustment policies since the early 1980s. Thailand had three episodes of adjustment: one following the oil price rise of 1979, a second in 1985, and another following the East Asian crisis of 1997. Burkina Faso, Zimbabwe, and India began implementing adjustment policies in 1991. While in the 1980s most loans or credits were either structural or geared toward sectors such as trade, agriculture, and finance, in latter years the education, health, and social security sectors gained prominence. The classical adjustments of the early 1980s were characterized by a severe tightening of public spending, whereas post-1987 adjustments tended to protect social sector spending, with a pro-poor inclination. Adjustment in the 1990s, influenced by the birth of the WTO, also had a high dose of globalization and liberalization.

The forms of adjustment varied greatly among countries, supporting the adage that there are as many adjustments as there are adjusting countries. Two major policy changes implemented in most countries were cuts in public spending and devaluation of the currency, both as part of demand management. The magnitude of these cuts and devaluations varied across the countries. The sequencing of policy changes also differed across the countries: some had many episodes of devaluation (Mexico, India), while others had fewer. Monetary policy liberalizations have also been rapid in recent years, with a definite move toward independence of the central banks and less monetary expansion. A general trend observed in the last 20 years is decentralization, arrived at through various streams of thought and political initiatives, such that it cannot be attributed to adjustment. Country experiences of decentralization have also varied widely, as demonstrated in these six cases. Colombia initiated a radical political, fiscal, and administrative decentralization in the 1980s, followed by the adoption of a new Constitution in 1991. India amended its Constitution in 1992, heralding a shift from a two-tier to a three-tier government.

Since 1991, all MAPs have included at least one condition related to the health sector, and, by the end of 1996, more than 100 World Bank adjustment operations had an HNP (health, nutrition, and population) component. Thus, most countries under adjustment either undertook or completed a health sector reform. While these reforms were partly in response to causes which could be considered an extension of each country's economic problems, the reforms were most often carried out independently of the MAPs and aimed at issues specific to the health sector. This explains the great diversity of reforms, not only between countries, but even within the same country over different periods.

THE ABOUNDING HETEROGENEITY OF HEALTH SECTOR REFORMS

Certainly, the health sector reforms carried out were inspired by the overall context and by common principles promoted by international institutions, aimed at increasing health system efficiency and continuity. The experiences presented here thus subscribed to the sectoral reform model that typically includes policy initiatives geared toward: (i) increasing health funding by raising public funding and community financing through cost recovery; (ii) reallocating public spending to primary care and to the poor; (iii) improving quality of care; and (iv) supporting decentralization and liberalization—the latter aimed at promoting the private sector. Beyond these general principles, however, the reforms we describe here present, in their specific implementation modalities, very diverse configurations. While some are motivated primarily by a rationale of economic efficiency, as in Zimbabwe and India, others take on aspects that are more in line with a "pro-equity" approach. This is obviously the case in Colombia. However, in certain countries—such as Burkina Faso, Mexico, or Thailand—it is difficult to classify unambiguously reforms which, according to the elements observed, draw upon both motivations. The reforms are the result of many social compulsions and political pressures, and their heterogeneity reflects the diversity, and even the contradictions, inherent in their underlying social objectives. This heterogeneity is further increased to the extent that the reforms are integrated into medium- and long-term processes, and by the fact that they arise from a variety of choices made at different moments, and are subject to the circumstances and political orientations of the time, internal and external power relationships, and, of course, lessons drawn from policies then in effect.

If there is one area that best demonstrates the heterogeneity of the reforms, it is in the evolution of public expenditure on health. At the national level, the adjustment may be accompanied by an increase in public expenditure on health, as in Burkina Faso, or by a contraction in spending, as occurred in both Zimbabwe and Mexico in the 1980s. In Zimbabwe, the reduction in public spending in real terms has undermined the functioning of the health sector, whereas in Burkina Faso, the strengthening of the public contribution not only covered, but largely exceeded, the losses inherent in the major devaluation of the CFA franc. Our study therefore supports neither the opinion of those who believe the erosion of public expenditure on health is a characteristic feature of adjustment, nor of those who hold the opposite view. All we can do here is to note the existence of marked differences among the countries in our sample; we are in no position to draw any lesson whatsoever, nor to adopt any position in the debate on the effects of macroeconomic and sectoral reforms on the commitment of public authorities to health. On the other hand, we consider it particularly instructive to look at the evolution of public expenditure on health in the states of federations such as India and Mexico. In these two countries, public expenditure on health differs markedly from one state to another. Of course, these findings come from only two federations. Nevertheless, the case of India demonstrates that in such a political configuration, public involvement in health—apart from situations of major crises in public finances or so-called "stabilization" periods—is more dependent on political choices and allocation decisions taken by the states than on adjustment policies *per se* implemented by the central government.

If we look at outcomes, we must conclude that the reforms, in themselves, are not impressive. In many cases, the system was poorly managed and remained so. On the whole, decentralization was only partial and not very conclusive. In Mexico, decentralization was incomplete because financial and allocative powers were not completely transferred to the state level. The states' margins of manoeuvre were severely limited, giving them only the capacity to implement policy directions dictated at the central level and to use other state funds to finance local initiatives. Kerala devolved administrative control of the public health facilities to the local self-government institutions. In Burkina Faso, decentralization led to the designation of 53 health districts, managed by "district management teams" responsible for planning and implementing activities and services. Teams were created and trained, facilities were built and equipped, and the districts then had the ability to generate certain financial resources. Nevertheless, power remains strongly concentrated at the level of the central government, district teams have limited margins of manoeuvre, health budgets have not been devolved, and the transfer and recruitment of personnel still rest with the central government. The central political bodies and administration tend to be unwilling to transfer power to the local level, where there is, in any case, insufficient managerial capacity—the latter phenomenon partly legitimizing the former.

With regard to implementation, the reforms come up against some strong areas of inflexibility which, paradoxically, seem to be accentuated by decentralization. In Colombia, the transfer of power from the central government to the municipalities, in practice, negatively affected public health programs and activities. In Mexico, the authors conclude that the reforms, "although often sweeping, have remained within the framework of the pre-existing health system, leaving untouched the inequities inherent in an institutionally fragmented structure of unequal benefits." Thus, the reforms remain largely those of administrators and decision-makers at the central level. As is shown in the case of Burkina Faso and Mexico, the involvement of those running the system, and particularly of health professionals, is extremely reduced and limited. Health-care staff know very little of what is going on, unless it has a direct impact on their work.

Overall, then, the institutional changes are not very impressive and the results do not measure up to the current faith in the intrinsic benefits of decentralization, nor to the active promotion it continues to receive. Beyond decentralization, the reforms are even less convincing when it comes to the performance of health authorities in regard to regulating the health sector. While most countries have actually implemented measures aimed at liberalizing the health sector and opening it to the private sector, none seems really prepared to deal adequately with the needs for regulation imposed by such changes. Growth in the private sector stems essentially from a model of spontaneous development, following an exclusively market-based logic. In countries such as Burkina Faso or India, the corollary to this is an enormous concentration of private services offered in urban areas, leaving rural areas to the public sector. There is, however, one issue which remains worrisome—that of quality. In a context where power relationships do not favour the citizen, and the impunity of professionals is the rule, competition and the commodification of health tend to occur to the detriment of ethics in the medical profession. The boom in the private sector thus creates an enormous need for regulation and quality assurance. However, clearly, no one seems to have anticipated and prepared for this need. In countries where resource constraints are still very severe, as in sub-Saharan Africa, the concept of quality still tends to be reduced to very simplified expressions having to do with the availability of health resources—drugs, facilities, personnel. One consequence of this focus on resource availability is that it draws attention away from other questions having to do with the quality of processes and the appropriateness of resource utilization, and clearly does not encourage the emergence of a quality assurance culture. Even in intermediately developed countries, quality assurance remains embryonic. Monitoring agencies, whether public or professional, are virtually ineffective with regard to professional practices, protection of citizens, and imposing sanctions on deviant practices.

TOWARDS THE COMMODIFICATION OF HEALTH CARE

Beyond regulatory and organizational functions, we have been unable to establish any tangible link between the changes implemented and the overall performance of health systems. Even where reforms were accompanied by substantial increases in resources allocated to the health sector, as in Colombia, or in capital expenditures, as in Burkina Faso, the impact on the population remains to be demonstrated. With regard to the performance of health services, there is no clear improvement in allocative or technical efficiency and no significant change in resource productivity or in the quality of health services. The total increase in public investments did not translate into measurable improvements in the allocation of resources, and in particular, there continue to be important inequalities in favour of specialized establishments and urban centres. The case of Burkina Faso is a good example of this. Although there was a significant increase in government expenditure on health during the reform, the allocation of resources at different levels of the hierarchy is still unbalanced, without any notable reallocation of funding from public hospitals to the primary care level, nor from the centre to the periphery. Neither have India or Zimbabwe been able to resolve the problems of over-concentration of health facilities and personnel in large urban centres. In India, 45% of health facilities are concentrated in three states. In Zimbabwe, despite a formal commitment on the part of the authorities to primary health-care services, more than half of public funds continue to be allocated to central and provincial hospitals.

In terms of technical efficiency, the results are scarcely more conclusive. In India, the performance of the reforming states was not really very different from that of non-reforming states, and high transaction costs were observed in Colombia and Burkina Faso. Poor service quality is the norm in sub-Saharan African countries and in India, whose populations consistently emphasize the poor performance of government services and the inhospitability of the public employees. The most important benefits of the public sector appear to lie in its capacity to offer services locally and at prices which, while not always affordable, nevertheless are still much lower than those charged in the private sector. On the other hand, very little is known about the performance of services offered by the private sector. Even in a country like Mexico, the private sector and its capacity are not well known, and there are no good estimates of the population covered by it. Nevertheless, in general, the private sector is usually concentrated in urban centres where higher profits can be expected. Our information suggests also that it is better perceived, more appreciated, and more attractive than the public sector. However, as we can see from the example of Kerala, recourse to the private sector is not entirely motivated by its inherent qualities; rather, it must be understood in relation to the mediocrity of the alternative, which is the public sector. Thus, the private sector seems to have taken advantage of the failures of the public sector, as well as of the deregulation which made it possible to recruit high-quality staff away from the public sector. However, as we have seen in Burkina Faso, Colombia, and Kerala, this has been accompanied by a worrisome commodification of health, whose effects on professional practice and quality of care are open to question.

WIDENING INEQUALITY IN ACCESS TO CARE

Reducing inequality in access and removing financial barriers to utilization are central objectives in the poorest countries in this study (Burkina Faso, India, Zimbabwe), but also in those (Colombia, Mexico, Thailand) that are committed to implementing systems of universal coverage. Have inequalities in access to health care been reduced? The experience has been mixed. In Colombia and Thailand, the poor have benefited more and inequalities in access have been substantially reduced. In Mexico, the poor have been offered access to primary care but access to secondary care was still very unequal at the time of the study. In Zimbabwe, as well, the poor have received more benefits. In Burkina Faso, access to care is still unequal. India has shown no concern to improve access to health care for the poor. In these latter three countries, our household surveys revealed that for many, access to health care remains greatly limited by the capacity to pay for services. Whether for user fees or for the costs of treatments that must be purchased outside, the cost of using public services still too often exceeds the capacity for payment among those in the poorest strata of society. The application of user fees, strongly promoted by donors in both Zimbabwe and Burkina Faso, reduced the utilization of services and increased inequalities in access.

Analysis of the impacts of out-of-pocket expenditures in Burkina Faso shows that the economic burden of illness remains excessive and that direct expenses on health are a source of collective impoverishment. There, as in many other countries, the economic burden of health care is unevenly distributed, and this inequality is more pronounced in cities, where the offer—public as well as private—is more dense and income more unevenly distributed. Inequalities related to illness are greater than inequalities in overall well-being, and the health-care system has failed to carry out its redistributive responsibilities.

ENCOURAGING SIGNS FOR THE FUTURE

Despite the poor performance of services, ineffective regulations, inconclusive institutional reforms and regressive modes of financing—despite all this, there are some encouraging signs of a potentially better future.

The first of these signs is the increased commitment of governments worldwide to the health arena. Of course, our sample of case studies is far from representative of the many situations encountered. Also, the evolution of the public commitment, measured in terms of government expenditures in health, is far from being systematic or regular. But public spending on health shows a generally increasing trend. In Burkina Faso, public expenditures in health have increased in both nominal and real value terms. The proportion of health expenditure within overall public expenditure increased by nearly five percentage points between 1995 and 2000. These amounts include contributions from external partners, who played a key role in the expansion of public contributions. In Zimbabwe, allocations to the Ministry of Health, as a proportion of total expenditure, increased to 10.4% in 1995–96 and further to 11.5% in 2001. The trend in health expenditures as a percentage of public expenditure has been one of dramatic increases year after year. In Colombia, public expenditure on basic health activities increased from 0.53% of GNP in 1980 to 1.41% in 1996, and per capita expenditure more

than doubled over a period of eight years (1987–1995), going
from 24.7 USD to 58.7 USD. Expenditure per person among
the poor tripled, going from 58.5 USD to 192.4 USD. In Thailand, since the 1970s, the growth rate in health expenditures has
consistently outpaced the GDP growth rate, and consequently
the relative share of health expenditure in the GDP has steadily
increased, being now close to 4%. Further, the ratio of public to
private expenditures has also increased over time, and at present,
close to 60% of health expenditures are public. Within our
sample, India is the exception. Public capital expenditure in the
Indian health care sector shows a general decline since the early
1980s. Recurrent spending of the health sector as a proportion
of the total recurrent spending of the government in the states
also shows a falling tendency, although milder for the reforming
states. Despite the availability of the World Bank loan for capital
spending, the reforming states have not enhanced the share of
the health care sector in their total spending.

However, even in difficult economic circumstances, and even
when adjustment exerts strong pressure on public resources, the
situation does not necessarily lead to a reduction in public efforts
or in governments' expenditures in health. There is often a sharp
dip in spending in extreme crisis situations, such as in 1995 in
Mexico, or in the central government's spending in 1991 in India,
or in 1992 in Zimbabwe following a severe drought. But in these
three cases there was a quick recovery. In Mexico, public expenditure in health was negatively affected by adjustment policies;
the expenditure for social insurance agencies and services for the
uninsured declined by 3% annually in real terms between 1982
and 1994. However, in subsequent years it recovered, reaching 4%
of GDP in 1995. The year 1995 saw a sharp fall in public spending,
owing to the macroeconomic crisis, with a slow recovery over the
next five years. In Thailand's major economic crisis of 1997, the
authorities managed to save the sector through a series of measures
which led to the protection of recurrent expenditures. Of course,
this protection entailed a massive reduction in investments that

had originally been planned, but this was temporary and ultimately did not have major consequences on services. As a result, the contraction of the government's overall budget after the crisis and the structural adjustment policy that was implemented had very little impact on the reform underway, nor on the availability, quality, and affordability of the services offered to the public.

In Colombia, Mexico, and Zimbabwe, poor economic growth was not seen to be a constraint on health spending. Even if the proportion of public spending allocated to health within the total collective resources remains—with the exception of Colombia—much below those of wealthier countries, several countries (Burkina Faso, Colombia, Thailand) have, over the long term, maintained and increased government spending on health. An examination of the situations in India and in Mexico, however, shows that trends at the central government level can mask important variations among states, and that state policies can play a key role as buffers in getting through difficult economic circumstances or restrictive central government policies.

The second positive sign is the pro-poor orientation of public policies. In the three intermediate countries in our sample, this commitment is manifested in efforts to extend insurance coverage, particularly to the poor. The Thai Medical Welfare Scheme and, later, the Universal Coverage Scheme fall into this category and seek to address the needs of the poor. In Mexico, the strategy adopted in 1996 was to expand the social insurance coverage to non-salaried workers and to reduce employers' contributions. In Colombia, Law 100 in 1993 sought to integrate social security with public health and create universal access to the system. The Law also set the framework for a national health insurance system with the goal of increasing insurance coverage from 20% to 100% by 2001, ensuring entitlement to a basic package of services to all. While these orientations unfortunately did not result in very significant or rapid results in these countries, nevertheless, in all three cases, progress was made and access to health-care services among the poor did improve. In Thailand, the results are clear:

steady improvement in the provision and coverage of preventive and primary health-care services, and then the expansion of coverage—initially targeting the poor, the aged, the handicapped, and children—set the foundation for a system of universal insurance. Colombia saw dramatic improvements in insurance coverage and in the reduction of the enormous inequalities of access that had existed. To a certain extent, the reform helped to sever the link between access to care and the households' ability to pay. In Mexico, access for the poorest to health-care services was improved by means of special funds targeting the poor, rather than through any actual reform itself.

As seen in the previous section, the situation is different and more worrisome in the African countries and in India because, on the one hand, the concept of universal coverage is still remote, and on the other hand, reforms have had little impact on the poor. In sub-Saharan African countries, the integration of health policies into poverty-reduction strategies, the intensification of primary care resources, and the reform of fee mechanisms, all currently underway, can be regarded as conditions which, while not yet sufficient, nevertheless are positive precursors of success for health care policies that ultimately will mainly benefit the poor.

The third sign is probably the most encouraging: the growing tendency to enshrine health as a constitutional right of the citizen. Access to care and equity in health have increasingly been viewed as human rights and global values. Politicians and policymakers are becoming sensitive to this dimension and are either bringing about institutional amendments to enshrine them as rights or building administrative processes to met people's aspirations. The General Health Law (1984) in Mexico and the new Constitution (1991) in Colombia are the best examples. Under Colombia's new Constitution, health and social security became rights, and a concrete system was introduced for their attainment. In Thailand, while not referring to it as a fundamental right, the National Health Security Act (2002) sought to provide universal coverage for health care. There is a certain minimum consensus among political parties that no one shall be denied access to health care of reasonable quality. This was turned into an election promise by the Thai Rak Thai Party, which on coming to power began implementing it in 2002. In India, health is contained in the Directive Principles of the Constitution adopted after independence in 1950, but is not considered a fundamental right of the citizen, and unlike the right to food or to education, there has been no real attempt to make it one.

POLITICAL WILL FOR SAFEGUARDING HEALTH SYSTEMS

Clearly, the macroeconomic environment affects health-care systems. The evolution of the health sector, while certainly affected by adjustment, is ultimately shaped by a whole host of internal and external macroeconomic factors and processes. Thus, many examples demonstrate that inputs, and particularly investments, are very sensitive to the macroeconomic environment in the short term. These influences have quite variable repercussions on the offer of health services, but the experiences reported here suggest that, except in extreme cases such as "first-generation" structural adjustment programs or violent economic shocks, the macroeconomic environment does not necessarily have a lasting and determining impact on the inputs affecting health, nor on the performance of the offer of services (i.e., on productivity, efficacy, or efficiency). With regard to inputs and service performance, the macroeconomic environment and adjustment policies do not fully explain, or explain poorly, the various experiences reported here.

On the other hand, the impact of sectoral reforms appears more significant. First, however, it must be noted that this impact actually is of limited scope, as can be seen from the comparative analysis of adjusting and non-adjusting states in India. Second, results obtained from countries such as Burkina Faso, India, or Zimbabwe are hardly definitive with regard to short- and medium-term efficacy. Their reforms could be described as orthodox, based on relatively stereotypical formulas: decentralization, plus liberalization of the health sector with promotion of the private sector, plus the financial involvement of communities. The Thai and Colombian reforms were primarily determined by factors in the national context and fed by internal political processes, rather than by the orthodox prescriptions of international financial institutions. Whether these characteristics explain the better results observed is a difficult question to answer, because the two groups of countries also have very different levels of development, capacities for governing, and sociopolitical environments. At this stage, we can only point out the poor performance of "turnkey" models and the disappointing results of their key elements.

So, why do certain systems react better than others when faced with the risks presented by economic crises, growth deficits, or the implementation of adjustment policies, while some appear to be more vulnerable? We have yet to discover the answers to these questions. Perhaps part of the explanation lies in the original robustness of the health systems and their capacity to react in situations of stress created by cycles of crisis and adjustment.

The robustness of health systems and of the mosaic of institutions of which they are made up depend largely on political choices and long-term development strategies. Everything that contributes to defining health as a right and making it a development priority brings greater legitimacy to the health system as a social institution, promotes investments in health, and ultimately reduces its vulnerability. In Thailand, since 1975, except for brief periods of time, all governments, irrespective of their ideology, have increased or at least maintained the amount of financing for schemes aimed at covering the poor. In Colombia, embedding the public contribution in the Constitution made it possible to ensure a long-term commitment to the health sector and was essential in creating an improved system of social protection. It also shielded the sector from any fluctuations of support that might occur with changes in political leadership.

Strengthening the foundations of the health sector can prepare it better for weathering the storms of turbulent macroeconomic environments, but does not necessarily make the sector more resilient. Stable resources, well-governed institutions, effective decentralization, and more flexible levers of control and action allow for more rapid and effective response, thus limiting the impacts of future crises. Here again, the Thailand case is particularly instructive. The analysis carried out by our colleagues over nearly 30 years has led them to conclude that economic crises have constituted, *a posteriori*, opportunities for structural changes in the health sector. In effect, the crises have orchestrated the reforms and have led, each time, to a series of adaptations that have transformed the health sector for the better.

The best prepared health systems might also be those that succeed, as well, in conceiving and deploying effective strategies for adaptation and in drawing lessons for the future. These adaptive strategies may take different forms. In India, for example, the central government has protected social spending during adjustment and certain states have judiciously increased their efforts in health during this period. In Thailand, as mentioned earlier, the government has protected recurrent spending during crises. With judicious steering and clear foresight, it has been possible to create an effective buffer and minimize the impacts of crises on the stocks of medicines, as well as on the quality and utilization of services. This experience demonstrates that, in an appropriate context and seen over the long term, good policies, even if adopted in difficult times, can lead to improved access and expanded coverage.

Still, it is important to point out that these adaptive strategies have limits. Their effectiveness in the face of repeated shocks, or when the problems are more structural than circumstantial, is uncertain. Moreover, the example of Thailand cannot readily be generalized; while the crises were intense, they are more like "accidents" along the course of a long-term road of impressive growth and economic development, and the country benefited from favourable conditions that cannot be compared with those of other countries. There are also situations where an accumulation of unfavourable conditions (Zimbabwe), a decline in government (Burkina Faso), or the intensity of the crises (Mexico, 1995) will limit considerably the effectiveness of these adaptive strategies, reduce the capacity to safeguard existing benefits and to protect health-care systems, or prevent them from taking full advantage of existing opportunities for development.

Finally, if the recipes for effectively safeguarding and perpetuating health-care systems remain to be found, there are certain ingredients which might prove indispensable. The first is certainly the favourable environment inherent in long-term economic growth. The second is the political will that makes it possible to strengthen health-care systems and to take full advantage of existing opportunities for development. The third is found in the size and regularity of public investments and the resulting accumulations of capacity. Ultimately, it is in the performance of the system itself that we will find the conditions for its durability and resilience.

CONTRIBUTORS

Enis Barış, Senior Public Health Specialist at the World Bank, is a physician with graduate degrees in public health (MSc) and epidemiology (PhD), with specialization in health services. Previously, he served at the World Health Organization (WHO) Regional Office in Europe and at the International Development Research Centre of Canada, where he was Chief Scientist and Senior Scientific Advisor – Health. Dr. Barış has a wide range of experience in development and research in over 30 countries. He has initiated and managed multiple single and multi-country research and development projects on macroeconomic adjustment policies and health sector reform, decentralization and access to care, health-care reform, and tuberculosis control.

Stephen Chandiwana, PhD, was, until his death in June 2007, Personal Professor and Assistant Dean responsible for research and postgraduate studies in the Faculty of Health Sciences at the University of the Witwatersrand, Johannesburg. His research interests were in the field of HIV and AIDS epidemiology, and he was active in research training and in developing research databases. Dr. Chandiwana was also interested in issues of access and utilization of health services under varying socioeconomic conditions related to the capacities of modern and traditional health-care systems, and was often consulted on emerging international health issues, especially as they related to North–South and South–South cooperation models.

Luis Durán-Arenas is Head of the Health Systems Division of the Health Care Services Directorate at The Mexican Institute of Social Security. Dr. Durán-Arenas is a physician specialized in epidemiology, and holds graduate degrees in public health, health services administration (MPH), sociology (MA), and in health services organization and policy and sociology (PhD). He has conducted and directed numerous research projects, many with funding from international organizations, mainly in the areas of quality of health care, health-care services utilization, and technology assessment. He has taught extensively on health systems research in several universities and other institutions, and is an Academic Numerary of the National Academy of Medicine of Mexico.

Slim Haddad, PhD, is a physician specialized in public health and a health economist. He is a Professor in the Department of Social and Preventive Medicine at the *Université de Montréal*, where he teaches planning and evaluation of public health programs, health economics, and health and social justice. Dr. Haddad has coordinated numerous studies in low- and middle-income countries. His areas of expertise include health services research and the evaluation of health policies and services. His work has focused particularly on evaluating the impacts and analyzing the distributive effects of health policies, health sector reform, and health-financing mechanisms such as micro-insurance.

Jeannie Haggerty, PhD, Assistant Professor in the Department of Community Health Sciences at the *Université de Sherbrooke*, currently holds a Canada Research Chair on Population Impacts of Health Services. Dr. Haggerty trained in epidemiology and biostatistics at McGill University and did a post-doctoral fellowship in health policy analysis with the *Groupe de recherche interdisciplinaire en santé* at the *Université de Montréal*, where she subsequently worked five years in the Department of Family Medicine. Her domain of research is accessibility and quality of primary care, both in Canada and in developing countries, and particularly the impacts of clinical guidelines, physician practice patterns, and health system policies and reforms on population health.

Katherine S. Mohindra holds a Global Health Research Fellowship (Canadian Institutes of Health Research) at the Department of Health Care and Epidemiology, University of British Columbia and is currently a visiting scholar at the Institute of Women's Studies, University of Ottawa. She holds a PhD in public health from *Université de Montréal* and has been a research associate at the International Development Research Centre (IDRC). Her main research interests are gender and women's health, evaluating health impacts of public policies and local development interventions, and social justice and global health.

Delampady Narayana is Professor, Reserve Bank of India Development Studies Chair, at the Centre for Development Studies (CDS), Thiruvananthapuram, Kerala, India. Dr. Narayana received his PhD from the Indian Statistical Institute, Kolkata, and has taught at the CDS for 25 years. In 1994–95, he was a Fulbright scholar at the Harvard Centre for Population and Development Studies. From January to June, 2006, he was Visiting Professor at *Unité de Santé Internationale*, Montreal, Canada. His areas of current interest are decentralized governance and health care services. He is also actively involved in capacity building at the level of the local government and with women's self help groups in Kerala.

Sanguan Nittayaramphong is Secretary-General of the National Health Security Office, Thailand, a position he has held for three years. Prior to that post, he was the Deputy Permanent Secretary, Ministry of Public Health, and served as Committee Secretary to the Thai Parliament in drafting the National Health Security Act (2000) which led Thailand to implement universal health-care coverage. Dr. Nittayaramphong, author of several publications on health-care system development, obtained his medical degree from Mahidol University (Thailand), a Master's in Public Health from Prins Leopold Institute of Tropical Medicine (Belgium) and a Certificate in Health Economics from the London School of Hygiene and Tropical Medicine (UK).

Adrien Nougtara, MD, MSc (Maternal and Child Health) has occupied several positions at the Ministry of Health of Burkina Faso, where he has coordinated projects in primary care and reproductive health. He also participated in decentralization and the setting up of health districts under the country's health system reform. Since 1991, as national researcher, he has coordinated a research program on service utilization and access to care, conducted in the district of Nouna in cooperation with the University of Heidelberg and the European Union. He has worked with different agencies such as GTZ and has been involved in reproductive services assessment in Burkina Faso, Ivory Coast, and Mali, with UNFPA and Family Care International.

Francisco José Yepes is a professor at Javeriana University, Bogotá, and a researcher in health policy and systems. Dr. Yepes was the director of the Colombian National Health Survey (1975–78), the Colombian Hospital Study (1986), and the Colombian Health Sector Analysis (1988–89). He is currently executive director of the Colombian Health Association – ASSALUD and director of its Health Policy and Systems research group. Formerly, he was General Secretary at the Ministry of Health and Vice-president at the Social Security Institute. He received his MD and MPH degrees from Universidad de Antioquia, Medellin, and an MSc (Health Services Administration) and PhD from Harvard University, Boston. His current research is on governance and evidence-based decision-making.

INDEX